AI for Gig Workers

Essential Strategies to Transform Your Freelance Career

SAIPH SAVAGE

PAMELA CERDEIRA

LILIANA SAVAGE

WILEY

Published by John Wiley & Sons, Inc., Hoboken, New Jersey.

Library of Congress Cataloging-in-Publication Data: 2026933071

ISBN: 9781394379712 (Paperback)
ISBN: 9781394379736 (ePDF)
ISBN: 9781394379729 (ePub)

Cover Design: Wiley
Cover Image: @YumizuArt

SKY10149566_031326

To my family, whose faith in me has never wavered and whose love quietly carried this book into existence.
To the freelancers who have collaborated with me: thank you for your honesty, your creativity, and your courage.

—Saiph

To everyone who has been generous with their knowledge and taught me something new. And to my family, for putting up with my intensity whenever a subject ignites my passion—and for enduring the fact that once it does, I simply can't stop talking about it, just like with AI.

—Pamela

To my parents, Alberto and Araceli, my greatest advocates and steady believers. And to my partner, Steven, a constant source of encouragement and equilibrium throughout this project.

—Liliana

Contents

Introduction: The AI Sidekick for Gig Workers

This book is your roadmap to thriving in the gig economy with AI. It's not a jargon-heavy tech manual or a motivational pep talk. It's a practical guide with strategies, tools, and examples to help you:

- Work more efficiently
- Earn more consistently
- Build credibility by showcasing your AI skills

Whether you're freelancing, side-hustling, or working full time, the goal is to meet you where you are and give you actionable steps to level up.

Practice and Gain Your Credentials Along the Way

Every chapter in this book comes with a Badge Achievement Plan: short, hands-on exercises where you'll put new tools and strategies into action right away. These sessions are about experimenting, practicing, and discovering what works best for your style of gig work. Not everything will be perfect on the first try, and that is part of the process.

Here is the exciting part: if you complete the exercises for a chapter and submit them, you will have the chance to *earn digital badges from Northeastern University*. Each badge highlights the specific AI skills you gained in that chapter. These badges are not just for you. You can add them to your portfolio or share them with clients and future employers as proof that you have validated, real-world AI expertise. This way, you are not only learning how to use AI but also building a visible record of your skills that helps you stand out in the gig economy.

The journey doesn't end when you close your laptop. The bonus chapters show how AI can transform both your personal life and your professional future. Bonus Chapter I helps you reclaim time, reduce stress, and find balance beyond work. Bonus Chapter II explores the human side of technology, showing how gratitude toward your AI can help you stay mindful, balanced, and creative in an automated world. Bonus Chapter III looks ahead to 2030, imagining what the next decade of freelancing might bring and how to stay creative, ethical, and irreplaceably human in a world of intelligent machines.

Picture this: It's 11 p.m., and you're on your laptop, juggling a client email, a half-finished project, and a mental to-do list that feels never-ending. You're a gig worker, maybe a freelance designer in New York, a rideshare driver in Chicago, a tutor in Mexico City, or a content creator in Caracas. You do love the freedom of your hustle, the ability to set your own hours, and the thrill of landing a new gig. But let's also be real: it's exhausting. You're not just doing the work you love. You also have to be the accountant, the marketer, and the scheduler all rolled into one. The gig economy is a wild, exhilarating ride, but it often feels like you're navigating it without a map, blindfolded, in a storm. Sound familiar? You're not alone.

Welcome to *AI for Gig Workers*. This book isn't about just surviving the gig life: it's about *thriving* in it, with a powerful ally at your side: artificial intelligence (AI). Whether you're a seasoned freelancer or just getting started in gig work, AI can completely transform the way you hustle. It can make you faster, smarter, and more confident in every job you take on. Think of AI as your assistant in a taco truck. While you focus on your craft—designing the flyers, cooking the tacos, and making deliveries—AI takes care of the rest: mapping the best routes, taking orders, managing your schedule, and even translating for customers who speak different languages. AI is not here to replace you. It's here to help you serve more people, earn more money, and reduce stress. In the chapters ahead, you'll learn how to use AI to automate repetitive tasks, increase your income, and build a freelancing career that's not just sustainable, but epic. Ready to trade the late-night chaos for a smarter, smoother hustle? Let's dive in.

The Gig Worker's Challenge: Navigating Without a Roadmap

The gig economy is booming. According to Upwork's *Future Workforce Index 2025* (2024), more than 70 million Americans participated in freelance or contract work in 2025, and the number continues to grow as independent professionals take on roles across every major industry. Globally, the gig economy has become a multitrillion-dollar force connecting millions of workers through platforms like Fiverr, Upwork, and Freelancer. Analysts project that by 2028, freelancers will make up nearly 60% of the U.S. workforce, with similar growth trends emerging worldwide. It's a world of opportunity: work when you want, where you want, for whom you want.

But with all that freedom comes a catch: you're often a one-person show, wearing every hat in the business. You pitch clients, chase invoices, and update your portfolio, and somehow you also have to find time to actually *do* the work. It's like being the owner of a taco truck who has to source the ingredients, prep the meat, set up the cart, serve customers, handle money, and clean up, all while competing with five other taco stands and taco trucks on the same street. You're the chef when you're grilling, the marketer when you're shouting specials to passersby, the accountant when you're counting your cash box, and the janitor when you're scrubbing down at closing time. Some days nobody's hungry for what you're selling, but you still have to spend hours getting ready and putting in the work.

Examples of this difficult dynamic show up with different types of freelancers around the globe. Let's take a freelance designer who focuses on user experience (UX). She absolutely loves designing user-friendly websites for her clients, but she spends hours staying current with the latest web development techniques, writing proposals to land new web page projects, and managing a constant stream of client emails. Those emails alone are exhausting: progress updates on the websites she is doing, small revision requests, back-and-forth questions about project details. By the time she actually sits down to design and build her clients' websites, she's already drained.

Or consider a freelancer who works as a content strategist. He has to juggle multiple clients but loses sleep worrying about late payments and endless rounds of revisions. Then there's a yoga instructor who dreamed of scaling her freelancing business but found herself drowning in scheduling conflicts and social media marketing.

These gig workers aren't failing at what they do. They're actually thriving in their craft. But the gig economy's demands can feel like having to run that taco truck alone. Maybe you're amazing at making the most delicious carnitas in town, but you're so busy sourcing ingredients, cleaning equipment, and chasing down customers who haven't paid their catering bills that you barely have the energy left to cook the food you love making.

These challenges are real. First, there's the time-suck problem: all those admin tasks like emails, invoicing, and research eat into your billable hours. Then you've got income uncertainty: some months you're rolling in cash, and others you're scraping by, making budgeting feel like a total nightmare. On top of that, there's client overload, because keeping multiple clients happy while somehow finding new ones becomes an exhausting balancing act. The skill pressure doesn't help either, because clients expect cutting-edge work with data insights, polished branding, and lightning-fast turnarounds, all while wanting to pay you less. And honestly, the burnout risk is huge when you're doing everything alone and have no time left for rest or actually growing your business.

If you've nodded along, you know the gig life is a hustle that tests your grit. But here's the good news: you don't have to do it alone anymore. Enter your new sidekick: AI.

Why AI Is Your Ultimate Sidekick

AI isn't just for tech bros or sci-fi movies. It's for you, the gig worker hustling to make your mark. Think of AI as your personal assistant who just keeps going and going—an assistant that's available 24/7, costs nothing to almost nothing, and learns to fit your workflow perfectly. Tools like ChatGPT, Jasper, Figma AI, and Notion AI are transforming the gig economy, turning all that chaos into real opportunity. You can think of AI as the great equalizer because it lets you, working solo, deliver results that can compete with those big, fancy agencies that have entire teams and massive budgets.

Here's what makes this so powerful: those big agencies have copywriters, data analysts, designers, project managers, and researchers all working on client projects. But with AI, you can access those same capabilities right from your laptop. You can generate professional content like their copywriters, analyze data like their analysts, create stunning visuals like their design teams, and research market trends like their strategy departments. This AI transformation is happening at lightning speed, and the gig economy is evolving right along with it. By 2030, half of gig tasks could involve AI in their work, from content creation to analytics. That means early adopters like you have a huge advantage right now. By integrating AI into your workflow, you have the potential to be able to command higher rates, win premium clients, and build the kind of stability that turns those unpredictable income swings into steady growth. Your AI sidekick is here to make that happen.

AI is your ultimate sidekick because it can tackle the exact challenges you're dealing with as a gig worker. First, AI can save you a crazy amount of time by automating those tedious emails, researching the market, and dealing with scheduling headaches in just minutes. We'll see how freelancers have used tools like ChatGPT to quickly research and understand the new web development trends, which gave them back hours to focus on what they actually love doing.

Second, AI can boost your income by helping you figure out smarter pricing and negotiate better contracts. By using AI tools such as Perplexity to research what's happening in the market, freelancers can enjoy multiple benefits, such as increased client inquiries.

Third, AI can make managing clients so much easier by handling communication and onboarding without you having to think about it. By automating signups with Notion AI, the yoga instructor saw her enrollment jump by 30%.

Fourth, AI can help you level up your skills so you can deliver impressive data insights or gorgeous visuals even if you don't have years of training. Maya, a freelancer translator, used Midjourney to create stunning visuals for foreign clients and landed a $3,000 project because of it. And finally, AI can help you avoid burning out by giving you back precious time for rest or actually growing your business. A freelance videographer used Fireflies.ai to automatically summarize his client meetings and got back 5 hours every single month.

AI doesn't have to replace your creativity. In this book you'll learn how to use AI to amplify your creativity and amplify your work. Think about working with AI like having a cooking assistant at your taco stand who dices all the onions, shreds the cheese, and chops the cilantro so you can focus on perfecting your secret salsa recipe and grilling the meat just right. Whether you're writing blogs, driving passengers, or planning events, AI can adapt to whatever gig you do, helping you save time and boost results. And here's the best part: you don't need to be a tech expert to use it. This book will help you feel confident with AI, no matter your background. We'll guide you step by step so you can unlock its full potential in your freelance journey.

Note that this book will teach you about AI and how you can use it for gig work, but it also goes a step further. As you move through each chapter, you'll have the chance to earn digital badges from Northeastern University. These badges are proof of the skills you've learned, and you can add them to your portfolio or show them to your clients.

We understand that freelancers often learn new things but struggle to show they've really mastered the skill. That's why we're offering these badges. Each chapter will guide you on how to earn the related badge so you can clearly demonstrate your abilities with recognition from Northeastern University. By the time you finish, you'll have not only new knowledge but also a set of badges that make your skills visible and valuable to others.

How the Book Is Organized

Part 1. Learning About AI

Before you start building your business, you need to understand the equipment.

This section gets you comfortable with what AI really is, how it works, and how to make it work for you.

Chapter 1. What Is AI, and How Are Gig Workers Like You Already Using It?

Discover what AI actually does, why it matters for freelancers, and how gig workers around the world are already using it to boost income and reduce stress.

Chapter 1 explains how the digital badges work and how to obtain them. Submission instructions are also available at `https://civicai.khoury.northeastern.edu/ai-for-gig-workers`.

Chapter 2. Under the Hood: How Your AI Sidekick Actually Thinks

Learn how AI learns, from recognizing patterns to making predictions, so you can understand its logic, communicate better with it, and work with confidence.

Chapter 3. Mastering AI Communication: The Art of Prompt Engineering

Get hands-on with prompt engineering and learn to "talk" to AI effectively so it delivers useful, creative, and personalized results for your freelance projects.

Chapter 4. Agentic AI

Explore how to create and manage specialized AI agents that work together to handle your daily freelance tasks and expand your capacity.

Chapter 5. AI and Creativity on Steroids

Find out how AI can spark new ideas, speed up your creative process, and help you push your work to new levels without losing your personal touch.

Chapter 6. Choosing the Right AI Sidekick for Your Work

Learn how to evaluate AI tools, compare free and paid versions, and build a toolkit that fits your workflow and budget.

Chapter 7. Using AI Without Losing Your Voice

Understand how to keep your unique style, tone, and authenticity intact, making AI sound like you, not like everyone else.

Chapter 8. AI and Ethics

Learn how to use AI safely, ethically, and transparently. Understand data privacy, bias, and accountability so you can innovate without losing trust.

Think of this part as learning your kitchen setup before you start cooking.

Part 2. AI-Powered Strategies for Solving Gig Work Challenges

Once you know the tools, you're ready to run your freelancing business with them.

This section focuses on using AI to eliminate busywork, find better clients, and grow your income sustainably.

Chapter 9. Freeing Gig Workers from Unpaid Labor with AI Automation

Automate repetitive tasks like invoicing, scheduling, and expense tracking so you can reclaim your time for paid, creative, and strategic work.

Chapter 10. Networking with AI

Use AI to discover high-quality clients, personalize your outreach, and manage long-term relationships that turn one-time gigs into ongoing work.

Chapter 11. AI for Personal Branding

Use AI to write stronger cover letters, optimize your online profiles, and build campaigns that make clients come to you.

Chapter 12. AI for Smarter Scheduling and Efficiency

Streamline your time management and productivity with AI tools that help you prioritize, focus, and balance deep work with daily demands.

Chapter 13. Using AI to Set Your Rates

Stop guessing your prices. Use AI to analyze market data, justify your value, negotiate confidently, and take control of your finances.

Chapter 14. AI for Deep Work and Specialized Tasks

Turn simple gigs into high-value projects by using multiple AI agents to plan, execute, and refine complex, creative, or data-driven work.

Chapter 15. Scaling Your Gig with AI

Move from freelancer to founder by using AI to systematize your business, attract clients automatically, and build sustainable income streams.

This part helps you move from survival mode to growth, not just getting clients but building your gig worker empire.

Conclusion. Your AI-Powered Gig Empire

Bring everything together and plan your next steps. Learn how to sustain long-term success, balance growth with well-being, and use AI to keep evolving as your career expands. Here, AI becomes less of a tool and more of a trusted business partner, helping you scale your impact, not just your workload.

Bonus Chapters

Bonus Chapter I. AI in Your Personal Life: More Time for You, More Space to Grow

Learn how to use AI to simplify everyday routines, from school schedules to meal planning, freeing up more time for creativity and rest.

Bonus Chapter II. Thanking Your AI

Explore why small acts of gratitude toward your AI can help you stay mindful, humble, and connected to your creative humanity.

Bonus Chapter III. The Future of the Gig Worker (2030)

Take a glimpse into the future of freelancing, where AI collaboration is the norm and your human creativity is your ultimate edge.

PART 1

Learning About AI

CHAPTER 1

What Is AI, and How Are Gig Workers Like You Already Using It?

We are stepping into the thrilling world of artificial intelligence (AI), where machines are no longer just tools, but intelligent partners capable of learning, reasoning, and even creating alongside us. The future where computers adapt to new challenges, provide insightful solutions, and generate new ideas is no longer science fiction; it is happening right now.

And it matters for you, because AI is not only changing how we live, it is transforming the very future of work. Every example you'll see in this chapter connects directly to how careers are shifting, what skills will matter most, and how you can prepare to thrive in the new economy.

What Exactly Is AI?

At its core, AI is a branch of computer science focused on creating systems that perform tasks typically requiring human intelligence. These include learning from data, reasoning through problems, adapting to new situations, and providing innovative solutions.

Think of it as teaching a computer to recognize patterns, learn from experience, and make decisions, much like humans do. The more data AI processes, the better it becomes, just as humans improve with practice.

Why This Matters for Work

AI's ability to learn and adapt means that many tasks that once required human effort can now be automated or accelerated. For workers, this does not mean replacement; it means that routine work will shift to AI, whereas humans will increasingly focus on strategy, creativity, and problem-solving.

AI in Your Daily Life

What makes AI remarkable is how seamlessly it has blended into everyday life. Most of the time, it operates quietly in the background, making our experiences faster, safer, and more personalized.

Here are some common examples and what they mean for work:

1. Understanding language

   Voice assistants like Siri and Alexa use *natural language processing* (NLP) to understand and respond to human speech.

   - *Work connection:* NLP is the foundation of chatbots, transcription tools, and translation systems. This means jobs in customer service, administration, and global collaboration are already being reshaped by AI that can process language instantly.

2. Learning preferences

   Netflix, Spotify, and Amazon use *recommendation systems* to analyze behavior and suggest personalized content.

   - *Work connection:* The same technology powers job-matching on labor platforms like Upwork and LinkedIn. Workers who understand recommendation systems will know how to optimize their profiles to be discoverable.

3. Filtering and classification

   Spam filters learn what unwanted messages look like and adapt as new threats emerge.

   - *Work connection:* This same logic is used in cybersecurity and fraud detection, fields that are rapidly growing as AI-powered systems protect data and digital identities.

4. Perceiving and acting

   Self-driving cars use sensors and AI to make split-second decisions.

   - *Work connection:* Autonomous systems are expanding into logistics, delivery, and manufacturing. Workers in these industries will increasingly shift toward supervising, maintaining, or designing such systems.

5. Curating information

   Social media platforms use AI to decide what content you see.

   - *Work connection:* This has created new career paths in digital marketing, content strategy, and algorithmic literacy. Professionals must now understand how AI "feeds" audiences to ensure that their work reaches the right people.

6. Finance and security

   Banks use AI for fraud detection, credit scoring, and chatbots.

   - *Work connection:* AI is transforming financial services and auditing. Professionals who can interpret AI-driven insights will have an edge over those who only understand traditional systems.

7. Healthcare

   AI analyzes X-rays, predicts risks, and supports doctors in diagnosis.

   - *Work connection:* Healthcare workers who learn to collaborate with AI tools will be able to deliver faster, more accurate care, making AI literacy a competitive advantage in medicine.

Activity: AI in Your Own Life

- Write down three ways AI has influenced you today.
- For each, ask: *What does this example teach me about how work is changing?*
- Share with a partner and compare how AI shapes different professions.

The Current Landscape: Artificial Narrow Intelligence (ANI)

Most of today's AI falls under ANI. These systems are experts at a single task, like translating text, analyzing scans, or recommending songs.

Why This Matters for Work

ANI is what powers the tools workers use daily. Even if you don't "work in AI," chances are you already rely on ANI in spreadsheets, search engines, or online platforms. Careers today require knowing how to use ANI as leverage, just as earlier generations had to master email, spreadsheets, and the internet itself.

The Technology Behind ANI

ANI systems often rely on two key technologies:

- *Machine learning:* Computers learn patterns from data, similar to how a child learns to recognize animals.
- *Neural networks:* Modeled after the brain, they process information in layers to recognize complex patterns (like faces, speech, or medical images).

Together, these systems power translation apps, recommendation engines, fraud detection, and much more.

Why This Matters for Work Understanding the basics of machine learning and neural networks isn't just for engineers; it helps professionals across industries know what AI can and can't do. This knowledge makes you better equipped to adopt AI tools into your workflow without fear of being replaced.

The Creative Revolution: Generative AI

Unlike traditional ANI systems that mainly analyze or classify, Generative AI creates. It can write stories, compose music, generate images, and even code. Think of it as a digital collaborator that can brainstorm, draft, and refine your work.

How Generative AI Works

At the heart of Generative AI are advanced forms of machine learning. Instead of being programmed with strict step-by-step rules, these systems learn by studying massive amounts of data. The more examples they process, the better they get at spotting patterns and predicting what should come next.

One of the most important breakthroughs powering Generative AI is the language model. A language model is trained on huge collections of text: books, articles, websites, and conversations. And it learns how words, sentences, and ideas fit together. The model doesn't "understand" language the way humans do, but it becomes very good at predicting which word is most likely to follow another. Imagine finishing the sentence "Once upon a. . .": you probably thought of "time." That's how a language model works, except it can do this billions of times in a row to generate entire essays, stories, or reports that feel natural and human-like.

Beneath language models are neural networks, which are specialized machine learning structures inspired by the human brain. Neural networks are made up of layers of artificial "neurons" that pass information to each other. Each layer processes a different level of detail:

- Early layers might detect very simple features, like letters in text or edges in an image.
- Middle layers combine those into more complex features, like phrases in a sentence or shapes in a picture.
- Deeper layers put it all together to capture meaning, tone, or even artistic style.

A Helpful Analogy: A Team at Work

You can think of a neural network like a team of workers in a publishing house:

- The first worker looks at a draft and marks basic spelling and grammar.
- The next worker builds on that, checking sentence flow and clarity.
- Another adds style, making sure the writing sounds engaging.
- Finally, the editor at the end reads it all together and decides what the finished product should look like.

Each worker specializes in one part of the task, and together they produce a polished piece. Neural networks function in a very similar way: layer after layer, each one builds on the work of the previous one until a complex and realistic result emerges.

Connection to ANI

Generative AI is still part of ANI. A language model is outstanding at generating text, but it cannot drive a car. An image generator can create art, but it cannot diagnose medical conditions. Each system is narrow and specialized.

Yet within its narrow scope, Generative AI is incredibly powerful. This power comes from the combination of three elements, each playing a different role:

- Massive datasets provide the raw material. Just as humans learn by experiencing the world, AI learns from enormous collections of text, images, audio, or code. The more examples it sees, the richer its "knowledge" becomes.

- Machine learning algorithms are the methods for finding patterns in that data and making predictions. They give the system the ability to learn from examples instead of following rigid, preprogrammed rules.
- Neural networks are a special type of machine learning model designed to handle very complex patterns. They process data in layers, which allows the system to recognize structures such as grammar in sentences, harmonies in music, or objects in images.

A helpful way to imagine this is as a recipe. The datasets are the ingredients. Without high-quality and diverse ingredients, you cannot prepare a great dish. Machine learning is the cooking process, the set of techniques that transform raw ingredients into something new. Neural networks are the specialized kitchen tools, like a blender or a pressure cooker, that make it possible to handle recipes that are far more complex than what you could do with only a basic pan.

When all three come together, AI moves beyond analysis into creation. That is why Generative AI feels like such a leap forward within ANI.

This creative shift is also why Generative AI is one of the most important technologies shaping the future of work. It makes professional-level writing, design, and coding available to everyone, and it is redefining the skills that will matter most in the new economy.

Why This Matters for Work

Generative AI democratizes creativity. Anyone, regardless of their artistic or technical background, can now produce high-quality outputs. This opens opportunities for freelancers, entrepreneurs, and professionals who can use AI to scale their work and reach larger audiences.

Reflection Question: What task in your work would benefit most from having a digital creative partner?

Case Study: Freelancers in Marketing

Imagine a freelance marketer. With Generative AI, they can:

- Generate dozens of ad slogans in seconds.
- Create visuals for campaigns with image generators.
- Draft blog posts tailored to a client's brand.

By combining AI speed with human judgment, they can serve more clients and charge higher rates.

Workflow: How Freelancers Use AI

1. Brainstorm: AI suggests campaign ideas.
2. Draft: AI produces first versions of text or visuals.
3. Refine: Human expertise polishes the output.
4. Test: Different AI-assisted variations are shared with clients.
5. Deliver: A polished final product is delivered faster than ever before.

This workflow highlights the future of work: humans plus AI are more powerful than either alone.

Looking Ahead: From ANI to AGI

Right now, we live in the age of ANI. But researchers are working toward artificial general intelligence (AGI), which could perform across many domains like humans. Beyond that lies artificial superintelligence (ASI), which could surpass human capabilities entirely.

Although these remain future possibilities, even today's ANI and Generative AI are enough to reshape industries, redefine jobs, and demand new skills from workers everywhere.

Navigating Challenges and Responsibilities

AI is not perfect. It learns from human data, which means it can also inherit human biases. Workers and companies need to remain alert, ensuring that AI is used ethically and responsibly.

Why This Matters for Work

Employers are increasingly seeking people who can not only use AI tools but also question their outputs: who can spot bias, ensure fairness, and make human-centered decisions. This is one of the fastest-growing career niches in AI ethics, auditing, and governance.

Embracing the Intelligent Future

AI is already transforming the way we live, work, and create. From narrow systems that recommend movies to generative models that design entire campaigns, the future of work is being rewritten by these tools. For freelancers, businesses, and professionals across industries, those who learn to collaborate with AI will find themselves more productive, more innovative, and more resilient. The story of AI is also the story of work. And those who embrace AI, not as a replacement, but as a partner, will be best positioned to thrive in this intelligent future.

As you can see, AI is no longer just background technology. It is becoming a true collaborator, changing the way work gets done and how opportunities are created. For freelancers, this shift is especially exciting. By learning how to use AI tools, you can work faster, scale your services, and compete with larger teams while keeping the personal creativity and flavor that make your work unique. Think of it like running your own taco stand in a world of big restaurant chains. With the right tools and a bit of imagination, you can serve something they never could.

To take full advantage of these opportunities, it helps to understand the key concepts behind AI, such as language models, machine learning, and neural networks. These are the ingredients behind the tools you will use. Knowing how they work allows you to use them more effectively, ask smarter questions, and recognize their limits.

Understanding the foundations of AI, including both its strengths and challenges, gives you confidence and direction. The future of work is not about competing with machines; it is about learning to work alongside them. The goal is to blend human creativity with the speed and intelligence of AI, creating something better than either could do alone.

In the chapters ahead, we will explore these ideas in depth, practice hands-on activities, and apply AI directly to your freelance journey. You will see how to use these tools not just to keep up but to thrive, creating a business that feels smarter, faster, and a little more flavorful, too.

Unleashing Your Potential: How AI Empowers the Modern Freelancer

Right now, you have had a nice overview of what AI is. Let's next connect with why you as a freelancer would even want to learn about AI. The world of freelancing is constantly evolving, and at the forefront of this transformation is AI. Far from being a futuristic concept, AI is already an indispensable tool that can revolutionize how freelancers operate, from streamlining business processes to enhancing client interactions and opening doors to new opportunities. For the modern independent professional, understanding and leveraging AI isn't just an advantage; it's a pathway to greater efficiency, increased income, and sustainable growth.

AI offers a comprehensive suite of tools and capabilities that can help freelancers streamline their work, dramatically increase productivity, and accelerate business growth. By embracing these intelligent solutions, independent professionals can transcend the limitations of manual processes and position themselves for continued success in an ever-evolving digital landscape.

Mastering Your Freelance Business with AI

One of the most significant ways AI assists freelancers is by optimizing the foundational elements of their business. Think of AI as your dedicated and tireless business consultant, helping you refine your approach and maximize your impact across every aspect of your professional journey.

Strategic Business Planning and Market Intelligence Before a single project begins, AI can help freelancers articulate their unique value proposition with unprecedented precision. By analyzing market trends, competitive landscapes, and industry data, AI tools can assist in identifying profitable niches, defining a clear set of services, and suggesting optimal pricing strategies based on real-time industry benchmarks and the perceived value of your skills.

This data-driven approach moves beyond guesswork, empowering freelancers to make informed decisions about their offerings and target audience. AI can analyze successful competitors in your field, identify gaps in the market, and even predict emerging trends that could present new opportunities. For instance, a graphic designer might discover through AI analysis that there's growing demand for sustainable packaging design, allowing them to pivot their services accordingly. Similarly, a freelance accountant could use AI to identify that most small businesses in their city are struggling with crypto tax compliance, leading them to launch a highly specialized and premium service. Or a video editor might use trend analysis to realize that short-form educational content is generating 40% more engagement than long-form documentary work, prompting them to restructure their service packages around high-volume, quick-turnaround educational videos.

Cultivating an Entrepreneurial Mindset Through Intelligent Support Although AI doesn't directly address self-doubt, it provides tools that foster confidence and a proactive approach to business growth. By automating tedious tasks and providing valuable insights, AI frees up mental energy, allowing freelancers to focus on strategic thinking, problem-solving, and continuous improvement.

The ability to quickly iterate on ideas, analyze performance metrics, and adapt to client feedback, all facilitated by AI, naturally builds resilience and a growth-oriented mindset. When you can see clear data about what's working and what isn't, making strategic adjustments becomes less intimidating and more empowering.

Building a Powerful Personal Brand with AI Optimization In the crowded freelance marketplace, a strong personal brand is paramount to standing out and attracting ideal clients. AI plays a crucial role in optimizing your online presence across multiple platforms and touchpoints.

AI-powered tools can analyze the effectiveness of your LinkedIn profile, suggesting specific keywords and content improvements that attract your ideal clients. These tools can examine successful profiles in your industry and recommend modifications that increase visibility in search results and professional networks.

AI can also help in crafting compelling narratives about your expertise, generating engaging social media posts that showcase your personality and skills, and even assisting in the design of professional portfolios that visually communicate your accomplishments. Advanced AI tools can analyze which types of content generate the most engagement from your target audience, helping you refine your messaging strategy over time.

Effective Sales and Value Proposition Development The art of selling as a freelancer isn't about aggressive tactics; it's about presenting solutions that genuinely address client needs. AI excels at helping freelancers understand client pain points by analyzing their communications, industry trends, and past project outcomes.

With these insights, you can craft proposals that precisely address specific client challenges, positioning your services not just as tasks performed but as valuable solutions to their business problems. AI can analyze successful proposals in your field and suggest language, structure, and pricing models that have proven effective.

Furthermore, AI can assist in developing sophisticated pricing strategies, helping you structure your fees to reflect the true value you deliver rather than simply quoting an hourly rate. By analyzing project outcomes, client satisfaction, and market rates, AI can recommend pricing that maximizes both competitiveness and profitability.

Strategic Client Acquisition and Relationship Nurturing

Although AI isn't a substitute for genuine human connection, it significantly enhances the client acquisition and retention process. AI can help identify potential leads by scanning job boards, professional networks, and industry publications for opportunities that align perfectly with your skillset and experience.

More importantly, AI excels at supporting existing client relationships through intelligent automation and insights. By automating follow-up emails, scheduling regular check-ins, and providing insights into client preferences and communication patterns, AI helps maintain consistent, professional communication that builds loyalty and trust.

Because a significant portion of successful freelance work comes from repeat clients and referrals, AI ensures that these valuable relationships are nurtured effectively. AI can track client project histories, remember important details about their business, and suggest personalized approaches for future engagements.

Upholding Professionalism and Service Excellence

Delivering exceptional customer service is the cornerstone of a thriving freelance career, and AI tools can significantly enhance your ability to maintain high standards consistently. AI-powered project management tools can track timelines, monitor progress, and provide automated reminders and status updates that ensure deadlines are met without constant manual oversight.

AI can also assist in drafting professional communications, ensuring clarity, consistency, and appropriate tone in all client interactions. Advanced language models can help you communicate complex ideas clearly, address client concerns diplomatically, and maintain professionalism even in challenging situations.

By handling the organizational heavy lifting, AI allows freelancers to dedicate more time and mental energy to the quality of their work and the satisfaction of their clients, solidifying their reputation for reliability and excellence in their field.

AI as Your Intelligent Assistant: Boosting Productivity and Innovation

Beyond strategic business planning, AI is becoming a smart and adaptable assistant that fits naturally into your daily routine. This is where the real benefits begin. It takes care of repetitive tasks and background details so you can focus on the creative and strategic work that matters most. Think of it as having a trusted extra set of hands in your taco stand, quietly handling the prep work while you focus on perfecting the recipe. AI helps you protect your most valuable resource: your mental energy.

By handling tasks like summarizing long meeting notes, organizing your inbox, or quickly drafting routine email replies, the AI sidekick allows you to focus your intellectual efforts entirely on the specialized, high-value work clients pay you for. For a coder, this means more time solving complex architectural problems; for a writer, it means more time crafting the perfect narrative. AI acts as a foundation of efficiency, opening new avenues for productivity and creativity across all freelancing domains.

Advanced Task Management and Organization Imagine having an assistant who never forgets a detail and can intelligently prioritize your workload. AI-powered productivity tools can create intelligent to-do lists that automatically prioritize tasks based on deadlines, importance, client value, and your personal work patterns.

These systems can track the progress of multiple projects simultaneously, manage complex content calendars, organize research materials, and even predict potential bottlenecks before they occur. From managing editorial calendars for content creators to organizing research materials for consultants, AI ensures that freelancers stay organized, focused, and on top of their commitments while reducing stress and increasing overall output.

Automation of Routine and Repetitive Tasks One of AI's most transformative applications for freelancers is its ability to automate repetitive and time-consuming tasks that previously consumed hours of valuable time. This automation spans multiple areas:

Email management and communication: AI can summarize lengthy email threads, draft polite and professional responses that match your communication style, filter out irrelevant messages, and even schedule emails to be sent at optimal times. Some advanced AI tools can manage entire email conversations for routine inquiries, saving hours each week.

Data entry and organization: For freelancers dealing with large datasets, client information, or research materials, AI can automate data extraction from various sources, categorize information intelligently, and perform accurate data entry with minimal human oversight. This dramatically reduces manual effort and potential errors while ensuring consistency.

Content generation and creative assistance: Although it does not replace human creativity and insight, AI can significantly assist writers, marketers, and designers by generating outlines, drafting initial content blocks, brainstorming creative ideas, and creating multiple versions of ad copy, social media captions, or marketing materials. This jump-starts the creative process and provides a solid foundation for human refinement and personalization.

Video and content production: For video editors and content creators, AI can handle initial video cuts, generate thumbnails, create subtitles, and even suggest editing improvements. A video editor could use AI to handle routine editing tasks, allowing them to take on more projects and focus on creative storytelling elements.

Enhanced Content Creation and Social Media Management AI tools have revolutionized content creation and social media management, offering freelancers powerful capabilities to scale their output while maintaining quality. These tools can assist in generating fresh ideas, creating engaging drafts, and producing high-quality content for blogs, social media platforms, and websites.

Specialized AI tools can help create visually appealing social media carousels, generate short-form video content optimized for different platforms, and enhance your presence on platforms like Twitter, LinkedIn, and Instagram. AI can analyze trending topics, suggest optimal posting times, and even create content variations to test what resonates best with your audience.

For freelancers managing multiple client accounts, AI can maintain consistent brand voices across different clients while adapting content for various platforms and audiences.

Advanced Data Analysis and Business Intelligence Many freelancers work with data, whether it's client analytics, market research, project performance metrics, or industry trends. AI tools can analyze complex datasets from spreadsheets, databases, and other sources, extracting key insights, identifying patterns, and generating clear, professional visualizations.

This capability allows freelancers to make data-driven decisions, demonstrate measurable impact to clients, and uncover new opportunities that might otherwise remain hidden in raw data. For consultants and analysts, AI can process vast amounts of information quickly and identify trends that would take humans days or weeks to discover.

Sophisticated Information Processing and Research AI's capabilities extend to understanding and manipulating various forms of information, making research and information processing incredibly efficient.

Document analysis and research: AI can quickly scan lengthy documents, research papers, and reports to identify key information, create comprehensive summaries, and extract specific data points. This makes literature reviews, competitive analysis, and client research significantly more efficient.

Image and visual content processing: From identifying objects and text in images to extracting information from handwritten notes or photographs, AI can digitize and process visual information. This is invaluable for researchers, designers, content creators, and anyone who works with visual materials.

Audio transcription and processing: For freelancers working with interviews, meetings, podcasts, or legacy audio documents, AI can accurately transcribe speech into text, identify different speakers, and even summarize key points from long recordings. This saves countless hours of manual transcription work.

AI-Enabled Skill Development and Continuous Learning The freelance landscape constantly evolves, demanding continuous skill upgrades to remain competitive. AI offers personalized learning experiences, recommending courses, tutorials, and resources tailored specifically to a freelancer's goals, current skill set, and learning style.

Whether you're mastering new software, learning a programming language, or staying updated on industry trends, AI acts as a personal tutor and learning coordinator. AI can assess your current knowledge, identify skill gaps, and create customized learning paths that fit your schedule and learning preferences.

Enhanced Client Communication and Collaboration AI can significantly improve client relationships through better communication and collaboration tools. Some platforms are integrating AI to allow clients to iterate on projects with an AI system before the freelancer adds final touches, streamlining the revision process and improving client satisfaction.

AI-powered chatbots can handle routine client inquiries, schedule meetings, and provide project updates, ensuring that clients feel supported even when you're focused on deep work. These systems can maintain your professional voice and provide consistent, helpful responses to common questions.

Strategic Planning and Problem-Solving Support Advanced AI tools like sophisticated language models can serve as virtual business advisors for strategic planning and problem-solving. Freelancers can use these tools to brainstorm new service offerings, create detailed action plans, analyze business challenges from multiple angles, and develop innovative solutions to complex problems.

AI can help you think through different scenarios, identify potential obstacles, and develop contingency plans. This strategic support is particularly valuable for solo freelancers who don't have traditional business partners or advisors to bounce ideas off.

Reputation Management and Online Presence Maintaining a positive online reputation is essential for freelancers, and AI can help you manage this important part of your business. Think of it as a friendly team member who keeps an ear out for what people are saying about your tacos while you focus on improving the recipes. AI tools can track mentions of your name or business across the internet, analyze the tone of client reviews, and even help respond to feedback on platforms such as Google, Facebook, and specialized industry sites.

These systems can craft thoughtful, consistent replies that protect your professional image while notifying you of anything that needs a personal touch. AI can also help you proactively gather positive reviews by identifying satisfied clients and suggesting optimal times to request testimonials.

The Future Is Freelance, Powered by AI

For freelancers, AI represents not a threat but an incredible opportunity for growth, efficiency, and innovation. By embracing AI tools strategically, independent professionals can transcend the traditional limitations of manual processes, dramatically elevate the quality and scope of their services, and position themselves for continued success in an ever-evolving digital landscape.

The integration of AI into freelance workflows enables professionals to compete more effectively with larger agencies by leveraging technology to scale their capabilities. A single freelancer equipped with AI tools can often deliver results that previously required entire teams while maintaining the personal touch and flexibility that clients value.

As AI continues to evolve, early adopters in the freelance community will gain significant competitive advantages. Those who learn to effectively collaborate with AI systems will be able to take on more complex projects, serve larger clients, and command higher rates for their enhanced capabilities.

The future of freelancing is intelligent, efficient, and infinitely more capable, thanks to the transformative power of AI. By viewing AI as a collaborative partner rather than a replacement, freelancers can unlock new levels of creativity, productivity, and business success that were previously impossible for independent professionals to achieve.

The key to success in this AI-powered future lies not in fearing technological change but in embracing it strategically and learning to leverage these powerful tools to amplify human creativity, insight, and professional expertise. The freelancers who thrive in the coming years will be those who successfully integrate AI into their workflows while maintaining the human elements that make their services unique and valuable.

Digital Badges

Throughout this book, you will encounter sessions to earn digital badges. These are hands on activities designed to help you apply AI tools directly to your gig work and build practical skills as you move through each chapter.

Readers who complete these Sessions have the opportunity to earn digital badges that recognize specific AI for work competencies. These badges are designed to help gig workers document and signal skills that are often developed through practice but are difficult to demonstrate through traditional resumes or credentialing systems.

To obtain a digital badge, complete the corresponding Session and follow the submission instructions available at: `https://civicai.khoury.northeastern.edu/ai-for-gig-workers`.

After successful review, readers may receive a Northeastern University issued digital badge that can be shared on professional profiles, portfolios, or with clients and platforms.

Badge Achievement Plan: AI Foundations

Complete the following missions to demonstrate your skills and earn your badge!

You've just learned what AI actually means: not science fiction, but systems that learn from data, recognize patterns, and make predictions. You've explored how AI powers the tools you already use, from recommendation engines to writing assistants, and how this technology is reshaping every kind of freelance and creative work. Now it's time to turn that big-picture understanding into personal insight. This session will help you reflect on what AI already does in your life, where it might fit into your work, and how you can start thinking like someone who uses technology with strategy and confidence.

Time Required: 40 minutes

Goal: Identify how AI already touches your daily routine, and discover the first opportunities to integrate AI into your freelance or creative workflow.

What You'll Need:

- Access to a free AI tool (ChatGPT, Perplexity, or Notion AI)
- A notebook or digital document for notes
- Curiosity, and maybe a snack, because learning is better with tacos

Mission 1: Define the Core Concepts (10 minutes)

- Let's start simple. You're going to use your favorite AI tool, such as ChatGPT, to test what you've learned about how AI "thinks."

- Secret prompts to try:

  Prompt 1: "Explain the difference between Artificial Narrow Intelligence and Generative AI using tacos as an example."

  Prompt 2: "Use a cooking recipe to explain how datasets, machine learning, and neural networks work together."

- Your task:

  Write down what the AI says in your notebook.

  Then explain the same idea in your own words, short and simple.

  Reflection: What surprised you about how AI learns?

Mission 2: Discover AI in Your Everyday Life (10 minutes)

AI is already around you; you just might not notice it.

Step 1: Look around your daily routine. Write down three AI tools or apps you used today. Examples:

- Spotify → recommends songs using AI.
- Google Maps → plans routes and avoids traffic using AI.
- Gmail → finishes your sentences using AI.

Step 2: For each one, write a sentence about how it makes your life easier.

Secret prompt to try: "List five everyday apps that use AI and explain how they help freelancers."

You'll start realizing you've been using AI all along, just without calling it that.

Mission 3: Try AI as Your Helper (10 minutes)

Now for the fun part: time to let AI give you a hand with your work. Choose one of these "secret prompts," paste it into your AI tool, and see what it creates for you.

Prompt for writers: "Give me three creative post ideas for my social media about [your topic]."

Prompt for designers: "List five design trends in [your field] and explain how I could use them in my work."

Prompt for anyone: "Write a short, friendly email introducing my freelance services to a potential client."

Your task:

Pick one output and personalize it. Add your tone, your humor, your human touch.

Reflection: Did the AI save you time or spark new ideas?

Mission 4: Reflect and Plan Your Next Move (5 minutes)

You've now used AI like a pro. Let's plan how you'll keep experimenting.

Secret prompt to try:

"What are three small ways freelancers like me can use AI every week to save time or attract more clients?"

Your task:

Write down one small action you'll try this week. Maybe it's using AI to plan content, summarize research, or write emails faster. The goal is progress, not perfection.

Mission 5: Knowledge Check Quiz (5 minutes)

1. A freelance marketer uses an AI tool to generate slogans for a client. According to the chapter, what kind of AI system is she using?
   a. Artificial general intelligence (AGI)
   b. Artificial narrow intelligence (ANI)
   c. Generative AI
   d. Machine learning
2. Why is it important for non-engineers to understand the basics of machine learning?
   a. Non-engineers must be able to code and train their own foundational models
   b. Understanding how AI learns (from data and patterns) is crucial for crafting better prompts and identifying bias in the output
   c. It is only important for non-engineers if they plan to work directly on hardware optimization
   d. Understanding machine learning basics helps reduce the cost of using cloud-based AI services
3. Why does the chapter emphasize learning how AI works before using it in your freelance business?
   a. Because understanding the basics helps freelancers use AI tools strategically and confidently
   b. Because freelancers need to learn programming before using any AI tool
   c. Because AI tools are too complex to be used without professional training
   d. Because knowing how AI works eliminates the need for creativity

Answer Sheet

1. **C: Generative AI**

   Generative AI creates new content like text, images, and music based on patterns it has learned, unlike ANI systems that simply classify or analyze information.

2. **B: Understanding how AI learns (from data and patterns) is crucial for crafting better prompts and identifying bias in the output**

   Non-engineers don't need to code, but understanding how AI "thinks" helps them communicate more effectively with tools and recognize potential bias or inaccuracy in results.

3. **A: Because understanding the basics helps freelancers use AI tools strategically and confidently**

   The chapter stresses that understanding AI's foundations helps freelancers use it intentionally, not fear it, and apply it effectively to real work.

Congratulations!

By completing these four missions, you will have demonstrated a strong foundation in AI. You will be able to define key terms, connect AI concepts to your own life and career, and explain the strategic implications of this powerful technology. Once you finish, mail your responses to the address at the end of the book to receive your AI Foundations Badge, issued by Northeastern University.

This badge is more than just a symbol of completion. It is proof that you can speak the language of AI and apply it in real-world contexts. For freelancers, it is especially powerful because clients often wonder whether you truly understand how AI works or if you are simply using tools without depth. Showcasing your badge on LinkedIn, in your portfolio, or on freelance platforms signals that you have taken the time to build genuine expertise. It helps you stand out in a competitive market, reassures clients of your credibility, and positions you as someone who can confidently deliver AI-powered solutions.

What You Have Gained

You've taken your first real step into the world of AI for freelancers. In this chapter, you learned what artificial intelligence actually is: not science fiction, but practical tools that already power everyday work. You saw how gig workers around the world use AI to save time, stay organized, and grow their income.

Most importantly, you now understand that AI isn't just for engineers; it's a creative, accessible sidekick that can help you work smarter right now.

In Chapter 2, we will lift the lid and peek under the hood to see how machines actually learn. You will uncover the logic behind algorithms and start building the confidence to use AI like a pro. Think of it as learning the recipe behind your favorite salsa before you start adding your own creative twist.

CHAPTER 2

Under the Hood: How Your AI Sidekick Actually Thinks

Welcome back! In the last chapter, we met your new AI sidekick, the powerful assistant that can automate routine tasks, boost your income, and free you to focus on the work you enjoy most. We also began to explore a key question: *what exactly is AI?*

In this chapter, we will go deeper. We will move beyond the surface and get into the technical details that explain how AI actually works. This is not about turning you into a computer scientist. Just as you don't need to be an engineer to drive a car, you don't need an advanced degree to understand AI. But having a clear sense of what is happening under the hood makes you more confident, better prepared, and able to use these tools strategically.

We will demystify the core technologies that give AI its power. You will see how it learns from data, how it makes predictions, and how it creates new content. By the end of this chapter, you will have a solid foundation in the key concepts that will help you work alongside AI more effectively and take advantage of the opportunities it is creating in the future of work.

Why You, a Creative Human, Should Care About the Robot Brain

Let's get the biggest question out of the way first: Why should you, a talented freelancer, be it a writer, designer, driver, or consultant, care about the technical jargon behind AI? Isn't that for the tech bros in Silicon Valley?

The simple answer is that AI isn't the future anymore; it's the tool you're competing against (or working with) right now. Ignoring AI today is like a taco truck owner in the early 2000s ignoring the internet. Sure, you could keep handing out paper flyers, but your competitor who built a simple website and got on Google Maps is suddenly getting all the customers.

- *It's already everywhere:* You're already using AI every single day. The algorithm that decides which of your posts your followers see on Instagram? That's AI. The spam filter that keeps your inbox clean? AI. The GPS that reroutes you around traffic? AI. These systems are the new infrastructure of the digital world. Understanding the basics helps you navigate this world more effectively instead of just being pushed around by algorithms you don't understand.
- *It's a tool for efficiency and creativity, not just a threat:* The biggest shift is seeing AI not as a replacement for you, but as your new coworker. You have Generative AI, which acts as a creative partner that can brainstorm ideas with you when you're stuck. And you have other forms of AI that are like the world's best operations manager, handling the boring, repetitive parts of your job so you can focus on the strategic, creative work that you love and that clients pay you the big bucks for.
- *The landscape is changing, fast:* The pace of AI development is incredibly fast. Industries are not going to change in a decade; they're changing *this year*. Freelancers who understand the shift can adapt, offer new services, and thrive. Understanding the technology allows you to ride the wave of change instead of being swept away by it.

Ultimately, you should care about AI for the same reason a chef cares about their ingredients. You don't need to be a farmer, but you need to know the difference between a fresh tomato and a rotten one. A little bit of knowledge about the core concepts of AI will give you the power to choose the right tools, get better results, and build a more successful and future-proof freelance business.

So, let's start by looking at the most important ingredient in the entire AI kitchen: the concept of "learning."

Your Brain Is a Machine Learning Model (You Just Didn't Know It)

Before we dive into the different types of AI, let's get one thing straight: you are already an expert in the fundamental process that powers modern AI. You use it every single day.

Think about a simple, almost magical task you can perform: telling the difference between a cat and a dog. How did you learn to do that?

Did your parents sit you down with a technical manual and a set of rules?

- *Rule 1: If the creature has four legs, fur, and a tail, it is a dog.* (But wait, cats fit this rule too.)
- *Rule 2: If the creature barks, it is a dog. If it meows, it is a cat.* (What if it's silent? Or what if it's a Basenji, a dog that doesn't bark?)

Trying to define a complex reality with a strict set of "if-then" rules is incredibly difficult and quickly falls apart. This is how old-school computer programs worked, and it's why they were often so rigid and easily confused.

Now, think about how you *actually* learned. It was through experience.

From a young age, you were exposed to countless examples. Your family pointed at the fluffy creature in the park and said, "Look, a dog." You saw a sleek animal in a cartoon and were told it was a "cat." You saw big dogs, small dogs, loud dogs, and quiet dogs. You saw black cats, orange cats, and cats with stripes.

With each example, your brain wasn't memorizing rules; it was building an intuitive *pattern*. It was learning the thousands of subtle visual cues, movements, and sounds that, when combined, create the *concept* of "dog" or "cat." You were training your own internal model on data from the real world.

After enough examples, a magical thing happened. You could see a breed of dog you had never encountered before—say, a Corgi—and instantly know, "That's a dog." You didn't need a rulebook. You made a prediction based on the patterns you had learned from all your past experiences.

This is the secret of machine learning.

At its heart, machine learning works the exact same way. Instead of feeding an AI a list of rigid rules, developers feed it a massive number of examples. To teach an AI to recognize dogs, they don't write code about "fur" or "tails." They show it millions of pictures that have been labeled "dog." The AI processes all these examples and, just like your brain, starts to build its own intuitive understanding of the patterns.

Back at the taco truck, this is the difference between giving your new cook a 500-page manual on every possible taco combination versus showing them 1,000 pictures of your best-selling tacos and saying, "Make them look like this." One relies on rules; the other relies on learning from examples. The second method is not only more efficient but also allows the cook to handle a new, unexpected order with confidence because they've learned the underlying *principles* of what makes a great taco.

So when you hear the term "machine learning," don't let it intimidate you. It's simply a technical version of the most natural learning process in the world: learning by experience. You've been doing it your whole life. Now, let's look at the two main ways we can guide that learning process.

The Two Main Flavors of Machine Learning

Flavor 1: Supervised Learning, the Great Taco Sorter

The most common type of machine learning is called supervised learning. The "supervision" just means we're giving the AI examples that have already been labeled correctly. We're the supervisor, teaching the student with an answer key.

Back at the taco truck, imagine that your ingredients arrive all mixed up in big bags. You have bags of jalapeños, habaneros, and bell peppers. You want to build a machine to sort them. Using supervised learning, you would

1. *Create a labeled dataset:* You take thousands of peppers and label each one. This one is a "jalapeño." This one is a "habanero." This one is a "bell pepper."
2. *Train the model:* You feed all these labeled examples into your AI sorting machine. The AI analyzes them, learning the patterns of color, shape, and size associated with each label.
3. *Make predictions:* Now, when a new, unlabeled pepper comes down the conveyor belt, the machine can look at it and make an educated guess: "Based on the patterns I've learned, this looks like a jalapeño with 98% confidence."

You see this everywhere. When your email automatically sorts a message into "Spam," it's because it's been trained on millions of emails labeled by users as "spam" or "not spam."

- *Why this matters for your gig:* The platforms you use to find work, like Upwork, Fiverr, and even LinkedIn, are giant supervised learning machines. When a client posts a job for a "graphic designer for a startup logo" and successfully hires someone with those exact keywords in their profile, that creates a labeled data point. The platform's AI learns from millions of these successful matches to "predict" which jobs you would be a good match for. Understanding this tells you that the words on your profile are the labels you are feeding the machine. If your profile is vague, the machine can't sort you correctly. If it's specific and packed with the keywords your ideal clients use, you're making it easy for the AI to put you in the "high-quality candidate" pile.

However, this is also where we have to be careful, because an AI that learns from the real world will also learn our real-world biases. Imagine that you train an AI to suggest the "correct" price for a taco at a food festival by feeding it

20 years of sales data. If that historical data shows that, due to systemic biases, tacos sold by female vendors were consistently priced 15% lower than identical tacos sold by male vendors, the AI will learn that pattern. It won't understand the injustice; it will just see a correlation. This is a real problem in AI-driven tools that suggest salaries or project rates, as they can accidentally perpetuate historical wage gaps if they are not designed and audited carefully.

Flavor 2: Unsupervised Learning—Discovering Your Secret Customers

If supervised learning is about teaching with a labeled answer key, unsupervised learning is what happens when you tell the AI, "Here's a giant pile of stuff. Find something interesting." You don't give it any labels. The AI's job is to look at the raw data and find hidden structures or groups all on its own.

Let's go back to the taco truck. You have a spreadsheet with every single order you've ever sold. You could feed this to an unsupervised learning AI. Without any guidance, it might come back and say, "I've analyzed your 50,000 orders, and I've found three distinct customer groups you didn't know you had: The Weekday Lunch Rush, The Late-Night Crowd, and The Weekend Family Pack." You never told the AI to look for these groups. It discovered these customer "clusters" by finding patterns in the raw sales data.

- *Why this matters for your gig:* You can apply this thinking to your own freelance business. It's about looking at your past work for hidden patterns. A freelance writer might analyze all their past articles and discover that their pieces on "personal finance for millennials" consistently get the most shares, an unsupervised discovery of a profitable niche. A virtual assistant might look at client requests and find that their most successful clients consistently ask for a combination of "email management," "calendar scheduling," and "social media posting," which they can then bundle into a premium "Startup Executive Package."

Natural Language Processing (NLP): Teaching Your AI to Read and Write

Natural language processing, or NLP, is the field of AI focused on giving computers the ability to understand, interpret, and generate human language, both text and speech.

For decades, computers were great with numbers but terrible with words. They could calculate a million equations in a second but couldn't understand the difference between "I'm feeling blue" and the color "blue." That's because human language is messy, full of context, sarcasm, and slang.

NLP is the "magic" that bridges this gap. It's what allows your AI sidekick to not just process commands but also understand the *meaning* behind them.

You're already using NLP all the time:

- *Spell-check and grammar tools:* When Grammarly suggests a better way to phrase a sentence, that's NLP at work.
- *Translation apps:* Google Translate uses NLP to understand the grammar and context of one language and translate it into another.
- *Chatbots and smart assistants:* When you ask Siri or Alexa a question, NLP is what allows it to understand what you said and form a coherent answer.

At its core, the technology you're using in tools like ChatGPT is a very advanced form of NLP. It has been trained on a vast amount of text from the internet, allowing it to understand and generate human-like language with incredible sophistication.

Computer Vision: Giving Your AI a Pair of Eyes

NLP gives AI its "ears" and "mouth," and computer vision gives it "eyes." This field of AI trains computers to see, interpret, and understand information from images and videos.

Just like teaching a child to recognize a dog, computer vision models are trained on millions of labeled images. They learn to identify objects, people, places, and even complex scenes. It's the technology that allows a machine to extract meaningful information from visual data and take action based on it.

You probably use computer vision every day without thinking about it:

- *Unlocking your phone:* When your smartphone recognizes your face, that's computer vision.
- *Scanning QR codes:* Your phone's camera uses computer vision to identify the code and understand the information it contains.
- *Social media filters:* When Instagram or TikTok places a filter perfectly on your face, it's using computer vision to identify your facial features in real time.
- *Searching your photos:* When you search your phone's photo library for "beach," the AI is using computer vision to find all the images that contain sand, water, and sun.

How This Helps Your Freelance Hustle

Understanding these two concepts unlocks a whole new level of practical tools for your gig.

- *For freelancers who work with words (writers, marketers, VAs):* NLP is your new superpower. A writer can use an AI tool to summarize a 50-page research report into a few key bullet points in seconds. A marketer can use it to analyze customer reviews and get an instant summary of the overall sentiment (positive or negative). A virtual assistant can paste a long, rambling email from a client into an AI and ask it to "extract the key action items and deadlines," turning chaos into a clear to-do list.
- *For freelancers who work with visuals (designers, content creators, photographers):* Computer vision is changing the game. A graphic designer can now use AI tools to remove the background from a complex photo with a single click. A social media creator can use AI-powered image generators to create stunning, original visuals for their posts without hiring a photographer. An event planner could even take a photo of an empty venue, and an AI tool could use computer vision to suggest different furniture layouts. For any freelancer, the ability to instantly digitize receipts or the notes from a whiteboard meeting using your phone's camera is a simple but powerful time-saver powered by computer vision.

Data Science: Your Secret Recipe for a Thriving Business

So we have machine learning, the powerful engine that learns from examples. But who decides what data to feed the engine? Who asks the questions in the first place? That's where data science comes in.

If machine learning is the automated taco-making machine, data science is the work of the head chef. It's the human-driven, creative process of using data to ask smart questions and make brilliant decisions that grow your business. It's a simple but powerful four-step process: Ask, Gather, Analyze, and Act.

1. *Ask an interesting question:* This is the most important step. The chef doesn't just stare at sales numbers; they ask, "Why are we selling so few fish tacos?"
2. *Gather the data:* The chef then gathers relevant information like sales reports and customer feedback.

3. *Analyze and find the insight:* The chef looks at the data and discovers the "aha!" moment: "People aren't buying the fish taco because the menu photo is unappetizing."
4. *Take action:* Based on this insight, the chef takes a beautiful new photo and updates the menu.

How This Helps Your Freelance Hustle

You do not need to be a math genius or buy expensive software to start thinking like a data scientist. You just need to get curious about your own business. This mindset is what separates freelancers who are just getting by from those who are strategically building a profitable career.

- *It helps you price smarter:* Instead of just guessing what to charge, you can ask a data science question: "What is my *true* most profitable service?" You can then gather data from your last 10 projects in a simple spreadsheet (price, hours worked, unpaid hours on revisions/emails). When you analyze it, you might discover your high-ticket website design gigs actually have a lower effective hourly rate than your smaller logo design projects. Your action? You can now confidently raise your rates on websites or focus on finding more of that surprisingly profitable logo work.
- *It helps you find better clients:* Instead of just looking for any work, ask: "Where do my *best* clients come from?" Gather the source for each of your past projects (e.g., a referral, Upwork, a LinkedIn message). When you analyze the data, you might find that your referral clients pay more and are easier to work with. Your action? Spend less time bidding on low-quality jobs, and create a simple referral program to encourage your best clients to spread the word.
- *It helps you level up your skills:* Instead of wondering what course to take next, ask: "What skills are clients in my niche *actually* paying for?" Gather data by quickly analyzing 20–30 job descriptions for your ideal role. Analyze them to find the most frequently mentioned skills or software. Your action? You now know exactly which skill to learn next to make yourself more valuable in the marketplace.

Data science is simply the discipline of making decisions with evidence instead of just a gut feeling. It empowers you to become the head chef of your own business, designing the menu, optimizing the kitchen, and building an empire, one smart decision at a time.

Prompt Engineering: Learning to Speak Your Sidekick's Language

So, you now understand the concepts that power your AI sidekick. You know how it learns and the types of problems it can solve. But there's one more crucial piece to the puzzle: learning how to *talk* to it.

This is where prompt engineering comes in. If AI is a brilliant, powerful, and incredibly skilled assistant, a prompt is the instruction you give that assistant. And prompt engineering is the art of giving crystal-clear instructions to get the exact result you want.

Think about ordering food at your taco truck.

- *A bad prompt:* "I'm hungry, give me some food." You'll get something, but it's probably not what you were hoping for.
- *A good prompt:* "Give me two al pastor tacos on corn tortillas with extra cilantro, no onions, and a side of your spiciest salsa." You get precisely what you wanted on the first try.

Generative AI works the same way. It's an incredibly capable chef, but it's also very literal. It can't read your mind. The quality of what you get out of it is directly proportional to the quality of what you put in.

The Recipe for a Perfect Prompt

A great prompt isn't about using fancy code; it's about providing clear context and constraints. Although there are many ways to structure a prompt, most effective ones contain a few key ingredients.

1. *The role (who is the AI?):* Start by telling the AI who it should be. Giving it a role, like "expert copywriter" or "social media strategist," focuses its response and elevates the quality of the output.
2. *The task (what should it do?):* Be very specific about your goal. Don't just say "write a post"; say "write three headlines for a blog post" or "create a bulleted list of marketing ideas."
3. *The context (what's the background?):* Give the AI the necessary background information to do the job well. Who is the target audience? What is the product or service? What is the key message?
4. *The format (how should it look?):* Define the rules and constraints. Should the output be a paragraph, a table, or a list? Should it be under 200 words? Should the tone be professional, friendly, or witty?

How This Helps Your Freelance Hustle

Mastering prompt engineering isn't a "nice-to-have" skill; it is arguably the single most important skill for effectively using Generative AI in your freelance business. It is the difference between treating AI as a novelty toy and wielding it as a professional-grade tool.

- *It saves you massive amounts of time:* A well-crafted prompt can give you a 90% finished product on the first try, turning what used to be a 2-hour task into a 10-minute one. A vague prompt will give you a generic result that you have to spend 45 minutes rewriting, defeating the purpose of using AI in the first place.
- *It improves the quality of your work:* By telling the AI to "act as an expert," you can leverage its vast training data to produce work that is better structured, more insightful, and more professional. It can help you brainstorm angles you hadn't thought of or phrase something more eloquently, effectively "leveling up" the quality of your deliverables.
- *It unlocks new services you can offer:* As a freelancer, the better you get at prompt engineering, the more valuable you become. A graphic designer who masters prompting AI image generators can start offering concept art and mood boards as a new service. A writer can offer "AI-assisted content strategy" or "prompt library creation" for businesses that want to use AI but don't know how. It becomes a marketable skill in its own right.

Here's a quick example:

- *Bad prompt:* "Write a social media post about my VA services."
- *Good prompt:* "Act as a social media marketing expert. Write a 150-word LinkedIn post targeting busy entrepreneurs. The post should highlight my virtual assistant services, focusing on how I save them 10+ hours a week on administrative tasks so they can focus on growing their business. End with a question to encourage comments."

The second prompt will deliver a piece of content that is specific, targeted, and almost ready to publish, saving you time and delivering a better result for your business. We'll take a deeper dive into prompt engineering in Chapter 3.

The Big Question: So, Will AI Take My Job?

It's impossible to talk about these powerful concepts without addressing the fear of being replaced. The honest answer is that AI is changing the job market, but it's not a simple story of replacement.

AI is not replacing the chef. It's replacing the onion-chopper. This fear of being replaced by a machine is a story as old as technology itself. In the early 1800s, English textile workers known as the Luddites famously smashed the new weaving looms that threatened their jobs. They were right that their specific tasks were being automated, but they couldn't have imagined the millions of new jobs the Industrial Revolution would create. Every major technological leap has followed a similar pattern: some tasks become obsolete, freeing up human ingenuity to invent entirely new roles. Think about the early automotive industry: the job of the master wheelwright, who painstakingly crafted wooden carriage wheels, vanished entirely. But in its place came a massive industry requiring designers, mechanics, assembly line workers, and supply chain managers, all new roles focused on the complex, higher-level task of building, selling, and maintaining the automobile. This means the competition is not between you and the AI; the competition is between you and the freelancer who uses AI better.

Think about it. The most tedious, repetitive, and rule-based parts of your gig are the most vulnerable to automation. But what about the uniquely human parts of your work?

- *Strategic thinking:* AI can analyze data, but it can't decide what a business's goals should be. That's the chef's job.
- *Empathy and client relationships:* AI can't understand a client's frustration or build the kind of trust that leads to long-term partnerships.
- *True creativity:* AI can generate ideas based on patterns, but it can't have that flash of inspiration that changes the game. That's the soul of the artist.

The future of freelance work belongs to those who focus on elevating these human skills, using AI as a powerful assistant to handle the rest. Your value is no longer just in your ability to *do* the task but in your ability to *direct* the task. You are the creative director, the strategist, and the final quality control.

By understanding the concepts in this chapter, you're preparing yourself for this future. You're learning to speak the language of your new AI partner, allowing you to stay in the driver's seat and command the entire kitchen.

Badge Achievement Plan: Understanding Your AI Sidekick

Complete the following missions to demonstrate your skills and earn your badge!

You've just explored how machines *learn*, from supervised learning that follows examples to unsupervised learning that finds patterns on its own, and how concepts like NLP let AI understand and respond to human language. Now it's time to connect those ideas to your daily hustle. This session will help you apply what you've learned to redesign your workflow, using AI to reduce repetitive work, spark insight, and open time for meaningful projects.

Time Required: 30 minutes

Goal: Use the core concepts from this chapter—machine learning, NLP, and the data science process—to map where AI can help you work smarter, faster, and more creatively.

What You Need:

- Access to a free AI tool (ChatGPT, Perplexity, or Notion AI)
- A notebook or digital document
- One real task from your weekly routine

Mission 1: Identify Your Top Three Time-Sinks (5 minutes)

First, let's find the opportunities. Think about your typical work week, and write down the answers to these questions:

1. What task eats up the most time every week (e.g., manually creating social media posts, sorting client emails, data entry)?
2. What type of work do I dread doing repeatedly (e.g., analyzing market trends, brainstorming new service ideas, creating visuals)?
3. What would I delegate if I had a smart assistant (e.g., finding new clients, managing my project pipeline, onboarding new customers)?

Now pick one task that feels like the perfect target for AI help. That's your "test case."

Mission 2: Meet Your Learning Mindsets (10 minutes)

Your AI learns in different ways. Let's test them with "special secret prompts."

Supervised Learning Mindset AI learns from examples. Show it what "good" looks like with past material you have written or with successful examples that you find online.

> Secret prompt: "Here are three examples of [great client emails / social posts / proposals I've written/ found]. Learn my style and write a new one for a [specific situation]."
> Reflection: Did the AI match your tone and format?

Unsupervised Learning Mindset AI can find hidden patterns without examples.

> Secret prompt: "I'm going to paste some client feedback. Group it by themes and tell me what main issues or opportunities you see."
> Reflection: Did it find insights you hadn't noticed?

NLP AI understands and summarizes language.

> Secret prompt: "Summarize this long document or meeting note into three bullet points with clear next steps."
> Reflection: How much time did it save you?

Mission 3: Reflect and Refine (10 minutes)

Ask yourself:

- What worked surprisingly well?
- What do I want to try next week?
- How can I keep improving my prompts to get better results?

> Secret prompt: "Suggest three small ways I can improve how I use AI in my daily freelance work."

Mission 4: Knowledge Check Quiz (10 minutes)

1. According to the chapter, why should a nontechnical freelancer care about the "robot brain" of AI?
   a. Because all freelancers will eventually need to become coders
   b. Because AI is the new infrastructure of the digital world, and understanding it helps you use it more effectively
   c. Because AI tools are expensive and require technical knowledge to purchase
   d. Because you need to be able to build your own AI from scratch to stay competitive
2. The chapter explains machine learning by comparing it to how a human learns to tell a cat from a dog. What is the core idea of this analogy?
   a. Learning is a slow process that requires a detailed rulebook
   b. AI learns by building an intuitive understanding from thousands of examples, not by memorizing a strict set of "if-then" rules
   c. Only humans can truly learn, and machines just pretend to
   d. The most important part of learning is having a good teacher
3. How can a freelancer use their understanding of supervised learning to their advantage on a platform like Upwork or Fiverr?
   a. By creating a very simple and vague profile to appeal to a broader range of clients
   b. By supervising the AI to make sure it doesn't make mistakes in its recommendations
   c. By packing their profile with specific, searchable keywords that act as "labels" to help the platform's AI match them with the best gigs
   d. By reporting other freelancers who use AI-generated profile descriptions
4. A writer analyzes all of their past articles and discovers that their posts about "sustainable technology" consistently get the most engagement. This process of finding a hidden, profitable niche is an example of applying which mindset?
   a. The supervised learning mindset
   b. The AI agent mindset
   c. The unsupervised learning mindset
   d. The computer vision mindset
5. What is the primary function of natural language processing (NLP)?
   a. To give computers the ability to see and interpret images and videos
   b. To give computers the ability to understand, interpret, and generate human language
   c. To create autonomous AI agents that can manage entire projects
   d. To analyze sales data and find hidden customer groups

6. The chapter describes data science as the work of a "head chef." What is the most important first step in the data science process for a freelancer?
   a. Gathering as much data as possible from every source
   b. Asking a smart, human-driven question about their own business (e.g., "Where do my best clients come from?")
   c. Buying the most advanced AI analytics software available
   d. Creating a beautiful chart to present to potential clients
7. What is the key difference between a standard AI chatbot and an AI agent?
   a. An AI agent is free to use, whereas a chatbot requires a paid subscription
   b. A chatbot answers single prompts, whereas an agent can take on a complex, multistep goal and work autonomously to achieve it
   c. Only coders can build AI agents
   d. An AI agent can see and hear, but a chatbot cannot
8. The chapter uses the phrase "AI is not replacing the chef. It's replacing the onion-chopper." What is the main point of this analogy?
   a. AI is primarily a threat to workers in the food service industry
   b. Freelancers should avoid all tasks that are repetitive, like chopping onions
   c. The creative and strategic parts of a job (the "chef") become more valuable, and the tedious, repetitive parts (the "onion-chopper") are what get automated
   d. Only chefs will be able to find work in the future
9. The chapter warns that an AI trained on historical sales data might suggest lower prices for female-run businesses. This is an example of what critical concept?
   a. An AI hallucination
   b. Unsupervised learning discovering a new pattern
   c. An AI agent going rogue
   d. Inherited bias, where an AI learns and reproduces the systemic biases present in its training data

Answer Sheet

1. **B: Because AI is the new infrastructure of the digital world, and understanding it helps you use it more effectively**

   The chapter makes the case that AI is already everywhere, from the algorithms on social media to the GPS in your car, and understanding the basics helps you navigate this new landscape.

2. **B: AI learns by building an intuitive understanding from thousands of examples, not by memorizing a strict set of "if-then" rules**

   The "cat and dog" analogy is used to show that modern machine learning is about pattern recognition from vast amounts of data, just like our brains learn from experience.

3. **C: By packing their profile with specific, searchable keywords that act as "labels" to help the platform's AI match them with the best gigs**

   The chapter directly connects supervised learning to freelance platforms, explaining that a well-optimized profile with clear "labels" makes it easier for the matching algorithm to recommend you.

4. **C: The unsupervised learning mindset**

   This is a perfect example of unsupervised learning: analyzing a pile of unlabeled data (your past articles) to discover hidden "clusters" or patterns (a profitable niche).

5. **B: To give computers the ability to understand, interpret, and generate human language**

   The chapter defines NLP as the "mouth and ears" of AI, responsible for bridging the gap between human language and computer processing.

6. **B: Asking a smart, human-driven question about their own business (e.g., "Where do my best clients come from?")**

   The "head chef" analogy for data science emphasizes that the process always starts with human curiosity and a strategic question.

7. **B: A chatbot answers single prompts, whereas an agent can take on a complex, multistep goal and work autonomously to achieve it**

   The chapter defines an agent's key capability as its ability to plan, execute, and self-correct to achieve a high-level objective, not just respond to one-off commands.

8. **C: The creative and strategic parts of a job (the "chef") become more valuable, and the tedious, repetitive parts (the "onion-chopper") are what get automated**

   This analogy summarizes the chapter's core argument about the future of work: AI handles the grunt work, making the strategic human role even more critical and valuable.

9. **D: Inherited bias, where an AI learns and reproduces the systemic biases present in its training data**

   The chapter uses this specific example to warn readers that because AI learns from real-world data, it can accidentally learn and perpetuate historical injustices, like wage gaps, if not carefully designed.

Congratulations!

By completing these missions, you've moved beyond surface-level AI use and started to understand *how* it really works. You can now explain the difference between supervised and unsupervised learning, describe how natural language processing allows AI to understand and generate human language, and apply the data science process to your own projects. These are the building blocks of true AI literacy, the kind that helps you not just *use* tools but also *think* like someone who can design smarter workflows and solve complex problems.

Once you finish, submit your responses by following the badge submission instructions listed in Chapter 1 or at `https://civicai.khoury.northeastern.edu/ai-for-gig-workers`. This badge shows that you understand the inner mechanics of AI, a skill few freelancers can claim. It demonstrates that you can translate technical concepts into practical solutions, making you not only efficient but also trustworthy in the eyes of clients and collaborators. Add it to your portfolio or LinkedIn to highlight that you don't just follow AI trends, you understand them.

What You Have Gained

You have just completed a full tour of your AI sidekick's engine room. You now understand the core concepts that power the tools transforming the gig economy. You have seen how machine learning allows your AI to learn from examples, much like your own brain, and how its different flavors, supervised and unsupervised learning, help you master platforms and uncover new opportunities in your business. By adopting a data science mindset, you have learned how to stop guessing and start making smart, evidence-based decisions.

More than just theory, you now have a strategic advantage. You know that understanding these principles is the key to turning your freelance hustle into a truly profitable and sustainable business. You are no longer just driving the taco truck; you are learning how to tune the engine, read the road, and plan the next big destination.

Now that you understand how AI learns and thinks, it is time to focus on how you communicate with it. Using these tools effectively is not only about knowing what they can do, but about how you ask, guide, and collaborate with them. In the next chapter, “Mastering AI Communication: The Art of Prompt Engineering,” you will learn how to turn your ideas into clear, powerful prompts that bring out AI’s best work while keeping your unique voice and creative style at the center.

CHAPTER 3

Mastering AI Communication: The Art of Prompt Engineering

Running your gig is like commanding a taco truck at the world's busiest food festival. You've got your AI tools lined up like kitchen equipment, but here's the thing: even the best sous-chef needs clear instructions to make your signature tacos shine. The magic isn't just in the tool, it's in *how you talk to it*. That's where prompt engineering comes in: it's the art of talking to AI tools so they actually understand what you want.

Think of prompts as the way you place your order at the taco truck. If you just say "Give me food," you might get something edible, but probably not what you wanted. If you say "One al pastor taco, extra salsa, no onions, and make it to go," suddenly you're walking away with exactly what you pictured.

Why This Matters for Your Hustle

Here's the deal: the freelance world is competitive as hell. Everyone's fighting for the same clients, the same gigs, the same opportunities. The difference between landing that dream project and watching it go to someone else often comes down to speed and quality. And that's exactly where prompt engineering becomes your secret weapon. When you know how to communicate clearly with AI, you can turn a 2-hour task into a 20-minute one. You can create content that actually sounds like you, draft emails that get responses, and produce work that makes clients think "damn, this person really gets it."

The best part? You don't need to be a tech genius to master this. It's more like learning to order at a restaurant in a foreign country: once you know the right phrases, you get exactly what you want every time.

The Four Ingredients of a Perfect Prompt

Just like your perfect taco needs the right balance of ingredients, a great prompt has four essential elements. Miss one, and your AI output will be as disappointing as a taco truck that runs out of hot sauce.

1. *Be specific (tell it exactly what you want):* Vague prompts are like ordering "some food" at a restaurant. You might get a salad when you wanted a burger. Instead of asking AI to "write an email," try "write a professional but friendly email to reschedule our Tuesday meeting to Friday, keep it under 100 words, and include an apology for the short notice." See the difference? The first one gives you generic mush. The second gives you something you can actually send to a client without cringing.
2. *Give context (paint the picture):* AI isn't psychic. It doesn't know you're a freelance graphic designer talking to a startup client versus a tutor explaining math to a confused parent. Give it the background story. Instead of "create a social media post," try "I'm a freelance marketing consultant posting on LinkedIn to attract small business owners who need help with social media strategy. Write a post about common Instagram mistakes, keep it professional but approachable, under 200 words." Context is like telling your taco truck cook whether you're serving lunch rush workers who need food fast or late-night party-goers who want something Instagram-worthy.
3. *Set boundaries (give it rules to follow):* Constraints aren't limitations, they're lifesavers. Tell AI exactly what format you need, how long the result should be, and what tone to use. It's like giving your kitchen clear portion sizes and plating instructions. "Write a proposal" becomes "Write a 500-word project proposal for redesigning a small business website, include timeline and pricing structure, professional but warm tone, formatted with clear sections and bullet points."
4. *Choose your flavor (set the tone):* This is where your personality shines through. Do you want the AI to sound corporate and buttoned-up? Casual and friendly? Enthusiastic and energetic? The tone you choose should

match your brand and your audience. Think about it like seasoning your tacos. The same base ingredients can taste completely different depending on whether you add mild ranch or ghost pepper sauce.

Common Mistakes That Kill Your Prompts

Let us save you some frustration by pointing out the mistakes we see freelancers make all the time. It's like watching someone put ketchup on a perfectly good taco: technically possible, but why would you do that to yourself?

- *The "throw everything at the wall" approach:* Don't cram every detail into one massive prompt. Some people write prompts longer than the content they want created. If you find yourself writing a novel to explain what you want, break it down into smaller, clearer requests.
- *The "figure it out yourself" problem:* AI isn't your mind reader. If you don't give it context, it'll make assumptions, and those assumptions are usually wrong. It's like expecting your taco truck employee to know that the customer wants extra spicy sauce when they just said "make it good."
- *The "one size fits all" trap:* A prompt that works great for writing social media captions might be terrible for drafting client emails. Different tasks need different approaches, just like different customers need different levels of spice.

Advanced Techniques (Once You've Mastered the Basics)

Once you're comfortable with basic prompting, here are some pro techniques that'll make your AI work like a seasoned chef who knows your preferences by heart:

- *Chain your requests:* Break complex tasks into steps. Instead of asking for a complete marketing campaign in one go, start with "create five headline options for a social media ad targeting small business owners." Then, "expand the best headline into a full ad copy, 150 words, conversational tone." Finally, "suggest three calls-to-action that would work with this ad." It's like prepping your taco ingredients in order: meat first, then toppings, then assembly. Each step builds on the last.

- *Iterate and improve:* Don't expect perfection on the first try. If the output is close but not quite right, tell the AI what to adjust: "make it more casual," "add specific examples," "shorten the introduction." Treat it like taste-testing and adjusting your recipe.
- *Prompt engineering for admin life:* Prompts aren't only for creative work; they can run your admin life, too. Try asking: "Pretend you're my virtual assistant. I need a workflow for onboarding new clients: contracts, invoices, follow-ups. Create a step-by-step checklist." "Act like a project manager. Organize my tasks for this week into priority order, and flag which ones I can delegate." AI responds better when you assign it a role and give it structure.
- *Give it a role:* One of the easiest tricks is the "pretend you are. . ." prompt, in which the AI wears that hat and speaks from that perspective. Here's a simple formula to remember: Pretend [who you are], [what you want], [how you want it], [where it applies]. Example: "Pretend you are a career coach. I want feedback on my LinkedIn bio, written in a supportive but professional tone, for the tech industry."
- *Show examples:* If you have a specific style in mind, show the AI an example of what you want. "Write a bio similar to this one, but for a freelance graphic designer instead of a photographer."
- *Define limits with prompts:* Just as important as telling AI what you want is telling it what you *don't* want. That's where negative prompting comes in. "Write a client proposal in plain English. Do not use corporate jargon or buzzwords." "Summarize this article in 150 words. Don't include emojis or hashtags." This is like telling the taco chef "Extra salsa, but please, no onions." It keeps your results closer to your taste.
- *Avoid hallucinations:* AI is powerful, but let's be real: sometimes it hallucinates. It invents dates and quotes, or even makes up entire studies. The good news? You can minimize this with a few simple habits:
  - *Be specific with time and place:* Instead of "Write an invite for an event on Monday," say "Write an invite for an event on Monday, March 3, 2026, at 7 p.m." Always feed your AI the exact details you know for sure (dates, numbers, names). It's like giving the taco guy your exact address instead of just saying "somewhere in town."
  - *Double-check facts:* If you ask for stats, always confirm the sources. AI is a great assistant, but it's not your fact-checker.
  - *Shorter steps, clearer results:* Break complex tasks into smaller prompts instead of asking for everything at once.

Keep It Real and Keep It Honest

Here's something important: be up front about using AI. You don't need to hide it like some dirty secret. Most clients actually appreciate the efficiency, as long as you're adding your own expertise and personal touch. Think of AI like any other tool in your kitchen. You wouldn't be ashamed of using a food processor to chop vegetables; it just makes you more efficient. The magic happens when you combine that efficiency with your skills, creativity, and understanding of what your clients actually need.

Fact-Checking AI Output

When it comes to fact-checking with AI, you can use a few key strategies to ensure accuracy. The first is to ask the AI directly about its sources, prompting it to "List the sources you used for this answer." You can also try a cross-examination approach by asking it to "Give me three alternative sources that confirm this statistic." Finally, you can force the AI to be transparent by telling it, "If you don't know, say 'I don't know' instead of inventing."

For data, research, or client-facing reports that require complete accuracy, always supplement your AI fact-check with a quick Google search or a trusted database. For example, a UX designer once asked an AI to write an email citing an industry trend. The AI confidently made up a "2023 Adobe UX Survey" that didn't exist. The designer caught the error by asking for a direct link to the report. When the AI couldn't provide one, they knew to double-check the information themselves. Don't serve a taco you haven't tasted. Before you pass information on to a client, make sure it's real. Use AI as your prep cook, but you are the final inspector.

Your Next Steps

Start simple. Pick one task you do regularly, maybe writing client emails, creating social media posts, or drafting project proposals. Spend a few minutes crafting a really specific prompt using the four ingredients we talked about. Test it, tweak it, and keep refining until you get output that actually sounds like something you'd be proud to send.

Remember, mastering prompt engineering is like perfecting your taco recipe. It takes a little practice, but once you nail it, you'll wonder how you ever worked without it. Your AI tools will go from being random kitchen gadgets to essential team members who help you serve up exactly what your clients are craving.

The goal isn't to have AI do all your work, it's to have it handle the time-consuming parts so you can focus on the creative, strategic, relationship-building aspects that actually grow your business. Now let's get you some practice with the real thing.

Badge Achievement Plan: The Art of Prompt Engineering

Complete the following missions to demonstrate your skills and earn your badge!

You have just learned how to communicate with your AI sidekick like a pro. You now understand how the quality of your results depends on the quality of your instructions, and how the four ingredients of a great prompt: specificity, context, boundaries, and tone, work together to produce professional, reliable outcomes. This session will help you apply those principles to real-world freelance situations so you can write prompts that get better results, save time, and strengthen your personal voice instead of losing it.

Time Required: 35 minutes

Goal: Use your new prompt engineering skills to write clear, structured, and context-rich instructions that improve your results and reflect your professional tone.

What You Need:

- A notebook, notes app, or simple document to write and test your prompts
- At least one real task from your freelance or creative work that you would like AI to help you with

Mission 1: The Reality Check (5 minutes)

First, let's show you why most gig workers give up on AI. Try one of these terrible prompts:

- Drivers: "Help me make more money"
- Content creators: "Write something for Instagram"
- Virtual assistants: "Make my emails better"
- Tutors: "Create a lesson plan"

What You'll Get: Generic garbage that's useless for real client work.

Mission 2: The Pro Gig Worker Fix (10 minutes)

Now try these secret prompts that actually understand the gig economy:

For drivers:

"I'm a rideshare driver working evening hours in [your city]. Write a professional text template thanking customers and mentioning I'm available for return trips. Under 160 characters, friendly but not pushy."

For content creators:

"I'm a [your niche] creator with 2K followers trying to reach 5K. Write an Instagram post about [topic] with a personal story, actionable tip, and engagement question. Under 200 words, casual tone, include 5 non-oversaturated hashtags."

For virtual assistants:

"I'm a VA managing social media for a [industry] client. Write a polite but firm email about work requests outside our scope. Acknowledge the request, remind them of our agreement, offer to expand services at current rates. Under 150 words, professional but warm."

For tutors:

"I'm an online tutor teaching [subject] to [grade level] over Zoom. Create a 45-minute lesson plan for [topic] with 3 interactive activities for short attention spans, quick assessment, and homework."

Test the one that matches your gig. Notice how much more useful this is?

Mission 3: Create Your Money-Making Prompts (10 minutes)

Make three prompts for tasks that:

- You do repeatedly
- Directly impact your income
- Currently waste your time

Template: "I'm a [gig type] in [location] working with [typical clients]. [Specific request]. [Your situation/challenges]. [Length, format, tone]. [Outcome you need]."

Your three prompts:

1. Income-booster: ________________
2. Time-saver: ________________
3. Client relationship: ________________

Test and rate: Try each prompt, and rate it:

- Money maker: Will definitely improve income/efficiency
- Potential: Good foundation, needs minor tweaks
- Needs work: Back to the drawing board

Action plan:

- This week: Use your best prompt for real client work and time the difference.
- This month: Build a library of 10 prompts for common gig tasks.
- Remember: In the gig economy, time = money. Every minute saved with better prompts is a minute you can spend earning. Master this skill and pull ahead of freelancers still doing everything manually.

Try these exercises to practice smarter prompting:

1. *Role-play:* Ask AI to "pretend" to be your project manager. Have it organize your tasks for the week into priorities, and then ask, "Which of these could I delegate?"
2. *Negative prompts:* Pick a piece of writing (email, proposal, post). Ask AI to rewrite it in plain English, and tell it explicitly *not* to use jargon, filler words, or clichés.
3. *Catch a hallucination:* Ask AI for a statistic in your field. Then immediately follow up with "Provide the source." Notice whether it can give you a real, verifiable link.
4. *Prompt formula practice:* Write three prompts using the "Pretend [who you are], [what you want], [how you want it], [where it applies]" formula. Compare the results with your usual way of asking.

Mission 4: Knowledge Check Quiz (10 minutes)

1. What is the main idea behind "prompt engineering"?
   a. It is the technical skill of coding a new AI from scratch
   b. It is the art of giving clear and specific instructions to an AI to get high-quality results

   c. It is a method for checking AI-generated text for plagiarism
   d. It is the process of selling prompts to other freelancers
2. The chapter compares a vague prompt like "write an email" to what kind of order at a taco truck?
   a. Ordering five beef tacos with extra cilantro
   b. Ordering "some food" and getting a salad when you wanted a burger
   c. Asking for the spiciest hot sauce available
   d. Complaining that the food is cold
3. Which of the following is *not* one of the "four ingredients of a perfect prompt" discussed in the chapter?
   a. Be specific
   b. Give context
   c. Set boundaries
   d. Be vague to encourage creativity
4. Why is it important to "give context" when writing a prompt?
   a. To make the prompt as long as possible
   b. Because AI is not a mind reader and needs the background story to provide a relevant response
   c. To confuse the AI and test its limits
   d. It is only necessary when asking for numerical data
5. A freelancer who tries to get a complete, complex project proposal from an AI by writing one single, massive prompt is making which common mistake?
   a. The "one size fits all" trap
   b. The "figure it out yourself" problem
   c. The "throw everything at the wall" approach
   d. The "keep it honest" mistake
6. Telling an AI to "Act like an experienced email marketer and write a subject line that gets opened" is an example of which advanced technique?
   a. Chain your requests
   b. Give it a role
   c. Show examples
   d. Iterate and improve
7. What is the "chain your requests" technique?
   a. Asking the AI the same question repeatedly
   b. Breaking down a large, complex task into a series of smaller, sequential prompts
   c. Linking your AI account to your social media accounts
   d. Using a prompt that was written by another freelancer

8. What is the chapter's advice on being honest with clients about using AI?
   a. You should always hide your AI usage because clients view it negatively
   b. You should be up front about using AI as an efficiency tool, as most clients appreciate it when you also add your own expertise
   c. You should only mention AI if the client specifically asks about your tools
   d. You should claim you built the AI yourself to impress the client
9. The "choose your flavor" ingredient of a perfect prompt refers to what?
   a. The specific data points you want the AI to include
   b. Setting the tone and personality of the AI's response (e.g., professional, casual, friendly)
   c. The color scheme for any visual output
   d. Telling the AI what topic to write about
10. Why is a prompt like "Help me make more money" considered a "terrible prompt"?
    a. It is too ambitious for an AI to handle
    b. It will cause the AI to give you incorrect financial advice
    c. It is generic garbage that is useless for real client work because it lacks any context or specificity
    d. It is a prompt that costs extra to use

Answer Sheet

1. **B: It is the art of giving clear and specific instructions to an AI to get high-quality results**

   The chapter introduces prompt engineering as the crucial skill of communicating clearly with AI to turn a 2-hour task into a 20-minute one.

2. **B: Ordering "some food" and getting a salad when you wanted a burger**

   This analogy is used to show how a vague prompt can lead to a result that is technically correct but not what you actually wanted or needed.

3. **D: Be vague to encourage creativity**

   The chapter's core argument is that specificity, context, and boundaries lead to better AI output. Vague prompts are listed as a problem, not an ingredient for success.

4. **B: Because AI is not a mind reader and needs the background story to provide a relevant response**

   The chapter states directly that "AI isn't psychic" and needs context to understand if you're a designer talking to a startup or a tutor talking to a parent.

5. **C: The "throw everything at the wall" approach**

   This mistake is defined as cramming every detail into one massive prompt instead of breaking it down into smaller, clearer requests.

6. **B: Give it a role**

   This advanced technique involves telling the AI to adopt the persona of a specific expert to make its response more focused and valuable.

7. **B: Breaking down a large, complex task into a series of smaller, sequential prompts**

   The chapter describes this technique as asking for headlines first, then the ad copy, and then the call to action, with each step building on the last.

8. **B: You should be up front about using AI as an efficiency tool, as most clients appreciate it when you also add your own expertise**

   The chapter advises against hiding AI use, comparing it to a chef using a food processor and noting that most clients appreciate the efficiency it brings.

9. **B: Setting the tone and personality of the AI's response (e.g., professional, casual, friendly)**

   This ingredient is where your "personality shines through," and it's compared to choosing the right seasoning for your tacos to match your brand and audience.

10. **C: It is generic garbage that is useless for real client work because it lacks any context or specificity**

    The "Reality Check" section (Mission 1) of the exercise uses this and other similar prompts to demonstrate how vague requests lead to generic outputs that are not helpful for a professional gig worker.

Congratulations!

By completing these missions, you have learned to speak the language of your AI sidekick with precision and purpose. You now understand how to transform vague ideas into powerful prompts that produce high-quality results, and how specificity, context, boundaries, and tone shape the outcome every time. You have moved from being a passive user to a creative director, guiding your AI with clarity and intent.

Prompt engineering is not about coding; it is about conversation. You have discovered that your words are the code, and that the clearer and more intentional you are, the better your AI becomes. Like a master chef commanding their kitchen, you now know how to give exact instructions that lead to consistent, professional results.

Once you finish, submit your responses by following the badge submission instructions listed in Chapter 1 or at `https://civicai.khoury.northeastern.edu/ai-for-gig-workers`. This badge shows that you have mastered one of the most valuable digital skills of the decade: the ability to communicate effectively with intelligent systems. Display it in your portfolio or LinkedIn profile to show that you do not just use AI tools, you collaborate with them.

What You Have Gained

You have learned how to place the perfect order and how to talk to AI so that it delivers exactly what you need. You now understand how to guide your sidekick using clear prompts that include context, structure, and tone, transforming it from a clever assistant into a reliable creative partner. You have seen how precision can turn a generic response into something useful, original, and uniquely yours.

This skill is more than a shortcut; it is a cornerstone of the future of work. By mastering prompt engineering, you have learned to collaborate with AI as an equal, one that listens, adapts, and amplifies your best ideas. You have also gained confidence in your ability to lead technology rather than follow it.

Now that you know how to communicate with AI, it is time to take the next step: delegation. In the next chapter, "Agentic AI," you will learn how to build a digital teammate that not only understands your goals but can act on them. You will move from giving perfect instructions to letting your AI take initiative, automating workflows, and scaling your one-person hustle into a powerful digital team.

CHAPTER 4

Agentic AI

AI Agents: Hiring Your First Autonomous Employee

You have learned how AI thinks and how to speak its language through prompt engineering. Now it is time to explore the next frontier: AI agents. If a regular AI chatbot is like a brilliant intern who can answer any question you ask, an AI agent is more like a project manager who understands your big goals and takes action to reach them. It is the difference between asking for a recipe and having someone who can plan the menu, shop for the ingredients, and start cooking while you focus on the next big idea. You give the AI agent a complex, multistep objective, and the agent itself will:

1. *Create a plan:* It breaks down the high-level goal into a series of smaller, actionable tasks.
2. *Execute the tasks:* It begins working through its own to-do list, which can involve actions like browsing the web, reading documents, or writing code.
3. *Self-correct:* It analyzes the results of its actions, learns from its mistakes, and adjusts its plan accordingly to stay on track toward the goal.

It's the difference between asking a chef, "What is the recipe for salsa?" (a simple prompt) and telling them, "Increase our salsa sales by 20% this month" (a goal for an agent). The agent would then independently research popular recipes, analyze your past sales data, draft a marketing plan for a new "Salsa of the Week," and schedule social media posts to promote it, all without you needing to manage every single step.

Although this technology is still emerging, it represents a monumental shift from using AI as a simple tool to using it as an autonomous teammate.

How AI Agents Actually Work

At a technical level, AI agents may seem complex, but the concept is surprisingly simple. Think of every agent as having three main parts: a goal, a brain, a toolbox, and memory.

The Goal This is the mission you give it: the result you want, not the steps to get there. Instead of telling it *how* to work, you tell it *what* success looks like. For example:

> *"Find five potential clients in the wellness space, gather their contact information, and draft personalized outreach emails."*

A basic chatbot would stop after generating the first email. An agent understands that it needs to research, verify, and create until the whole job is done.

The Brain

The "brain" is powered by a large language model (LLM) like the one that powers ChatGPT. What makes it special is that it can reason in loops. It doesn't just reply once and stop; it *thinks, acts, checks, and repeats* until it achieves your goal. For example, if it discovers that two of the five wellness brands no longer exist, it automatically finds replacements and continues the process.

The Toolbox The agent connects to the outside world through tools and data:

- It might use APIs to search the web or send emails.
- It might reference files you upload, like your client list or portfolio.
- It can use plug-ins or connected apps (like Notion, Slack, or Google Sheets) to get work done automatically.

Memory Basic AIs forget everything when the chat ends. Agents don't. They can remember your preferences, client details, or pricing updates across sessions. Over time, they adapt to your tone, workflows, and even your goals, becoming more efficient the more you use them.

Together, these elements form the agent's workflow loop:

1. Read your goal.
2. Break it down into steps.
3. Choose the right tools.

4. Execute the actions.
5. Evaluate results and improve next time.

This combination of autonomy and memory is what transforms an AI from an assistant into a reliable team member.

How This Helps Your Freelance Hustle

For a solo freelancer, AI agents are more than just a time-saver. They're a way to scale your abilities and transform your one-person gig into a mini digital enterprise.

Here's how they can help you level up.

Operations and Productivity

- *Become a one-person agency:* AI agents allow you to multiply your output as if you had a full team. You can act as the creative director and CEO, while your agents function as your research department, your marketing team, and your administrative assistants. This allows you to take on larger, more complex projects that were previously only possible for agencies with a big staff.
- *Manage complex client projects:* In the near future, you'll be able to assign an agent a task like this: "Monitor our client's social media for the week. Analyze their top-performing posts from the last month, find three relevant news articles in their industry, and draft five new posts based on that analysis." The agent will handle the entire content workflow, from research to creation, leaving you to simply give the final approval.
- *Simplify proposal and contract management:* Instead of spending hours rewriting proposals or chasing client approvals, an AI agent can automatically adapt your proposal templates to fit each client's tone and budget. It can track when clients open your proposal, follow up with a friendly reminder, and even draft contract updates as your scope evolves. You get to focus on closing deals, not formatting documents.
- *Track performance and analytics:* Imagine never having to open a spreadsheet again. Your AI agent can pull key performance data from your website, social media, or invoices, summarize the trends, and show what's bringing in the most revenue or engagement. You can review weekly performance insights like a business owner, not a data analyst. This frees your energy to plan smarter moves for growth.

Growth and Business Development

- *Automate high-level research:* Imagine giving an agent a goal like "Find ten potential clients in the e-commerce space who recently received funding. For each one, identify their head of marketing, find their contact information, and draft a personalized outreach email that references their recent funding announcement." An AI agent can perform that entire multistep research and outreach process autonomously while you focus on your paid client work.
- *Build passive income systems:* AI agents can help you create systems that earn while you rest. You can assign an agent to monitor your online course enrollments, update your digital shop with trending keywords, or post repurposed content on your social channels. It can even automate follow-up emails that nurture leads or recommend your services to past clients. Over time, your agent becomes your digital business partner, keeping your brand alive and active 24/7.
- *Upskill while you work:* Freelancers don't have a learning department, but with AI agents, you can have your own. Set an agent to track industry updates, summarize top YouTube tutorials or articles about your niche, and deliver a short "learning digest" every Friday. You'll grow your expertise and stay ahead of your competitors without ever having to go down a research rabbit hole.

Client Communication and Support

- *Streamline client communication:* Client communication is one of the biggest time drains for freelancers. An AI agent can monitor your inbox, summarize long email threads, flag the ones that need a response, and even draft quick replies that match your tone. It can schedule calls, translate messages, and prepare recaps after meetings. This gives you back hours of focus time each week while still keeping your clients impressed with your professionalism.
- *Deliver 24/7 client support:* Clients operate in different time zones, and being constantly "on call" isn't sustainable. An AI agent can act as your round-the-clock assistant, answering FAQs, sending project updates, and ensuring that no message goes unanswered. You can wake up each morning to a neatly organized inbox, where every client feels supported, even while you were asleep.

AI agents represent the ultimate evolution of the AI sidekick. Think of it like this: instead of being the solo street taco vendor doing everything by hand, you now run the whole taquería. Your AI agents are the crew prepping ingredients, managing orders, and restocking supplies, all so you can focus on the sauce: the big-picture vision, the creative heat, the empire-building moves. With AI agents, you're not just working the job; you're designing the system. They are the tools that will allow you to move from being a freelance *worker* to a freelance *business owner*, delegating complex tasks to your digital team and freeing you to focus on the highest-level strategy and creative vision for your growing empire.

A Simple Guide to Building Your First AI Agent (No Coding Required)

The idea of an "autonomous employee" sounds futuristic and complex, but you can create your own specialized agent *right now* without writing a single line of code. The easiest way to do this is by using features within the AI tools you're already familiar with, or with a few that take only minutes to learn.

Think of it this way: you're not building a brand-new robot from scratch. Instead, you're taking your brilliant, all-purpose assistant (like ChatGPT) and giving it a special promotion. You're training it to become an expert in one specific role, complete with its own unique instructions and knowledge.

Where to Start and What It Costs

The most user-friendly platform for a non-technical person to use to build an agent-like assistant is GPTs, a feature available in ChatGPT Plus.

- *Where:* The GPT Builder in ChatGPT.
- *Cost:* This is a premium feature, so it requires a subscription to ChatGPT Plus (currently around $20/month).
- *Why:* It's designed for beginners. You build your agent simply by having a conversation in plain English, and you can give it specific documents to learn from, making it incredibly powerful.

But ChatGPT isn't your only option. Several no-code platforms now allow you to build powerful agents visually, using drag-and-drop workflows or pre-built templates.

Alternative Platforms for Building Agents

1. *Notion AI (Free or Plus Plan):* If you already use Notion to organize your projects, this is the easiest way to create lightweight agents. You can automate actions like sorting leads, rewriting bios, and generating client follow-ups directly from your workspace.
   - *Best for:* Admin tasks, note summaries, client onboarding checklists.
   - *Skill level:* Beginner.
   - *Bonus tip:* Use Notion's database and AI features together to create agents that automatically update project timelines or generate reports when you finish tasks.
2. **Make.com** *(formerly Integromat):* **Make.com** lets you connect your favorite tools like Gmail, Google Sheets, Trello, and Slack to create automated workflows. Each "scenario" acts like an agent that runs on its own once triggered.
   - *Best for:* Automating repetitive tasks like sending invoices, scheduling content, and moving client data between platforms.
   - *Skill level:* Beginner to intermediate.
   - *Bonus tip:* Combine **Make.com** with ChatGPT or OpenAI to build smart workflows that "think" before they act.
3. *Zapier AI (free tier available):* Zapier's AI Actions feature lets you create a simple agent that triggers multiple steps based on one command, like "Send a thank-you email to all clients who paid this week" or "Draft a LinkedIn post based on my latest blog entry."
   - *Best for:* Busy freelancers who want instant automations.
   - *Skill level:* Beginner.
   - *Bonus tip:* Start with a premade template like "AI Content Generator" or "Client Follow-Up Bot" to get instant results.
4. *Relevance AI or CrewAI (emerging platforms):* These tools specialize in building full "multiagent" systems, meaning your agents can communicate with each other. For instance, one agent can research, another can write, and another can edit.
   - *Best for:* Freelancers ready to scale or experiment with more advanced workflows.
   - *Skill level:* Intermediate.
   - *Bonus tip:* You can start small (a single agent) and later link multiple agents for tasks like client research, proposal writing, and email follow-up.

Step by Step: Creating Your First Custom Agent on ChatGPT Plus

Let's build an agent whose mission is to help you write better proposals.

Step 1: Define your agent's mission. Before you start, get crystal clear on your goal. What is this agent's one, specific job? Let's say our mission is "To act as an expert proposal writer who helps me draft winning proposals for graphic design projects."

Step 2: Open the GPT Builder. In ChatGPT, find the option Explore GPTs, and then click Create. You'll see a simple interface with two sides: a Create panel where you'll chat with the builder, and a Preview panel where you can test your new agent in real time.

Step 3: "Train" your agent by chatting with the builder. This is where the magic happens. You simply tell the builder what you want, and it will configure the agent for you. The conversation might look like this:

- You: "I want to create an AI assistant that helps me write proposals for graphic design clients."
- GPT Builder: "Great! What should we call it? How about 'Proposal Pro'?"
- You: "Perfect. Its primary role is to act as an expert business proposal writer. When I give it details about a client and a project, it should draft a proposal that includes a project overview, a timeline, a pricing section, and a call to action. It should always use a professional and confident tone."
- GPT Builder: "Understood. I've updated its instructions. Should it ask any specific questions before it starts writing?"
- You: "Yes, it should always ask me for the client's name, the project goal, the budget, and the deadline first."

Step 4: Give your agent special knowledge. This is the most powerful step. In the Configure tab, you'll see a section called Knowledge. Here, you can upload files that only your agent can see and use.

For our Proposal Pro agent, you could upload

- A PDF of your three most successful past proposals
- A document outlining your standard pricing and packages
- A text file with your company's mission and brand voice

Now, when you ask your agent to write a proposal, it won't just use its general knowledge; it will write it in *your style*, using *your pricing*, based on *your past successes*.

If you prefer a more visual approach, platforms like **Make.com**, Zapier, and Relevance AI let you build "if this, then that" style agents. You connect simple steps like "get info," "analyze," and "send" like puzzle pieces.

Example:

- *Trigger:* New client fills out your inquiry form.
- *Action 1:* Agent summarizes the client's info and adds it to your customer relationship management (CRM) system.
- *Action 2:* It drafts a personalized welcome email.
- *Action 3:* It schedules a discovery call in your calendar.

With just a few clicks, you've automated the entire onboarding flow. No code, no tech degree, just smart design.

How This Helps Your Freelance Hustle

By taking a few minutes to build your first agent, you're doing more than saving time; you're creating leverage. You move from using a generic tool to commanding a specialized expert that is perfectly tailored to your business needs. You're not working harder; you're working *through* your technology.

Today, it might just be one Proposal Pro agent. Tomorrow, it could be a Client Finder, Social Media Assistant, and Project Tracker, all running quietly in the background, helping you grow your business while you focus on what only humans can do: create, connect, and innovate.

You can create a whole team of agents:

- A Market Research Agent that you've instructed to always analyze trends specifically for your niche (e.g., sustainable fashion startups)
- A Social Media Agent that you've uploaded your brand voice guide to, ensuring that every post it drafts sounds exactly like you
- A Client Onboarding Agent that has your welcome packet and can instantly draft kickoff emails and project timelines based on your proven process
- A Portfolio Curator Agent that you've trained with your past work, testimonials, and case studies so it can instantly select and organize the most relevant examples for each new client proposal
- A Follow-Up and Retention Agent that you've instructed to track client activity and send timely check-ins or renewal reminders, helping you turn one-time projects into lasting partnerships

Once you understand how these moving parts fit together, you stop seeing AI as just a clever assistant and start thinking like a team leader. You can design your own workflows, build toolkits, and assign each agent a clear role in your business. The beauty is that you don't need to start from scratch or learn to code. Modern tools now let you create AI agents visually, connecting simple actions like "search," "summarize," and "send email." What once required a full team of developers can now be done by a freelancer on a laptop over a cup of *café de olla*.

AI agents are the closest thing freelancers have to cloning themselves. Once you grasp this, you can design an entire network of agents, each focused on a task that helps your business run smoother, faster, and smarter. This is the first step toward true automation: building a team of digital employees that understand you and your business, allowing you to work faster, maintain quality, and scale your freelance operation like never before.

Case Study: Freelancers Who Built Their First AI Agents

The best way to understand what's possible is to see how freelancers like you are already using AI agents to turn chaotic workflows into simple, scalable systems. These are everyday creatives and gig workers who started small, experimented, and built tools that transformed their one-person businesses.

Here's how they did it.

The Illustrator Who Reclaimed His Creative Time A freelance illustrator loved bringing client ideas to life but felt buried under endless admin work such as invoices, file management, and client updates.

He built his first agent using Zapier and ChatGPT: a simple system that summarized new client emails each morning and logged tasks directly into his Notion workspace. When clients requested changes, the agent automatically updated his project tracker and deadlines.

Within a week, he freed up almost a full workday of time. He later expanded his agent to draft client update emails and progress reports, leaving him more space to focus on drawing. His agent handles the small stuff; now he only touches what actually needs his creative brain.

The Screenwriter Who Built a "Pitch Writer" Agent A screenwriter once spent hours crafting personalized pitches for film projects and writing contests. When ChatGPT's Custom GPTs launched, she created Pitch Pro, an AI agent trained on her past scripts, winning submissions, and signature writing style.

Now, she simply provides it a few key details, such as theme, length, and tone, and her agent drafts a full pitch complete with a logline and a tight summary in her exact voice. What once took 2 hours now takes 15 minutes. Her agent doesn't replace her creativity; it just clears the clutter so her ideas can shine through.

The Musician Who Built a "Track Pitching" Agent A guitarist and composer spent most of his time creating music for brands and indie films. His biggest challenge was not writing songs but finding new clients to pitch them to.

He built an agent using Relevance AI that connected his portfolio with online music databases. It automatically identified new venues, brands, and collaborators that matched his genre, drafted a personalized message, attached his demo link, and followed up three days later if there was no reply.

Within three months, he booked five new collaborations, all from outreach done by his agent. It's like having a manager who never sleeps and never asks for a cut.

The Event Planner Who Built a "Client Care" Agent A freelance event planner managed everything from corporate launches to weddings. Her problem was not finding clients but keeping up with them afterward.

Using **Make.com**, she built a Client Care agent that monitors her calendar and client database. Two weeks after each event, the agent automatically sends a personalized thank-you note, requests feedback, and offers a discount for future bookings. It even drafts social media captions using highlights from her event photos.

The result: 30% more repeat bookings and a smoother, more polished client experience. Her agent helps her stay present with clients. It keeps the connection alive even when she's planning three events at once.

Each of these freelancers started with the same question: "What's one repetitive task that drains my time or energy?" They each built one small agent to fix it. No coding, no complicated setup, just smart delegation. Over time, they added new layers such as better prompts, shared data, and connected tools. That's the real power of AI agents. You do not need a full tech team to think like one. You start with one digital teammate, give it one job, and then promote it.

Badge Achievement Plan: Building Your First AI Agent

Complete the following missions to demonstrate your skills and earn your badge!

You have learned what AI agents are and how they can transform your freelance business from a solo act into a one-person agency. You now understand how agents can plan, act, and self-correct, handling complex tasks like research, communication, and content creation while you focus on strategy and creativity.

This session will help you design and launch your first digital teammate. You will define its mission, choose the right platform, and teach it how to think and act in your style. By the end, you will have your first working AI agent ready to support your business goals.

Time Required: 1 hour, 20 minutes

Goal: Build and test your first no-code AI agent that can perform a useful task in your freelance workflow, such as writing proposals, organizing client data, or automating outreach.

What You'll Need:

- A computer with internet access
- A ChatGPT Plus account or access to a no-code tool such as **Make.com**, Zapier, or Notion AI
- A few reference files (such as past proposals, templates, or client data) to train or connect your agent
- A clear idea of one task you want your agent to handle for you

Mission 1: Identify Your First Agent's Role (10 minutes)

Think about one task that constantly eats up your time. It might be repetitive admin work, client communication, outreach, or research. Ask yourself: *If I could hire a digital assistant to take care of this, what would I want it to do?*

Write a one-sentence mission statement for your agent.

> Example: "Act as my Market Research Agent, finding five new potential clients for my writing business every morning."
>
> Example: "Act as my Project Tracker Agent, updating deadlines and client notes in Notion at the end of each workday."

Goal: Define your first agent's job description clearly enough that it could start working today.

Mission 2: Choose the Right Platform (10 minutes)

You don't need to code to build an AI agent; you just need the right environment. Pick a tool from the following list and note why it fits your goal.

Platform	Best for	Cost	Why you might choose it
ChatGPT (custom GPTs)	Writing, proposals, research	$20/month	The easiest place to start. Great for creative or written workflows.
Make.com	Workflow automation	Free to low cost	Connects your favorite tools, like Gmail, Notion, and Slack.
Zapier AI	Fast, practical automations	Free + paid plans	Ideal for task reminders and quick multi-step flows.
Notion AI	Admin and organization	Free + paid plans	Perfect for summarizing notes, client logs, and content ideas.

Goal: Choose your "workplace," the environment where your first digital employee will live.

Mission 3: Build Your First Agent (20 minutes)

Using your chosen platform, set up your first agent with a simple, clear instruction. If you're using ChatGPT, go to Explore GPTs, Create and walk through the setup process. For a more advanced exercise, if you're using **Make.com** or Zapier, connect one or two apps and define the trigger (for example, "When I get a new client email. . .").

> Example: "Create a Custom GPT named Proposal Pro that helps me write a full proposal in under 10 minutes."
>
> Example: "Build a **Make.com** scenario that copies every new client email into a Notion database."

Goal: Create a working prototype, even a simple one, of your first digital teammate.

Mission 4: Give It Knowledge and Test It (15 minutes)

Now give your agent context. Upload the files, data, or examples it needs to work like *you.* In ChatGPT, this means adding files in the Knowledge tab. In **Make.com** or Zapier, it might mean connecting spreadsheets or templates.

For example, upload

- A PDF of your best proposals or project briefs
- A document outlining your pricing and tone of voice
- A list of your standard workflows or brand guidelines

Then, test your agent by giving it a real-world task.

Example: Use your Proposal Pro Agent to draft a proposal for a new client in the fashion industry.

Example 2: Ask your Research Agent to find three recent startups hiring designers.

Goal: See your agent in action and refine it until the output feels personal, professional, and useful.

Mission 5: Reflect and Expand (15 minutes)

Once your first agent works smoothly, ask yourself: *What else could it do?* Write down two or three additional agent ideas you'd love to have in your freelance business.

Example: "A Social Media agent that drafts posts in my brand voice."

Example: "A Project Summary agent that creates weekly reports for clients."

Example: "A Learning agent that finds new tools or tutorials related to my niche."

Goal: Begin designing your future agent network—your own digital team of specialists working behind the scenes to help you scale your freelance empire.

Mission 6: Final Knowledge Check Quiz (10 minutes)

Before you move on, test your understanding of how AI agents work and how they can expand your freelance business.

Each question has one best answer.

1. What is the key difference between a standard AI chatbot and an AI agent?
   - **a.** A chatbot can answer questions, whereas an AI agent can act autonomously toward a goal
   - **b.** A chatbot can only use text, whereas an AI agent uses voice commands
   - **c.** A chatbot is faster than an AI agent
   - **d.** A chatbot can be used offline, whereas an AI agent requires internet access
2. According to the "Simple Guide to Building Your First AI Agent," what is the most powerful feature of creating a custom GPT?
   - **a.** It can access your email automatically
   - **b.** It can learn from specific files and knowledge you upload, allowing it to write in your tone and follow your process
   - **c.** It replaces all your admin software
   - **d.** It costs less than $5 per month
3. Which of the following best describes the *"think–act–check–repeat"* loop used by AI agents?
   - **a.** A cycle that allows the agent to reason through tasks, check results, and adjust its actions until it completes a goal
   - **b.** A process for designing better chat prompts
   - **c.** A security feature that limits what the agent can do
   - **d.** A method for improving AI graphics quality
4. Why is memory an important feature for an AI agent?
   - **a.** It allows the agent to remember your preferences, tone, and instructions across tasks.
   - **b.** It helps the agent generate faster responses without internet access
   - **c.** It limits how many files the agent can access at once
   - **d.** It reduces the cost of using AI tools
5. Which of the following is the best first step when designing your own agent?
   - **a.** Connecting as many apps as possible to test integrations
   - **b.** Writing a clear, one-sentence mission statement describing the agent's main job
   - **c.** Purchasing multiple premium subscriptions
   - **d.** Copying another freelancer's setup

6. According to the chapter, what kinds of platforms can freelancers use to build no-code AI agents?
   a. ChatGPT (custom GPTs), Make.com, Zapier AI, and Notion AI
   b. Photoshop, Canva, and TikTok
   c. Microsoft Excel and Google Docs
   d. Blender, Premiere Pro, and GarageBand
7. Which example best fits how an AI agent could help a freelancer scale their business?
   a. A graphic designer's agent that finds new clients, updates their portfolio, and drafts project proposals
   b. A chef's agent that cooks meals in their kitchen
   c. A student's agent that writes homework essays
   d. A driver's agent that fuels their car automatically
8. Why is it important to start with just one small agent instead of trying to automate everything at once?
   a. It's safer and easier to manage, and it lets you learn from small wins before expanding
   b. Most tools allow only one agent per account
   c. Building multiple agents at once is illegal
   d. AI agents work on only one type of project at a time
9. What is one ethical responsibility freelancers should remember when using AI agents with clients?
   a. Always disclose when automation is being used and review results before delivering final work
   b. Never tell clients you use AI
   c. Let the agent handle contracts without review
   d. Store all client data publicly to improve the agent's learning
10. When your first agent is running smoothly, what should you do next, according to the chapter?
    a. Build a network of agents, each handling a single, clear task that supports your freelance business
    b. Turn off your agent and start over
    c. Delete your files to save space
    d. Stop using AI entirely

Answer Sheet

1. **A: A chatbot can answer questions, whereas an AI agent can act autonomously toward a goal**

   A chatbot stops after one response. An AI agent keeps going, planning steps, checking results, and completing a goal on its own.

2. **B: It can learn from specific files and knowledge you upload, allowing it to write in your tone and follow your process**

   The power of Custom GPTs is personalization. Your agent learns from your materials so it can sound and think like you.

3. **A: A cycle that allows the agent to reason through tasks, check results, and adjust its actions until it completes a goal**

   This loop—think, act, check, repeat—gives agents autonomy. They don't just react; they self-correct and improve.

4. **A: It allows the agent to remember your preferences, tone, and instructions across tasks**

   Memory makes your agent smarter over time. It remembers how you like to work and gets better with every project.

5. **B: Writing a clear, one-sentence mission statement describing the agent's main job**

   Every effective agent starts with a clear goal. Defining one specific mission keeps it focused and easy to train.

6. **A: ChatGPT (Custom GPTs), Make.com, Zapier AI, and Notion AI**

   These are all no-code tools that freelancers without programming knowledge can use to build functional, automated agents.

7. **A: A graphic designer's agent that finds new clients, updates their portfolio, and drafts project proposals**

   This example shows an AI agent performing real, high-value freelance tasks that scale a creative business.

8. **A: It's safer and easier to manage, and it lets you learn from small wins before expanding**

   Starting small helps you understand your agent's behavior and limits before automating more complex workflows.

9. **A: Always disclose when automation is being used and review results before delivering final work**

   Transparency and human oversight build trust with clients and ensure that your automated systems maintain quality.

10. **A: Build a network of agents, each handling a single, clear task that supports your freelance business**

    Once one agent works well, the next step is scale: a digital team of agents, each focused on a different part of your business.

Congratulations!

By completing these missions, you have moved beyond using AI as a tool and learned to manage it like a true digital leader. You now understand how to build, configure, and train your own AI agents to think, plan, and act toward your goals. You have discovered how to delegate work to intelligent systems that can research, organize, write, and communicate while you focus on creativity, strategy, and growth.

You have also built your first working agent, proving that you can design automation that serves your unique workflow without needing to code. Whether you used ChatGPT, **Make.com**, Zapier, or Notion AI, you now have hands-on experience turning an idea into a functioning digital teammate. You are no longer simply prompting AI; you are directing it.

Once you finish, submit your responses by following the badge submission instructions listed in Chapter 1 or at `https://civicai.khoury.northeastern.edu/ai-for-gig-workers`. This badge recognizes your ability to create, manage, and lead autonomous systems. Display it proudly in your portfolio or LinkedIn profile to show that you can build and supervise AI-powered workflows that make your freelance business smarter, faster, and more scalable.

What You Have Gained

You've leveled up from tech user to team leader—from someone working the grill to the one running the whole taco stand. You now understand how AI agents function, how to give them clear missions, and how to hook them up with the right tools to power your business. You've seen how even one well-trained agent can take a repetitive task off your plate, freeing up precious hours for the juicy stuff: strategy, creativity, and client relationships.

This isn't just a skill. It's a turning point in your freelance journey. You've learned how to multiply your output, expand your reach, and lay down the tortillas for long-term, sustainable growth. You now have the recipe to build not just one agent, but a whole squad of digital collaborators—your own AI kitchen crew, working in sync under your guidance.

In the next chapter, "AI and Creativity on Steroids," you will explore how to use these tools to unlock new levels of innovation. You will see how AI can inspire, remix, and accelerate your creative process without replacing your unique style and voice. Get ready to combine automation with artistry and discover what happens when your imagination meets intelligent technology.

CHAPTER 5

AI and Creativity on Steroids

Freelancers have always been hackers of creativity, turning a kitchen table into a studio, a café into an office, a napkin into a storyboard. We've learned to stretch our tools, improvise solutions, and make art out of whatever scraps the day gives us.

Now we have a new tool in the mix, and it's creativity on steroids. AI doesn't just hand you a hammer or a brush; it opens a warehouse filled with every instrument, every color, every sample, and says "Go wild."

But here's the catch: steroids don't replace your muscles. They just make your efforts more explosive. AI won't do the creative work for you, but it can take your first sketches, your half-formed riffs, your scribbled ideas, and amplify them beyond what you could do alone.

Think of it like your taco truck: AI won't invent your grandmother's recipe, but it will give you access to every spice market in the world. What you cook is still on you.

The Musician's Playground

A guitarist and composer used to spend nights piecing together demos on GarageBand. He'd layer chords, record rough vocals, and still end up with sketches that sounded flat. Potential clients often struggled to imagine the full sound.

Then he started using AI music tools like Suno and Udio. Suddenly, he could generate a backing track in seconds, a full band behind his guitar. For the first time, he didn't just send a riff. He sent a polished demo that sounded like a finished song. Clients stopped asking, "Can you show me more?" because they already heard it.

But here's the twist: when he sent the AI track as is, some clients loved it, but others frowned. "It's good," one said, "but it doesn't sound like you." That's when he realized the trick. The AI band was just scaffolding. He still had to layer his guitar, his rhythms, his imperfections, to make it feel alive.

PRO TIP Use AI to sketch, not to finish. Think of it as humming into a recorder. The melody is there, but the concert is still yours.

Lights, Camera, AI

A freelance videographer always dreaded the first client meeting. Storyboards took days, and half the time the client would look at her hand-drawn frames and say, "Sorry, I don't see it."

Enter AI. With tools like Runway, Pika, and MidJourney, she could now generate mood boards and even short animated clips in hours. She showed one client a concept for a coffee brand: steaming mugs, golden light, close-ups of hands passing cups across counters. The client's eyes lit up. They finally saw the vision.

But not everything worked. When she asked AI for "a traditional wedding in Oaxaca," the results came back with generic Western décor and outfits. The tool had no clue about cultural context. She had to add her own knowledge—specific textiles, Zapotec motifs, real local traditions—to make it authentic.

The Writer's Turbo Pen

A screenwriter once felt stuck. Her script had a great premise, but her characters wouldn't talk. Every attempt at dialogue felt wooden. She stared at the blinking cursor until her burrito went cold.

On a whim, she typed, "Pretend you're Quentin Tarantino. Write a 1-minute argument between siblings over a stolen car." The AI spat out a scene in seconds: sharp, messy, alive. It wasn't perfect, but it jolted her brain out of its rut.

She didn't copy the scene. Instead, she rewrote it line by line, adapting the rhythm to her own characters. It was like sparring with a partner who never tires, who always throws something unexpected back at you.

PRO TIP Use AI as your "what if machine." Don't let it write the story, let it challenge the narrative. Ask: "What if the villain was the hero?" or "What if the ending happened in reverse?" Let AI throw the punches, and you decide which ones land.

The Visual Artist's Infinite Canvas

An illustrator had a folder of unfinished sketches: dragons half-formed, landscapes with blank skies, characters missing faces. His problem wasn't starting; it was finishing.

One night, he uploaded three of his sketches into Stable Diffusion. He asked the AI to "remix" them into new variations. The results were bizarre. One dragon had feathers, one landscape sprouted skyscrapers, but they revealed something Malik hadn't seen: a hidden obsession with symmetry. The AI exaggerated his natural patterns, showing him what he unconsciously leaned toward.

Now he uses AI to prototype ideas faster. Clients love his quick drafts. But he's careful. Sometimes clients point to the AI variation and say, "I want that style exactly." That's when he explains: "That's not mine. My work looks like this."

AI and the Simplicity Superpower

Some of the most successful creative works are not complex. They are bold, repeatable, and easy to remix. Simplicity scales. The same is true when using AI.

Whether you're creating a soundtrack, a mockup, or a visual concept, never underestimate the power of a clear, focused prompt. You bring the depth and nuance. AI helps you amplify it.

Start with something familiar. Then let AI stretch it into something surprising. Your creative fingerprint lives in the choices you make: the edits, the rhythms, the moments you say "yes" or "no." That's what makes it art.

You don't need to invent a new recipe every time. Sometimes you just need to serve your taco in a slightly different way. AI helps you plate it faster, but it's still your seasoning that keeps people coming back.

AI in the Niche: Big Wins in Small Spaces

The creative economy doesn't always reward the loudest voice. More often, it rewards the most specific one.

Many of the world's most viewed or shared pieces of content meet very focused needs. Think bedtime lullabies, study playlists, or hyper-targeted memes. These aren't general hits; they're the go-to favorites for people looking for something that speaks directly to their moment.

Your own work might shine not by going bigger, but by going narrower. AI can help you do that with speed and precision. You can storyboard a whole series for a specific cultural tradition. You can test packaging for a community-rooted product. You can remix logos that use the slang and colors of your local scene.

When you serve a niche, the audience feels seen. It's like making the one taco nobody else in town offers. The line may start small, but it's loyal, and it grows.

The Cultural Remix

AI is a remix machine. But it can't invent your culture. That's your superpower.

Your language, your textures, your childhood references, these are the ingredients that make your work taste like yours. When you collaborate with AI, don't erase them. Amplify them. Train the model on your flavor, not someone else's.

Ask AI to riff on your voice. Feed it your sketches, your phrasing, your oddball obsessions. Then watch what it spits back. It won't be perfect, but it will reflect patterns you didn't know you were repeating. That's gold. That's your signature.

Your culture, your quirks, your secret salsa, that's what makes your work unforgettable. AI can help you scale it, but only if you let your roots stay visible.

Other Creative Tools to Explore

By now, you've seen how AI can remix your sketches, unblock your writing, generate storyboards, and even spot your creative patterns. But the tools we've used so far are just the beginning. There's a whole buffet of AI-powered platforms designed to support visual artists, musicians, videographers, and cross-disciplinary freelancers like you.

Here are a few that have taken off in the creative world.

Suno

What it does: Generates original, royalty-free music based on your prompt.

Why use it: Whether you need background music for a client video or want to sketch out a song idea, Suno delivers a full audio track in seconds, no instruments required.

Runway

What it does: AI-powered video editing and content generation.

Why use it: Quickly create videos, edit footage, remove objects, or stylize clips with just a few clicks. Ideal for social media content, pitch videos, and visual storytelling.

MidJourney

What it does: Creates detailed, stylized visuals from text prompts.

Why use it: Perfect for concept art, product mockups or branding, or any time you need high-quality visuals fast. Known for its painterly, emotional aesthetic.

Stable Diffusion

What it does: An open-source image generation model you can customize.

Why use it: For freelancers who want more control or want to train AI on their own art style. Great for experimenting, batch-generating options, or integrating into creative workflows.

These tools are part of a growing ecosystem that allows you to move faster, prototype more freely, and test ideas at scale. You don't need to master them all. Just pick one that supports the kind of work you're already doing, or the kind you want to get paid for.

The Dark Side of Creative AI

Of course, steroids come with side effects. Creative AI is no different.

- *Homogenization:* If everyone uses the same tools, outputs start looking alike—a million "fast-paced startup videos" with the same stocky vibe.
- *Copyright gray zones:* Who owns an AI-generated song or image? The law is still catching up.
- *The shortcut temptation:* Delivering something fully AI-made may seem easy, but it risks your credibility. Clients don't pay you to push a button.

The danger isn't that AI replaces creativity, it's that it floods the market with mediocre creativity, drowning out the voices who dare to stay original.

Badge Achievement Plan: Designing with AI as Your Creative Partner

Complete the following missions to demonstrate your skills and earn your badge!

You've learned how AI can act as your creative amplifier: not a replacement, but a remix partner, a rough draft generator, and a pattern spotter that accelerates your process without diluting your style. Whether you're a writer, designer, musician, or multi-hyphenate creator, you now have the tools to sketch faster, test ideas more boldly, and stay grounded in your unique voice while scaling your impact.

This session will help you collaborate with AI in your creative workflow, identifying where it can boost your process without taking over your authorship. By the end, you'll walk away with custom AI-generated content that reflects your taste, your goals, and your creative fingerprint.

Time Required: 1 hour 20 minutes

Goal: Use AI to co-create, remix, and refine creative outputs while keeping full control of voice and vision.

What You'll Need:

- A computer with internet access
- A ChatGPT Plus account or another creative AI tool (e.g., MidJourney, Udio, Pika, Runway, Canva AI)
- 2–3 examples of your past creative work (writing, sketches, audio, mockups, etc.)
- A creative task you're currently stuck on or curious to explore (e.g., story idea, video mood board, character design, logo draft)

Mission 1: Remix Your Voice (15 minutes)

Choose 2–3 samples of your creative work, and upload or describe them to your AI tool. Ask the AI to "remix" or "generate variations" based on your input. Don't aim for perfection, just observe what comes back.

Special secret prompts:

1. "Here are three examples of my creative work: [paste or describe]. Analyze my tone, rhythm, and main themes. What patterns do you notice in my style?"

2. "Remix my voice! Create three variations of this piece—one bolder, one funnier, and one more emotional."
3. "If my creative style were a music genre, which would it be and why? How could I amplify that energy in future projects?"

Afterward, ask yourself:

- What did the AI exaggerate?
- What patterns does it reveal about your style?
- Which remix sparks a new idea?

Mission 2: Push the Prompt (20 minutes)

Now it's time to stretch your creative thinking. Take something you're currently working on: a story, a post, a pitch, a design. Ask AI to flip it upside down. You're not asking it to *finish* your idea, but to push you to see it differently.

Special secret prompts:

1. "Rewrite this piece so the ending comes first. How does it change the emotion or flow?"
2. "Transform this design as if it were made for a 10-year-old audience. How would colors, language, or layout shift?"
3. "What if my main character or target audience was from Oaxaca? Adapt the tone, imagery, and expressions accordingly."
4. "Turn this idea into its opposite. What would it look like if I took a completely different perspective?"
5. "Give me three unexpected twists for this concept that still fit my brand voice."

Then, use the results as raw material: cut, remix, or rebuild. You don't have to agree with AI's suggestions; the point is to explore directions you wouldn't have found alone.

PRO TIP Creativity grows in friction. Let your AI challenge you, and then prove it wrong with something better.

Mission 3: Ground the Generic (15 minutes)

AI can generate endless ideas, but only you can make them *real*. Let's bring your human touch back into the mix.

Start by asking your AI to create something totally generic. Choose one of these:

- A storyboard for a short video
- A tagline for a new brand
- A poem about love

Then, rewrite or expand it using details only *you* could add: your hometown, your favorite places, your cultural voice, your inside jokes.

Special secret prompts:

1. Prompt 1: Write a generic poem about love." → Follow-up prompt: "Rewrite this poem as if I grew up in [your city or region]. Include imagery, slang, or small details only locals would understand."
2. "Create five taglines for a new coffee brand." → Then ask: "Now make them sound like they were written by someone from [your country or neighborhood]."
3. "Generate a short storyboard for a 30-second video about starting a business." → Then follow up: "Add visuals inspired by [local architecture / street food / landscapes]."

When both versions are ready, compare them.
Ask yourself:

- Which version feels more alive or authentic?
- How does personal or cultural context change the energy?
- What unique flavor do I bring that no AI ever could?

PRO TIP Generic AI is like a plain tortilla. You make it delicious when you add your own salsa.

Mission 4: Build Your Creative Toolkit (10 minutes)

You've experimented, remixed, and rewritten. Now it's time to organize your creative power tools so you can use them again and again.

Do this:

- Pick 1–2 AI tools that helped you the most today. Add them to your creative workflow; bookmark or save them.
- Create a Remix Folder (in Notion, Drive, or your sketchbook) where you store your best AI variations and prompts.

- Save 3 "special secret prompts" that consistently spark ideas.
- Make a quick Creative Debug List: a note with your go-to steps when you feel stuck.

Secret prompt to wrap it up:

"Help me design a simple creative toolkit. I want a list of tools, saved prompts, and steps to get inspired when I feel blocked."

By the end, you'll have your first personal AI-powered creative system, one that learns with you and keeps your ideas fresh, grounded, and unmistakably yours.

Mission 5: Share + Reflect (Optional, 10 minutes)

Share one of your remixed pieces with a friend, client, or creative group. Ask:

- Does this still feel like me?
- What surprised you about it?

Reflect on the role AI played: assistant, challenger, amplifier, or all three.

Mission 6: Final Knowledge Check Quiz (10 minutes)

1. What is the main role of AI in creative work, according to this chapter?
   - **a.** To replace human creativity entirely
   - **b.** To amplify and expand initial human ideas
   - **c.** To make art without any human input
   - **d.** To guarantee original cultural accuracy
2. Why did the guitarist and composer's clients say his early AI demos "didn't sound like him"?
   - **a.** Because AI cannot generate music at all
   - **b.** Because the AI tracks were unfinished
   - **c.** Because he sent the AI output without layering his own guitar and style
   - **d.** Because the clients only wanted acoustic demos
3. What lesson did the freelance videographer learn when AI generated a "traditional wedding in Oaxaca" with generic Western décor?
   - **a.** AI is always right about cultural details
   - **b.** AI outputs require human cultural knowledge to be authentic
   - **c.** AI makes better storyboards than humans
   - **d.** Clients prefer hand-drawn sketches to AI visuals

4. The screenwriter used AI to write dialogue in Tarantino's style. What was the real value she gained?
   a. She copied the scene directly into her script
   b. It jolted her out of writer's block and gave her a rhythm to adapt
   c. It replaced her need to write dialogue herself
   d. It showed her that AI can't write dialogue at all
5. The illustrator discovered a hidden creative pattern (symmetry) when AI remixed his sketches. What does this illustrate?
   a. AI can expose unconscious tendencies in your work
   b. AI is better at drawing dragons than humans
   c. AI always produces bizarre, unusable results
   d. Clients always prefer AI-generated variations
6. Which of the following is *not* listed as a "dark side" risk of creative AI?
   a. Homogenization of outputs
   b. Copyright uncertainty
   c. Shortcut temptation
   d. Improved client communication
7. Why should you rewrite a generic AI storyboard with local details?
   a. To make it longer
   b. To test whether AI understands slang
   c. Because adding your personal and cultural knowledge makes the result feel alive
   d. To trick clients into thinking you did the work

Answer Sheet

1. **B: To amplify and expand initial human ideas**

   The chapter emphasizes that AI is like steroids: it amplifies your initial efforts, it doesn't replace creativity.

2. **C: Because he sent the AI output without layering his own guitar and style**

   The guitarist and composer's AI tracks lacked his unique guitar layers, rhythms, and imperfections.

3. **B: AI outputs require human cultural knowledge to be authentic**

   The videographer learned AI tools lack cultural context; she had to add Zapotec motifs and real traditions.

4. **B: It jolted her out of writer's block and gave her a rhythm to adapt**

   The screenwriter didn't copy AI's scene; she used it to break writer's block and adapt dialogue to her own characters.

5. **A: AI can expose unconscious tendencies in your work**

   AI revealed the illustrator's unconscious tendency toward symmetry, showing how it can expose creative fingerprints.

6. **D: Improved client communication**

   Improved communication is not a listed risk; the three risks were homogenization, copyright gray zones, and shortcuts.

7. **C: Because adding your personal and cultural knowledge makes the result feel alive**

   Adding personal details makes the output authentic and resonant, instead of hollow and generic.

Congratulations!

By completing these missions, you have moved beyond using AI for quick fixes and learned to collaborate with it like a true creative professional. You now understand how to use AI to explore ideas, remix your drafts, and uncover stylistic patterns that make your work distinct. You have discovered how to accelerate the creative process while keeping full ownership of your artistic voice and cultural identity. You have also created AI-enhanced versions of your work, proving that you can integrate intelligent tools into your creative workflow without sacrificing originality. Whether you used ChatGPT,

Make.com, Zapier, or Notion AI, you now have hands-on experience using AI to support the type of work you want to be known for. You are no longer simply prompting AI. You are shaping the vision.

Once you finish, submit your responses by following the badge submission instructions listed in Chapter 1 or at `https://civicai.khoury.northeastern.edu/ai-for-gig-workers`. This badge recognizes your ability to use AI as a responsible and skilled co-creator. Display it proudly in your portfolio or LinkedIn profile to show that you can use emerging technology to boost your creativity, expand your capabilities, and deliver high-quality work more quickly.

What You Have Gained

You have gone from blocked to bold. From struggling with blank pages and slow drafts to rapid prototyping and creative momentum. You now understand how to push AI to help you experiment, iterate, and refine while staying true to the flavors that make your work yours. Your taco truck is still cooking the same signature recipes, but now with a much faster engine under the hood.

In Chapter 6, "Choosing the Right AI Sidekick for Your Work," you will take the next step in building your modern freelance business. You will learn how to identify which tasks deserve your human touch and which tasks can be delegated to intelligent tools. You will discover how to select the best AI partners for your goals so that you can spend more time in your creative genius zone and less time on repetitive busywork. It is time to choose the right sidekick for the empire you are building.

CHAPTER 6

Choosing the Right AI Sidekick for Your Work

Your AI Toolkit Awaits

Running your gig is like steering a taco truck through a vibrant global food festival where you're serving up sizzling work to clients from Nairobi to New York. You're a rideshare driver weaving through rush hour, an influencer dropping viral Reels, a virtual assistant juggling client chaos, a tutor sparking minds, or an event planner crafting unforgettable moments. The hustle is thrilling, but the grind—admin tasks, late-night edits, endless scheduling—can leave you stuck in the kitchen instead of shining at the window.

In Chapter 1, you discovered how AI can save time, boost your income, and reignite your creative spark. Chapter 2 took you under the hood to understand how AI actually works, breaking down machine Learning into something useful, not intimidating. Chapter 5 showed you how to collaborate with AI as a creative partner, helping you remix ideas and accelerate your output without losing your style.

Now, it's time to get practical. This chapter will help you choose the right AI sidekick for your work, with tools that match your pace, your goals, and your taco flavor. Think of it as stocking your kitchen with the ingredients and gear that help you cook faster, better, and with more joy.

The AI tool market is like a sprawling food market, packed with ingredients from basic spices to premium equipment, each promising to make your taco truck the best in town. But not every tool fits your recipe for success. A delivery driver needs route optimization to find hungry customers, not video editing software. A food blogger wants design tools for mouth-watering posts, not complex accounting systems for restaurant chains.

Choosing the wrong tool is like buying a drill for your taco truck: it's useless if it doesn't serve your needs. This chapter is your roadmap to navigating the AI toolbox and finding tools that match your gig, budget, and lifestyle, whether you're working from a smartphone in a Jakarta café, a tablet in a Lagos market, or a laptop in a London co-working space.

We'll follow real gig workers' case studies to learn how they use AI tools to transform their work. You'll learn how to test tools without breaking the bank, spot red flags to avoid duds, and build a workflow that feels like a well-oiled kitchen. We'll dive into mobile-first tools for on-the-go hustlers, ecosystems that combine multiple tools, and strategies to ensure your AI sidekicks work seamlessly with your setup. A hands-on Badge Achievement Plan will have you comparing tools like a pro, finding your perfect match. Later chapters will explore setting rates, networking with global clients, and scaling your gig into a business, but for now, let's stock your toolkit. Ready to build your AI dream team? Let's fire up the grill.

Why the Right AI Tools Matter

Choosing the correct AI tools is like picking the perfect spices for your tacos: get it right, and your gig bursts with flavor; get it wrong, and you're left with a bland mess. According to Upwork's *Future Workforce Index 2025* (2024), more than 70 million freelancers now power the U.S. gig economy, with millions more driving growth across Southeast Asia, Latin America, and Africa. But every gig is unique. Influencers need tools to design eye-catching Instagram stories and analyze follower trends to land brand deals; virtual assistants need an AI that can handle client emails and scheduling so they bring quality to the workplace; delivery drivers rely on AI to optimize routes and track earnings to maximize their shifts; event planners seek AI tools that can create stunning event proposals for their clients, as well as manage vendors for high-stakes weddings; tutors need apps for lesson planning and student engagement to grow their online classes.

The stakes are high in today's gig economy. Clients expect lightning-fast delivery, whether it's a polished Reel, a perfectly timed food drop, or a seamless corporate event. Platforms like Uber, Fiverr, and Instagram reward efficiency and quality with higher ratings, better gigs, or more followers. A 2025 Freelancer.com blog post notes that freelancers using tailored AI tools report 30% higher earnings and 25% more job satisfaction than those stuck with manual methods (Freelancer.com, "The Future of Freelancing"). The right tools also future-proof your hustle. As we'll explore in later chapters, they can help you network with global clients—say, pitching a U.S. brand from Nairobi—or scale your gig into a business, like turning your tutoring sessions into online courses or your delivery routes into a logistics startup.

But the AI market is noisy, with YouTube gurus hyping tools like Claude and Zapier while X posts rave about free apps like Canva AI and Grammarly. How do you choose? The key is alignment. Your tools must fit your gig's demands, your tech comfort, and your wallet. A tutor once tried a pricey video editor before realizing free Quizlet AI was perfect for her lesson plans, saving her $40 a month. A driver ditched a clunky paid app for Waze's free AI routing, saving $50 monthly and adding an extra shift. This chapter will steer you clear of those missteps, ensuring that your AI sidekicks make your taco truck a hit, whether you're serving clients in Lagos, Los Angeles, or Lisbon.

Understanding the Needs of Your Gig

Listen, before you get distracted by all the shiny AI tools promising to change your life, let's get real about what you actually need. Think of it like planning your kitchen before a busy night at your taco truck. You wouldn't randomly buy equipment without knowing what you're cooking, right?

Start by sitting down with a cup of coffee and honestly assessing your daily work. This is where you put on your "Head Chef" hat and apply that data science mindset. What takes up most of your time? What makes you want to throw your laptop out the window? These pain points are your golden tickets to finding the right AI tools.

Here's how to figure this out: Grab a notebook or open a simple document and track your work for just three days. Don't overthink it. Just focus on writing down what you're doing every hour. You'll quickly see patterns. Maybe you're spending two hours daily on admin tasks that feel like busywork. Or perhaps you're burning entire evenings creating content that should take 30 minutes.

Next, think about your biggest frustrations. Are you constantly switching between apps? Struggling to keep clients happy? Losing potential income because you can't work fast enough? These frustrations point directly to the type of AI help you need.

Matching Tools to Your Reality

Once you know your pain points, it's time to match them with the right type of AI tool. Let's break down the main categories and how they actually work to help your gig:

AI Automation Tools: Your Digital Assistant

These tools use rule-based automation and simple machine learning to handle repetitive tasks. They work by recognizing patterns in your workflow and automatically triggering actions when certain conditions are met. Think of them as digital dominoes: when one thing happens, it automatically triggers the next action.

For scheduling, Calendly AI uses algorithms to analyze your calendar, consider time zones, and prevent double bookings. You set it up once with your availability preferences and then share your booking link with clients. When someone books a meeting, Calendly automatically sends confirmations, reminders, and even Zoom links.

For expense tracking, QuickBooks AI uses machine learning to categorize your spending by analyzing transaction descriptions and learning from your past entries. Connect your bank account, and it automatically sorts business expenses from personal ones, tracks mileage when you drive for work, and prepares tax-ready reports.

For workflow automation, Zapier connects different apps using "if this, then that" logic. For example, when a client fills out your contact form, it automatically creates a new project in your task manager, sends you a notification, and adds their info to your CRM. You can spend an hour setting up these "zaps" and then save hours every week as they run automatically.

Generative AI: Your Creative Partner

This technology uses LLMs and neural networks trained on massive datasets to create new content. As you learned in Chapter 1, these are the tools that create something new from scratch. These systems understand patterns in human language and visual styles and generate original content based on your instructions.

Tools like ChatGPT and Claude use transformer neural networks to understand context and generate human-like text. You use them by writing clear prompts like "Draft a professional email declining a project but suggesting an alternative timeline." The AI analyzes your request, considers appropriate business language, and creates a polished response you can customize.

For visual content, Midjourney uses diffusion models that understand how to combine concepts, styles, and compositions. Tell it "Create a professional headshot background with soft lighting and modern office vibes," and it generates multiple options. Content creators use this to create consistent branding without hiring a photographer. Canva AI combines predesigned templates with generative features. It suggests layouts based on your content type, automatically resizes designs for different platforms, and even generates color schemes that match your brand. You start with your content, and it handles the design heavy lifting.

Recommendation AI: Your Strategic Advisor

These systems use data analysis and predictive algorithms to spot patterns and suggest optimizations. They are often powered by the supervised learning models we explored in Chapter 2. They work by analyzing large amounts of data to find trends you might miss and predict what actions will get the best results.

For example, Grammarly uses natural language processing to analyze your writing style, tone, and clarity. It doesn't just check spelling; it understands context and suggests improvements to make you sound more professional or confident. Virtual assistants use this to ensure that client emails hit the right tone every time.

YouTube Studio AI analyzes millions of data points about viewer behavior, trending topics, and engagement patterns. It tells you which thumbnails perform better, when your audience is most active, and which topics are gaining traction. Content creators use this data to post at optimal times and create content that actually gets views.

For drivers, Waze AI processes real-time traffic data, accident reports, and historical patterns to predict the fastest routes. It continuously learns from millions of users to spot traffic patterns and suggest alternatives that save time and fuel.

AI Organization Tools: Your Personal Manager

These tools use smart algorithms to prioritize tasks, manage your calendar, and help you focus on high-value work. They analyze your work patterns and automatically organize your day for maximum productivity. Notion AI combines database management with natural language processing to help you organize information. Ask it to "Create a client tracking system with project status, payment due dates, and communication logs," and it builds a custom workspace. Freelancers use this to keep all their projects organized without switching between multiple apps.

Reclaim AI uses calendar analysis to automatically block time for important work. It learns when you're most productive, protects time for deep work, and even schedules breaks to prevent burnout. It's like having a personal assistant who knows your work style and guards your time accordingly.

Motion AI goes further by analyzing your task list, deadlines, and energy levels to create daily schedules that actually work. Instead of hoping you'll find time for important projects, it automatically blocks calendar time and adjusts when urgent tasks pop up.

The Diplomat in Your Pocket

Not every personal task is about groceries, school, or flights. Sometimes the hardest thing you face as a freelancer is hitting Send when you're furious. We've all been there: you open your inbox, read a client's email for the tenth time, and feel the heat rising in your chest. Your fingers hover over the keyboard, ready to fire off the perfect angry reply.

This is where AI becomes your personal diplomat. Tools like GPT are surprisingly good at understanding tone. Before you hit send, paste your draft and ask:

> *"Rewrite this email so it still makes my point clear, but in a polite and professional tone."*

For example, one freelancer once wrote back to a client: "You never sent me the files on time, and now you're blaming me for the delay. This is completely unfair." Valid? Absolutely. Productive? Not so much.

She dropped the message into her AI, and it came back as

> *"I understand there were delays with receiving the files, which affected the timeline. Let's discuss how we can avoid this in the future so the project stays on track."*

Same message, zero fire. Instead of burning the bridge, the freelancer crossed it.

> **PRO TIP** *Emotional filter taco:* Before sending an angry email, let AI season it with diplomacy. You'll still get your point across, but with salsa that cools instead of burns.

Matching Tools to Your Specific Work

The key is understanding which type of AI addresses your biggest challenge:

- *Drowning in admin work?* Start with an automation tool like Zapier or Calendly to handle the repetitive stuff.
- *Struggling with content creation?* Generative AI like ChatGPT or Canva helps you create professional work more quickly.

- *Making decisions blindly?* Recommendation AI gives you data to work smarter, not just harder.
- *Feeling overwhelmed and disorganized?* AI organization tools help you focus on what matters most.

But here's the thing: don't try to solve everything at once. Pick your biggest time-waster and tackle that first. Success with one tool builds confidence to add more later.

Testing Smart, Not Hard

Now comes the fun part: testing tools without breaking your budget or sanity. Start with the free versions or trials of AI. Seriously, try not to pay for anything until you've kicked the tires for at least a week.

Here's a testing strategy: Pick one specific task and test how different tools handle it. Time yourself. Note how you feel using each tool. Some will click immediately, others will feel like wrestling with a stubborn printer. Trust those instincts.

Test during your actual work conditions, not when you have all day to play around. If you work from your car, test on your phone. If you like working in coffee shops with spotty Wi-Fi, see how the AI tools handle poor connections.

Building Your Perfect Setup

The magic happens when tools work together, not when you have a dozen apps that don't talk to each other. Think of it like running a high-performing taco truck. The tortillas are warming, the fillings are prepped, the salsa is within arm's reach, and the orders keep moving. Every station is set up with purpose, and everyone (or everything) knows what comes next.

When your tools, from client messaging to file storage to AI automation, are connected and flowing smoothly, your digital kitchen runs like a dream. You're not just tossing ingredients together. You're serving fire with speed, precision, and style.

Start simple. Maybe pair a content creation tool with a scheduling tool. See how they play together. Most good tools integrate with each other or at least export data easily. If a tool isolates your work, that's a red flag.

Your setup should grow with your business. What works when you're handling 5 clients might not work when you're managing 20. Choose tools that can scale or at least export your data when it's time to upgrade.

Avoiding Expensive Mistakes

Here's what we've learned from watching freelancers waste money on AI tools: if it feels complicated in the first hour, it's probably not right for you. Good AI tools feel almost boringly simple once you get the hang of them.

Watch out for tools that promise everything. The best tools do one thing really well. Also, be wary of anything that requires extensive training or has customer support that's hard to reach.

Before committing to any paid tool, ask yourself: "Will this save me at least an hour per week?" If the answer isn't a clear yes, keep looking.

The goal isn't to have the most AI tools. It's to have the right ones that make your work feel less like work and more like running a smooth, profitable business. Your future self will thank you for taking the time to choose wisely now.

Badge Achievement Plan: Choosing the Right AI Sidekick for Your Work

Complete the following missions to demonstrate your skills and earn your badge!

In this chapter, you've learned how to move from being overwhelmed by AI options to confidently selecting the tools that actually support your work. You now understand how to evaluate your real needs, match those needs to tool categories, and test AI platforms in ways that are grounded in your daily freelance routine. The goal isn't to learn every app, it's to build a toolkit that fits your flow, solves the right problems, and makes your business smoother, smarter, and more sustainable.

Now it's time to build your personal AI toolkit, the set of tools that will help you move faster, stay organized, and spend more time on the parts of your work that truly matter. Whether you need help writing proposals, automating reminders, or generating client-ready mockups, the right AI sidekick can make your workflow smoother and your business stronger.

This session will guide you through identifying your real needs, choosing the right categories of tools, and testing them in your actual freelance setup. By the end, you'll have a go-to digital sidekick that works *for* you, not the other way around.

Time Required: 1 hour 15 minutes + 3 days of testing

Goal: Find your perfect AI match and share your journey with the freelancer community.

What You'll Need:

- A computer with internet access
- A list of 3–5 tasks that slow you down or feel repetitive
- Access to 1–2 AI tools (ChatGPT, Notion AI, Canva, Zapier, etc.)
- A current or recent client task to use as your test case
- A space to take quick notes (Google Doc, notebook, template)

Mission 1: Spot the Friction (10 minutes)

List 3–5 tasks that drain your energy, delay client work, or just annoy you. Examples:

- Rewriting the same email over and over
- Copying data between platforms
- Posting manually on multiple channels
- Forgetting to follow up with leads

Ask yourself:

If a tool could take this off my plate, what would I do with that time instead?

Mission 2: Match the Pain Point to the Tool Type (10 minutes)

Now brainstorm the type of tool that could help. Don't pick apps yet, just categories:

Pain point	Tool type	Example tools
Writing, editing	Text generation	ChatGPT, Claude, Notion AI
Planning, organizing	AI + notetaking/task management	Notion, Motion, Mem.ai
Design + branding	AI for visuals	Canva, Midjourney
Repetitive busywork	Automation tools	Zapier, Make.com, Bardeen

Choose 1–2 tools from the right category to test.

Mission 3: The 3-Day Test Drive

You're not just reading about tools, you're taking one for a spin.

Day 1: Setup + First Task (15 minutes)

- Sign up for the tool.
- Complete basic setup (should take <15 minutes).
- Use it for *one* pain-point task.

Note: How easy was it to get started? Did it actually help?

Day 2: Real-World Trial (15–20 minutes)

- Use the tool in *your* normal work setting (café, phone hotspot, between calls).
- Try a second task.

Note: Did it work in real conditions? Any surprises or frustrations?

Day 3: Integration Test (15–20 minutes)

- Try using the tool as part of your normal routine.
- See if it plays nice with your other systems.

Note: Would you miss this tool if it disappeared tomorrow?

Mission 4: Share Your Journey (5 minutes)

Reflect on your experience, and then share it with your community.

Use this template to post on social media or in a freelancer group:

> Just completed my 3-day AI tool challenge!
> Tool tested: [Name of tool]
> Problem it solved: [Your pain point]
> Biggest surprise: [What you didn't expect]
> Time saved: [Estimated hours per week]
> Would I keep using it? [Yes/No + why]
> One tip for other freelancers: [Your insight]

#AIForFreelancers #GigEconomy #ProductivityHack #FreelanceLife

Mission 4: Final Knowledge Check Quiz (10 minutes)

1. What is the main reason for a gig worker to start with the free version of an AI tool before paying for it?
   a. Paid versions are always too complicated for beginners
   b. To test whether the tool actually saves time and solves a real problem without any financial risk
   c. Free versions have better customer support than paid ones
   d. To get your name on the company's marketing list for future discounts
2. According to the chapter, if you are a freelance virtual assistant drowning in scheduling and email follow-ups, which category of AI tool should you explore first?
   a. Generative AI
   b. Recommendation AI
   c. AI automation tools
   d. AI organization tools
3. A tutor saved money by switching from a pricey video editor to a free tool that better suited her needs. What lesson does her story teach?
   a. Expensive tools are always the best
   b. All free tools are better than paid tools
   c. A tool's value is determined by how well it aligns with your specific tasks, not its price tag
   d. Video editing is not a valuable skill for tutors
4. What is the primary function of a Generative AI tool like ChatGPT or Midjourney?
   a. To analyze your existing data and recommend the best course of action
   b. To handle repetitive tasks by connecting different apps together
   c. To create entirely new content, such as text or images, based on your instructions
   d. To organize your calendar and prioritize your to-do list automatically
5. When testing a new AI tool, the chapter advises to "test during your actual work conditions." What does this mean?
   a. You should only test tools when you have a full, uninterrupted day to learn them
   b. You should test the tool in the environment where you actually work, such as on your phone in your car or with spotty coffee-shop Wi-Fi
   c. You should ask a friend to test the tool for you and report back
   d. You should only test tools that are recommended by famous YouTubers

6. What does the chapter identify as a "red flag" when evaluating a new AI tool?
   a. The tool integrates easily with other apps you use
   b. The tool does one thing really well
   c. The tool isolates your work and does not allow you to export your data easily
   d. The tool offers a free trial period
7. Before committing to a paid AI tool, what key question should a freelancer ask themselves?
   a. "Is this the most popular tool on the market?"
   b. "Does this tool have more than 20 features?"
   c. "Will this tool make my work look more creative?"
   d. "Will this save me at least an hour per week?"
8. Which of the following gig workers would get the most benefit from a recommendation AI tool like Waze or YouTube Studio?
   a. A writer who needs to draft articles faster
   b. A delivery driver who needs to find the fastest routes or an influencer who needs to know the best time to post
   c. A VA who needs to automatically send emails when a form is filled out
   d. A tutor who needs to create custom worksheets from scratch
9. What is the main goal of the "3-Day Tool Test Drive" in Mission 3?
   a. To sign up for as many free trials as possible in three days
   b. To find a perfect AI tool by testing it on a single, specific pain point and deciding whether it's worth keeping
   c. To become an expert in using one complex AI tool
   d. To spend money on a premium tool to see if it's better than the free version

Answer Key

1. **B: To test whether the tool actually saves time and solves a real problem without any financial risk**

   The chapter strongly advises starting with free versions or trials to validate a tool's usefulness for your specific tasks before investing any money.

2. **C: AI automation tools**

   The chapter specifies that automation tools like Zapier and Calendly are designed to handle repetitive administrative work like scheduling and follow-ups.

3. **C: A tool's value is determined by how well it aligns with your specific tasks, not its price tag**

   The tutor's story illustrates that the "best" tool is the one that fits your workflow and budget, proving that a free, well-aligned tool can be more valuable than an expensive, ill-fitting one.

4. **C: To create entirely new content, such as text or images, based on your instructions**

   The chapter defines Generative AI as technology that creates new, original content like text, images, or code based on user prompts.

5. **B: You should test the tool in the environment where you actually work, such as on your phone in your car or with spotty coffee-shop Wi-Fi**

   The book advises this to ensure the tool is practical and works effectively in your real-life, on-the-go work setting, not just in a perfect, controlled environment.

6. **C: The tool isolates your work and does not allow you to export your data easily**

   The chapter warns that a tool is a potential dead end if it traps your work, as your systems need to work together and be scalable.

7. **D: "Will this save me at least an hour per week?"**

   This question is presented as a simple, practical test to determine whether a paid tool provides a clear return on investment by saving you valuable, billable time.

8. **B: A delivery driver who needs to find the fastest routes or an influencer who needs to know the best time to post**

   The chapter explains that recommendation AI works by analyzing data to suggest optimizations, using Waze for drivers and YouTube Studio for creators as prime examples.

9. **B: To find a perfect AI tool by testing it on a single, specific pain point and deciding whether it's worth keeping**

   The challenge is structured to be focused and practical: identify one major problem, test one free tool to solve it over three days, and then make a clear decision.

Congratulations!

By completing these missions, you've taken a bold and strategic step in building your AI-powered freelance business. You didn't just read about tools, you rolled up your sleeves, tested them in the wild, and learned what actually works in your real-world setup. You've learned how to match your pain points to the right kind of AI support, run practical tool trials, and integrate your winning sidekick into your workflow.

This isn't about having the trendiest app. It's about building a tech stack that serves you. You now know how to experiment with confidence, discard what doesn't serve you, and double down on what does. Whether you landed on an automation tool, a creative assistant, or a smart organizer, you've made your first intentional hire for your digital team.

Once you finish, submit your responses by following the badge submission instructions listed in Chapter 1 or at `https://civicai.khoury.northeastern.edu/ai-for-gig-workers`. This badge celebrates your ability to evaluate, test, and deploy AI solutions that align with your freelance goals. Add it to your portfolio, LinkedIn, or personal website to show you're not just using AI. You're leading with it.

What You Have Gained

You've gone from exploring tools to building systems. From reacting to tech trends to making proactive, informed decisions. You now know how to choose AI tools that actually fit your daily hustle, tools that remove friction, save you time, and amplify your impact. You've started designing your AI kitchen: streamlined, efficient, and ready to serve up your best work.

This chapter wasn't just about finding the right tool. It was about developing the mindset of a digital problem solver: someone who doesn't wait for perfect conditions but experiments, iterates, and grows.

In the next chapter, "Using AI Without Losing Your Voice," we'll go deeper into how to collaborate with AI without compromising your creativity, values, or authenticity. You'll learn how to stay true to your tone and style, even as AI speeds things up behind the scenes.

Get ready to take the spatula. Your voice is still the chef. AI is just the turbo grill.

CHAPTER 7

Using AI Without Losing Your Voice

Freelancers are rushing to AI like it is the hottest new food truck on the block. It is fast, it is cheap, and it delivers. But here is the catch: if you are not careful, you end up serving the same bland taco as everyone else.

And that is a problem, because your voice is your signature recipe. It is the reason clients hire you again, the reason readers stick around, the reason your work stands out in a sea of generic content. Lose your voice, and you become just another freelancer on the menu.

Why Your Voice Matters

Your voice is your creative fingerprint, the flavor of your business. It is what makes a client choose you over someone faster or cheaper. Your voice is not just about word choice or phrasing; it is your credibility. It is the difference between a proposal that feels personal and one that feels like a recycled template.

AI can make your workflow more efficient, but your personality is what makes your work unforgettable. Across every field, freelancers are discovering that although AI can write faster, design cleaner, or analyze better, it cannot create an emotional connection. It cannot feel humor, joy, or curiosity. And those are the exact ingredients that make your work resonate with people.

Clients equate authenticity with trust. When your voice feels genuine, they believe the work will be, too. Authenticity is not just creative; it is currency. Your voice is the bridge between what you do and how people experience it.

An influencer once learned this the hard way. She leaned on AI to brainstorm captions for her posts. The words were smooth and polished, but when she pasted them without edits, her followers noticed something strange. They could not name it, but they felt it. The captions lacked her warmth and humor. That small gap of authenticity was enough to weaken trust.

That is the risk. AI can assist, but it cannot replace the spark that makes people believe you. Sometimes, losing your voice does not just mean fewer likes on a post. It can mean losing the connection that brings opportunity.

The Foundations of Your Voice

Your voice is more than the words you choose. It is the rhythm of your thoughts, the emotions between your sentences, and the worldview that quietly shapes everything you create. It is the personality of your work, that unmistakable flavor that makes someone read a few lines, glance at a design, or hear a sound and instantly know it came from you.

Every freelancer, whether they realize it or not, already has a voice. It shows up in the way you describe your work to a client, the tone of your messages, or even the color palettes and patterns you choose. Some voices are playful and quick, others are reflective and calm. Together, these traits create a creative fingerprint that no algorithm can reproduce.

When you collaborate with AI, that fingerprint becomes even more important. Because AI is trained to imitate patterns, it naturally leans toward the average. Its strength lies in coherence, not character. If you are not careful, the edges that make your work special—your phrasing, rhythm, or emotional tone—can fade until everything sounds a little too safe.

The foundation of your voice rests on three key elements: tone, perspective, and rhythm.

Your *tone* is how you make people feel: whether your work sounds confident, playful, warm, or bold. Your *perspective* is what you notice and choose to highlight: the themes, insights, and values that reflect your worldview. And your *rhythm* is the pacing and flow of your words, visuals, or design choices. When these align, they form your creative identity.

Understanding these elements allows you to communicate them clearly to AI. You can say, "Write this in my tone, calm but curious," or "Design this in my voice, bold colors with human warmth." When you know your foundation, AI becomes an amplifier instead of an eraser. It learns to echo your voice rather than flatten it.

Your voice is not static; it evolves as you do. It grows through every project, client, and late-night idea. When you keep that awareness, AI collaboration becomes a process of reflection, not imitation. Because voice is not something you find once; it is something you protect, refine, and evolve each time you create.

The Value of Imperfection

Here is the irony: before AI, nobody doubted we were human. Our writing had typos, awkward phrasing, and inside jokes that only made sense in context. That was normal. That was us.

Now, we live in a world where technology constantly asks us to prove we are not robots. We click on traffic lights, identify crosswalks, and type squiggly letters just to prove our humanity online. Strangely, the same test has slipped into our creative lives. Every email, every post, every proposal is now quietly judged: did a human write this, or a machine?

We used to create without thinking about that question. But now, the burden is on us to sound less like the tools we use. The paradox of working alongside AI is that the more powerful it becomes, the more we have to protect the fragile, imperfect edges that make us human.

Machines are excellent at sounding polished and neutral, but efficiency has no heartbeat. Neutrality has no fingerprints. Perfection has no story. Clients are not hiring you for clean sentences; they are hiring you for the spark behind them. The spark that shows up in the stumble, the odd metaphor, the typo that proves you were typing fast because you cared.

Many freelancers also confuse consistency with perfection. They think sounding "on brand" means sounding exactly the same every time. But the strongest voices have range. You can be serious in a proposal, curious in a blog, and playful in a caption, and still sound like you.

Perfection often hides authenticity. The small shifts in your tone, the different notes of confidence, warmth, or humor, are what make your voice human. Clients want to work with someone flexible enough to adapt while staying unmistakably themselves. Think of your voice like a taco recipe. The base stays the same, but the toppings change depending on the day, the season, or the audience. That variation is what keeps people coming back.

That is why your mistakes matter. They are brushstrokes on the canvas, proof that a hand was really there. AI can imitate the picture, but it cannot imitate the trembling hand that made it. No one comes to the taco stand for uniform tortillas. They come for the messy salsa, the uneven fold, and the flavor that happens only when a real person is behind the counter.

So when you catch yourself editing until everything feels too smooth, stop and ask: does this sound like me, or does it sound like everyone else? Because sounding like yourself, even with flaws, will always be more valuable than sounding like a perfect machine.

The Job Posting Story

Consider this: a small creative agency posted a job opening for a copywriter. The task was simple: write a short statement explaining why you would be a good fit. More than 100 applications landed in their inbox.

On paper, the answers looked fine. Too fine. The hiring manager noticed something odd: dozens of applicants wrote in the same rhythm. Sentences began with the same patterns, like "In today's fast-paced digital world" or "I am passionate about leveraging creativity to deliver impactful solutions."

Individually, each response seemed polished. Collectively, they read like clones. The manager joked, "It is like they all went to the same AI taco stand and ordered the 'Motivated Freelancer Special'."

Most of those applications were rejected, not because the candidates were unqualified, but because they lacked personality. They did not sound human. Ironically, by using AI as a shortcut, they erased the very thing that could have helped them stand out.

The candidate who got the job? Their application was not flawless. It had a typo, the tone was slightly uneven, but it felt real. It had a voice. And in a pile of sameness, that voice was what cut through the noise.

How to Keep Your Voice

To collaborate effectively with AI, treat it like a capable assistant who needs guidance. The more direction you give, the better it can help. Think of it as someone joining your creative kitchen, quick and efficient, but waiting for you to decide how spicy the recipe should be.

Always begin with your own ideas: your outlines, notes, and sparks of inspiration. This keeps the emotion anchored in your voice instead of the machine's rhythm.

When you are ready to collaborate, feed AI your flavor. Give it examples of your past work, and ask it to analyze your tone, rhythm, and humor. That becomes your recipe card, your personal style guide. Then train it. Provide a few samples, and ask it to write new content in that same style. You will be surprised how quickly it begins to echo your rhythm rather than flatten it.

Next, set boundaries. Tell AI what not to do. You might say, "Avoid corporate jargon," or "Keep this conversational." Defining what to stay away from is just as important as describing what you want.

Let AI help with structure or mid-process writing, but always begin and end human. Write or rewrite your openings and conclusions yourself, because those are the emotional anchors where your heart and personality shine most.

Once AI delivers a draft, edit like yourself. Rewrite until the words feel natural. Add your human layer: a story, a joke, a detail, or a small imperfection. Those touches are what make people feel you behind the words.

And for the love of tacos, watch out for clichés. If you spot phrases like "In today's fast-paced world," cut them. Replace them with your own metaphors, the funny, messy, human ones that only you would use. Sprinkle in your quirks. Maybe it is how you start messages with "Hey team," or how you drop food analogies into serious conversations. That is not noise. That is your brand DNA.

Finally, check the emotion. Read your work aloud. Does it sound alive? Does it sound like you? If it feels too polished or distant, add rhythm, warmth, or a human story until it carries your unique flavor again. Think of AI as a mirror, not a mask. It should reflect your voice, not hide it.

A VA once asked AI to help him with client communication. Instead of asking for a generic, polished response, he said, "Summarize this email in my tone: short, friendly, no fluff." The AI reflected his rhythm back to him, and the result sounded exactly like him, only faster. That is the goal, not to erase your voice, but to amplify it.

Pro Tips, Taco Truck Style

Here is the taco wisdom: AI can chop onions all day long, but only you decide how spicy the salsa should be. Always taste the taco before you serve it. If it does not sound like you, adjust. Test your work on a friend. If they say, "This does not sound like you," take that seriously.

Build a voice bank. Keep a small collection of your best work and feed it to AI regularly, like giving your sous-chef a reminder of your signature recipes. Over time, AI learns your rhythm, your punchlines, your quirks.

And remember, no matter how advanced AI gets, the secret sauce is still your story. Update your voice bank often, because your tone evolves with every project. AI should grow with you, not ahead of you.

Your voice is your calling card, your personality, and your business advantage. It is what turns a gig into a relationship and a task into trust. Use AI to help you express it more clearly, not to hide it. The goal is not to sound like a machine that learned to be human, but like a human who learned to use machines wisely, creatively, and with a little extra flavor.

Badge Achievement Plan: The Authentic Creator

Complete the following missions to demonstrate your skills and earn your badge!

In this chapter, you have learned how to use AI as a collaborator without letting it erase what makes your work unique. You now understand how to protect your creative fingerprint, how to make AI echo your rhythm instead of flattening it, and how to turn efficiency into authenticity. The goal is not to write like AI, but to make AI write like you.

This session will help you practice the art of keeping your human spark alive in every task. You will refine your voice, build your personal style guide, and train AI tools to sound more like *you*. By the end, you will have a clear process for maintaining your tone and emotion, no matter what tools you use.

Time Required: 1 hour 10 minutes + optional 1–2 days for refining your style guide

Goal: Create your personal "voice system" and train your AI tools to follow your unique creative rhythm.

What You'll Need:

- A computer with internet access
- A few writing samples, designs, or past projects that sound most like you
- Access to an AI tool such as ChatGPT, Notion AI, or any writing/design platform you use regularly
- A place to take notes or build your style guide (Google Doc, Notion page, or notebook)

Mission 1: The Voice Audit (10 minutes)

Choose two or three samples of your past work that sound the most "you." These could be emails, proposals, posts, or scripts. Read them carefully, and highlight what stands out: your tone, pacing, favorite phrases, or emotional rhythm.

Ask yourself: *What makes this sound like me?*

This reflection becomes the foundation for your creative identity, the essence of your voice.

Mission 2: The Style Guide Recipe (15–20 minutes)

Now, turn what you discovered into a mini style guide. Write 5–7 rules that define your tone and rhythm. For example:

- Use short, friendly sentences.
- Avoid corporate language.
- Add one metaphor or example per section.
- Keep humor light but real.
- End with warmth or encouragement.

> Special secret prompt:
> "Help me write a short tone and style guide based on this writing sample: [paste your example]. List 5 key rules that define my voice."

This guide is what you'll feed to your AI later so it learns how to sound like you.

Mission 3: AI Sidekick Session (20 minutes)

Now it's time to teach your AI your unique flavor.

Pick an old piece of writing: a client pitch, a blog post, or even a social caption. Feed it into your AI, and use your tone guide as the recipe.

> Special secret prompts:
> 1. "Rewrite this in my tone and voice. Use short sentences, friendly rhythm, and a conversational flow."
> 2. "Use my tone guide: [paste your rules]. Rewrite this to sound more natural and human."
> 3. "Which parts of this writing sound less like my tone? Suggest edits to make it more consistent with my voice."

Compare versions. Adjust your prompts until the output sounds natural. Save your best results; these become your AI templates for future work. The more you use your tone guide, the better AI becomes at mirroring your rhythm. What you've built is not just a style, it's a signature. You can now collaborate with AI confidently, knowing that every word still sounds like *you*.

Mission 4: The Voice Test (10 minutes)

Write something new with AI, using your style guide. Then read it out loud or share it with a trusted friend or colleague. Ask: *Does this sound like me?* If not, tweak your guide and try again. Each round makes your AI partner a better reflection of your true creative identity.

Optional: Record yourself reading your favorite piece aloud, and listen to the flow. That sound, your natural rhythm, is what you are teaching your AI to protect.

Mission 5: Reflection (10 minutes)

Think about how your voice has evolved during this process. Write one short paragraph answering this question:

> "What part of my voice do I want clients to always recognize, no matter how much I use AI?"

Mission 6: Knowledge Check Quiz (10 minutes)

Choose the best answer for each question.

1. According to the chapter's "Taco Truck" analogy, what is the primary risk freelancers face when using AI as a shortcut?
   - **a.** The cost of the AI subscription eventually outweighs the profit
   - **b.** The AI tool might fail a client's security audit
   - **c.** The work becomes generic, causing the freelancer to lose their unique voice and stand out in the marketplace
   - **d.** AI can introduce complex legal problems like copyright infringement
2. The chapter argues that a freelancer's "voice" is more than just word choice. What is the most important element of your professional voice?
   - **a.** The consistent use of industry-specific jargon
   - **b.** The ability to write perfectly smooth, grammatically flawless sentences
   - **c.** Your credibility, the unique spark that makes clients feel understood and builds trust
   - **d.** The speed at which you can generate and submit a final draft
3. In the age of AI, why does the chapter suggest that the "imperfect edges" of human work (awkward phrasing, odd metaphors, minor flaws) are becoming more valuable?
   - **a.** Because clients actively enjoy correcting typos
   - **b.** Imperfection is a sign of fast, efficient work
   - **c.** These flaws serve as fingerprints or brushstrokes, proving the presence of human effort, thought, and personality
   - **d.** Flaws make the content cheaper to produce and easier to replicate
4. In the "Job Posting Story," why were dozens of applications written by AI rejected?
   - **a.** The AI used outdated facts and figures in the applications
   - **b.** The applications were too short and lacked detail
   - **c.** They all sounded like clones, lacking personality, rhythm, and the voice necessary to cut through the noise of sameness
   - **d.** The hiring manager was legally prohibited from hiring anyone who used an AI tool

5. What is the recommended strategy for integrating AI, based on the analogy of using it as a "sous-chef"?
   a. The AI should handle the entire project, from concept to delivery (the whole meal)
   b. The AI should only be used for tracking time and managing the budget
   c. Let the AI prep the ingredients (research, draft, summarize), but the human must decide the final seasoning (add the unique voice and style)
   d. The sous-chef should always be kept secret from the client
6. What does the chapter mean by treating AI as a "mirror, not a mask"?
   a. The AI should only be used to create content about yourself
   b. The AI should reflect your unique style and rhythm back to you, not hide your authentic voice behind generic corporate language
   c. You must use the AI's output exactly as generated to avoid changing the reflection
   d. The AI should only be used for visual or image-based tasks, not writing
7. What is the most effective way to train your AI sidekick to sound like *you*?
   a. Buy the most expensive subscription plan available
   b. Feed the AI a large voice bank of your past work (emails, posts, pitches), and specifically ask it to analyze and replicate your style, rhythm, and humor
   c. Only use brand-new prompts that the AI has never seen before
   d. Use a wide variety of different AI tools for every task

Answer Sheet

1. **C: The work becomes generic, causing the freelancer to lose their unique voice and stand out in the marketplace**

   The chapter uses the "taco truck" analogy to warn that if you rely too heavily on AI for the final product, you end up serving the "same bland taco as everyone else." Your unique voice is your signature, and losing it makes you easily replaceable.

2. **C: Your credibility, the unique spark that makes clients feel understood and builds trust**

   Your voice is your credibility. It's the unique connection that makes a client feel, "This freelancer gets me," which is what ultimately builds the long-term trust necessary for repeat business.

3. **C: These flaws serve as fingerprints or brushstrokes, proving the presence of human effort, thought, and personality**

   In a world of perfect AI output, the small imperfections, the odd metaphor, the rough flow, become valuable human fingerprints. They are the proof, like a brush stroke on a painting, that a real, unique human mind was behind the creation.

4. **C: They all sounded like clones, lacking personality, rhythm, and the voice necessary to cut through the noise of sameness**

   The candidates were rejected not for lack of skill but because their cloned, sterile writing erased their personalities. The hiring manager noted they all sounded like they ordered the "Motivated Freelancer Special," proving that a lack of voice makes you invisible in a stack of sameness.

5. **C: Let the AI prep the ingredients (research, draft, summarize), but the human must decide the final seasoning (add the unique voice and style)**

   The core message is control: the AI can do the heavy lifting (prep the ingredients, drafting, researching), but the human worker must retain creative control and add the unique final seasoning (style, judgment, and voice) that defines the final product.

6. **B: The AI should reflect your unique style and rhythm back to you, not hide your authentic voice behind generic corporate language**

   Using AI as a mirror means you customize the AI's output to reflect *your* existing, authentic voice, your short, friendly rhythm, or your specific humor. Using it as a mask means letting the AI hide your identity behind generic, corporate robot-speak.

7. **B: Feed the AI a large voice bank of your past work (emails, posts, pitches), and specifically ask it to analyze and replicate your style, rhythm, and humor**

   The most effective way to protect your voice is to train the AI with it. By feeding it a voice bank of your own successful past work and explicitly detailing your desired style, you teach the AI to echo your unique flavor instead of flattening it.

Congratulations!

By completing these missions, you have learned how to protect the most valuable asset in your creative career: your voice. You now know how to guide AI with intention, how to make it echo your rhythm without erasing your spark, and how to transform efficiency into authenticity. You have trained your digital sous-chef to prep the ingredients while you create the flavor.

Your voice is your currency. Clients can get generic AI text anywhere. What they cannot get is *you*: your perspective, your phrasing, your sense of humor, your story. AI can organize your ideas, polish your grammar, or smooth your drafts, but the secret sauce that turns words into connection still belongs entirely to you.

Once you finish, submit your responses by following the badge submission instructions listed in Chapter 1 or at `https://civicai.khoury.northeastern.edu/ai-for-gig-workers`. This badge certifies that you know how to collaborate with AI while preserving what makes your work human. Add it to your portfolio or LinkedIn profile to show clients that you can use technology responsibly and still sound unmistakably like yourself.

What You Have Gained

You have discovered how to use AI as a mirror instead of a mask. You have learned to teach it your tone, set boundaries, and keep the emotion and rhythm that define your creative identity. You now have a personal style guide that can grow with you, one that ensures AI becomes an extension of your authenticity rather than a replacement for it.

More than that, you have learned a deeper truth about the future of work: technology should amplify humanity, not erase it. By staying true to your creative fingerprint, you stand out in a world that is starting to sound the same. Your imperfections, humor, and quirks are not flaws; they are proof of life. They are the brushstrokes, the spice, the flavor that remind your clients there is a real person behind every word and design.

In the next chapter, "AI and Ethics," we will explore how to use this powerful technology with integrity, respect, and responsibility. You will learn how to build a creative practice that not only sounds authentic but acts authentically, ensuring that your success never comes at the expense of others. Because your work, like your tacos, should always be made with care.

CHAPTER 8

AI and Ethics

AI is transforming freelance work more quickly than any trend before it. It helps us brainstorm, edit, automate, and deliver results in record time. But as the power of AI grows, so does the responsibility to use it wisely.

The big question is no longer *what* AI can do, but *how* we should use it. Can clients trust the results we deliver? Can collaborators trust us with their data? Can we use AI to help people without accidentally causing harm?

For freelancers, ethics is not an abstract concept. It is the invisible contract between you and the people who trust you. Every time you use AI to write, design, plan, or communicate, you make a choice that shapes how others see your professionalism and your humanity.

Why This Matters

Ethics is what turns technology into something people can believe in. AI without ethics is like a taco without tortillas: messy, unstable, and impossible to hold together.

In the gig economy, your reputation is your currency. Clients rarely meet you in person; they evaluate your work, reliability, and tone. When they see that you use AI responsibly, it strengthens their trust in you. Ethical freelancers keep clients longer, get better referrals, and avoid the misunderstandings that can derail a project.

Being ethical with AI means being mindful of our impact. It means using it with awareness, crediting its role when necessary, and reviewing its output with care. In a crowded market, trust becomes your competitive advantage.

The Trust Equation

The heart of ethical AI work is trust. Trust grows from four simple habits—transparency, accountability, fairness, and reliability:

1. *Transparency* means being open about how you use AI. If you rely on a tool to edit your photos or draft proposals, be clear about how you review and finalize the work. Under-promising is always better than over-promising. Don't claim that AI's ideas are your own; explain how you refine and personalize them.
2. *Accountability* means taking responsibility for your AI outputs. If an automated tool produces a biased image or sends the wrong message, own it. Clients value quick, honest fixes more than perfect technology.
3. *Fairness* means testing your tools with diverse prompts and scenarios. Many AI systems are trained on limited data, which can unintentionally exclude or misrepresent people. Balance your inputs so your work includes more perspectives.
4. *Reliability* means consistency. If your tools break or misbehave, have a backup plan. Treat AI like an assistant: capable, fast, and sometimes forgetful.

The Hidden Risks of Ignoring AI Ethics

Ignoring AI ethics doesn't just risk your reputation; it can cause real harm. AI systems have made hiring unfair, misidentified workers, and misjudged qualifications, not because of malice, but because nobody stopped to test for bias. No one stopped to ask questions.

As freelancers, we face the same responsibility on a smaller scale. A careless use of an image generator could spread stereotypes. An AI script might reflect cultural biases. Even an overconfident chatbot can cross emotional boundaries.

If you use AI to help write sensitive content such as emotional support posts, personal essays, or wellness guides, remember that AI can mimic empathy but does not feel it. For people struggling with mental health, a wrong response from a chatbot could have real consequences. Human review must always be part of the process.

Ethics begins with that pause, the moment before you hit Send, when you ask yourself, *Who could this affect?*

Security: Don't Feed the AI Your Secret Sauce

Every freelancer has a secret sauce: the recipe that makes their work unique. Maybe it's your pitch strategy, creative process, or hard-earned client list. But if you upload all of that into a public AI without thinking, you might be giving it away.

Not all AI tools treat your data equally:

- *ChatGPT (OpenAI):* Free users' data may train future models. Plus and Enterprise users' data isn't used for training, but chats are stored on servers. Turn off chat history to reduce retention.
- *NotebookLM (Google):* Files stay in your Google account and aren't used for model training, but remember that it's still cloud-based.
- *Notion AI:* Keeps your data within your workspace; privacy depends on settings.
- *Other tools (e.g., Canva AI, Jasper, Copy.ai):* Many use third-party APIs, meaning your data might travel through multiple systems.

A copywriter once uploaded a full client contract to an AI tool so it could generate a "summary." The AI stored it remotely, and trust was lost. Meanwhile, another freelancer summarized public blogs: same benefit, zero risk. The difference wasn't the tool; it was judgment.

Rule of thumb: Let AI cook your tacos, but don't hand over the recipe.

Never upload:

- IDs, contracts, client databases, or personal information
- Sensitive creative work without consent

Risks include:

- *Legal:* Sharing personal data without consent violates privacy laws.
- *Technical:* Cloud accounts can be hacked.
- *Exposure:* AI might reuse or surface private details in future outputs.

If you wouldn't print it on a flyer, don't paste it into AI.

Quick Check: Is Your AI Safe?

1. Google the tool's privacy policy.
2. Look for a line about "improving models," which means your data may train the system.

3. Check how long they keep your data and whether you can delete it.
4. Compare free vs. paid versions; privacy often costs.
5. Finally, ask yourself: *Would I email this to a stranger?* If not, keep it out of AI.

The Dark Side of AI: Hallucinations, Bias, and Overreliance

Hallucinations and False Confidence

AI doesn't know the truth; it predicts patterns. It can sound right while being completely wrong.

A translator once used AI to summarize a legal contract. It looked perfect until his client noticed two invented clauses.

> **PRO TIP** Always double-check facts, dates, and names before sending anything AI-generated to a client.

Bias in the Machine

A copywriter once asked AI for "top entrepreneurs to study." The list? Ten men from Silicon Valley. That's bias reflecting the data the AI learned from. Bias isn't just about inclusion; it affects money, too. In studies, AI salary tools advised equally qualified women to charge less than men.

> **PRO TIP** When AI gives advice, test it. Change details like gender, country, or age. If answers shift, bias is baked in.

The Creativity Trap

A social media manager used AI for every caption. Soon, engagement dropped. Every post sounded the same: polished but soulless.

> **PRO TIP** Let AI brainstorm, but keep your voice in the final cut. Add humor, emotion, or a personal touch.

Privacy and Intellectual Property

Your clients trust you with sensitive information: budgets, contracts, or designs. Uploading those to public AI tools risks leaks and breaches. Even paid tools store data.

Rule: If you wouldn't email it to a stranger, don't paste it into AI.

The Ethical Tightrope

Is it okay to deliver AI-generated work without saying so? A content freelancer, learned the hard way. His client found nearly identical phrasing elsewhere from another AI user. Transparency could have saved his reputation.

PRO TIP Say, "AI helped me brainstorm, but I finalized and reviewed everything." Clients respect honesty more than speed.

Quick Test: Spotting the Dark Side

Underline *Yes* or *No*:

1. I always fact-check information I get from AI. Yes No
2. I avoid uploading sensitive client data into AI tools. Yes No
3. I can spot when an AI answer shows bias or missing voices. Yes No
4. I rewrite AI drafts in my own style before delivering them. Yes No
5. I'm transparent with clients if AI played a role in the process. Yes No
   - If you underlined 4–5 "Yes" answers, you're using AI responsibly. Keep your gloves on.
   - If you underlined 2–3 "Yes" answers, it's time to tighten your safety net. Pick one area to improve.
   - If you underlined 0–1 "Yes" answers, you're playing with fire. Before using AI again, commit to building safer habits.

When Ethics Meets Everyday Decisions

Ethics might sound big, but it lives in small choices. Every time you use AI, you are shaping what kind of professional you become.

Do you credit the AI when it helps? Do you double-check your sources before quoting generated text? Do you stop and ask if automation is saving time or cutting corners?

Clients notice these things. They notice when you take ownership, when you admit a mistake, when you explain how your process works. Each moment of honesty adds up to something much bigger: long-term trust.

Here's the truth: ethics isn't about following a rulebook. It's about building a reputation that feels safe to work with. When clients know you care about fairness, accuracy, and respect, they trust you not only with their money but also with their brand, audience, and story. That is priceless.

Freelancer Ethics in Action

Let's look at how three freelancers handled AI responsibly.

A social media manager uses AI to generate ideas and draft captions. One day, her AI tool suggested hashtags that misrepresented a cultural event. Instead of posting blindly, she researched each term, replaced the ones that didn't fit, and added her personal context. The result wasn't just more accurate, it was more authentic. Her followers felt her voice, not a machine's.

A scriptwriter uses AI for brainstorming dialogue in her scripts. At first, she noticed that the AI defaulted to Western names and speech patterns. She took a step back and added context: "Use East African idioms, include local slang, and reflect Nairobi's rhythm." The rewrite sparkled with realism. Her client said it felt "alive again." That's the power of human editing paired with ethical awareness.

An event planner uses AI tools to design visual mockups for weddings and galas. When one program repeatedly suggested Western-style decorations for a Mexican celebration, she didn't ignore it. She trained the tool with examples of traditional Oaxacan textiles and colors. The result was both culturally accurate and emotionally powerful. Her clients felt seen.

These freelancers didn't avoid AI; they managed it. Each time they questioned a result, they strengthened their reputation as thoughtful, responsible professionals.

How to Build Ethical AI Habits

Ethical work habits are like cleaning your kitchen: not glamorous, but essential if you want to keep serving great tacos:

1. *Accountability:* Always review your AI's work before sharing it. Automation is fast, but it cannot understand tone or emotion as you can. If your AI writes something that feels off, rewrite it.

2. *Transparency:* Be clear about your process. Tell clients how you use AI to save time or test ideas. When people understand your methods, they respect your results more.
3. *Fairness:* Use prompts that include diverse voices and perspectives. If you design visuals, include people of different ages, abilities, and backgrounds. If you write, vary your cultural references. Fairness isn't just right; it makes your work richer.
4. *Reliability and safety:* Never use a tool in a client project before testing it yourself. Run small experiments to learn where it fails. Keep backups so a glitch never stops your workflow.
5. *Privacy and security:* Before uploading anything into a public tool, ask: *Would my client be okay with this?* If the answer is "I'm not sure," stop and anonymize the data. Treat privacy like the secret sauce of your business; once spilled, it's hard to get back.
6. *Inclusiveness:* Respect different experiences. If your AI generates language or images, ensure that they include diverse representation. Your work reaches farther when it welcomes more people in.

Your 15-Minute Freelance Ethics Check

Run this quick audit once a month to stay aligned with your values:

1. *Inventory:* List every AI tool you use and what data it touches.
2. *Risk rating:* Label each one as low, medium, or high risk.
3. *Bias test:* Try different prompts: gender swaps, cultural contexts, accessibility scenarios. Does anything change?
4. *Documentation:* Note what you find and how you fix it. These notes show professionalism if a client ever asks about your ethical process.

The Legacy of Digital Trust

One of the biggest lessons in the age of AI is that technology moves fast, but reputation lasts. Every project you complete contributes to your digital legacy. Clients remember who handled mistakes gracefully, who respected their data, and who sounded genuinely human in a world of templates.

AI tools will come and go. What remains is how you used them. Ten years from now, you might not remember the exact tools, but you'll remember the clients who came back because they trusted you.

Ethics is not about perfection; it's about care. Every thoughtful decision you make adds up, like slow-cooked salsa. It might not be flashy, but it's the ingredient that keeps people coming back.

Badge Achievement Plan: The Ethical Creator

Complete the following missions to demonstrate your skills and earn your badge!

In this chapter, you learned that ethics is not about avoiding AI but rather about using it with awareness and respect. You discovered how fairness, transparency, and accountability build strong, lasting client relationships. Now it's time to apply these lessons to your freelance work.

Time Required: 1 hour 35 minutes, plus a quick 15-minute monthly review

Goal: Build a personal ethics checklist for your freelance business, and strengthen your clients' trust in your process.

What You'll Need:

- A notebook or digital document
- A list of your AI tools or automations
- One current or recent client project to review

Mission 1: The Trust Check (15 minutes)

List all the AI tools you currently use. For each one, answer:

- Would my client feel comfortable knowing I use this?
- Do I review the AI's output before delivering it?
- Have I ever disclosed my process?

Write down one thing you could communicate more clearly in future proposals.

Mission 2: The Risk Map (20 minutes)

Give each tool a risk level: low, medium, or high. For high-risk tools, describe one action you can take to lower that risk, such as anonymizing data, adjusting settings, or adding a human review step.

Mission 3: The Bias and Hallucination Test (15 minutes)

Choose one piece of AI-generated content (like a caption, proposal, or summary).

1. Highlight three factual statements and verify them with Google or the original source.

   Prompt: "List three factual statements in this text. Mark which ones may need verification."
2. Ask AI the same question again, but change one variable (e.g., gender, age, or region).

   Prompt: "Now repeat your answer as if the subject was [change gender, age, or region]."
3. Compare the outputs; do they change in tone or quality? Write a few lines about what you discovered.

Mission 4: The Transparency Statement (15 minutes)

Write one short paragraph to include in proposals, such as

"I use AI tools to support creativity and efficiency. All outputs are reviewed and finalized by me, and no client data is shared without consent."

> Special secret prompt:
>
> "Help me write a short, professional statement that explains how I use AI ethically in my freelance work. Make it sound transparent, confident, and human."

Save your version and include it in your future client proposals. This builds credibility and sets you apart as a trustworthy professional.

Mission 5: The Safety Habit (10 minutes)

Create a checklist for every new project:

- I've tested this AI tool myself before using it on client work.
- I've reviewed privacy policies.
- I've anonymized or redacted client data.
- I've kept a local backup of important files.

Keep this checklist visible in your workspace.

Mission 6: Reflect (10 minutes)

Write a few sentences answering:

"What does ethical AI use mean to me, and how can I show it in my daily freelance work?"

Mission 7: Final Knowledge Check (10 minutes)

1. What builds the strongest client trust?
   a. Consistency and transparency
   b. Marketing and automation
   c. Profit and speed
   d. Complex tools
2. What should you do if a client worries about data privacy?
   a. Ignore the concern
   b. Be open about how data is handled and protected
   c. Promise AI is always safe
   d. Avoid answering
3. Why is it better to under-pitch your AI capabilities?
   a. It sets realistic expectations and prevents disappointment
   b. It hides what you can really do
   c. It keeps competitors guessing
   d. It makes clients pay less
4. What is one common freelance ethics mistake?
   a. Automating without client consent
   b. Asking for feedback
   c. Testing for bias
   d. Writing documentation
5. What is the purpose of your monthly AI audit?
   a. To slow your workflow
   b. To identify risks and maintain trust
   c. To impress clients with jargon
   d. To track subscriptions
6. What's the best rule before uploading anything into AI?
   a. If I wouldn't email it to a stranger, I shouldn't upload it
   b. Upload everything for speed
   c. Free tools are always private
   d. Paid plans can't store data

Answer Sheet

1. **A: Consistency and transparency**
   Trust grows from clear communication and reliability.
2. **B: Be open about how data is handled and protected**
   Transparency removes fear and builds credibility.
3. **A: It sets realistic expectations and prevents disappointment**
   Clients value honesty more than perfection.
4. **A: Automating without client consent**
   Always check what clients want automated before doing it.
5. **B: To identify risks and maintain trust**
   Small audits prevent large problems later.
6. **A: If I wouldn't email it to a stranger, I shouldn't upload it**
   Keep sensitive information private; safety first.

Congratulations!

By completing these missions, you've turned ethics into an everyday practice. You now know how to use AI to enhance your business while staying true to your values. You now know how to fact-check, spot bias, protect client data, and communicate your process with integrity. Additionally, you've built a system for fairness, accountability, and trust that clients can depend on.

Once you finish, submit your responses by following the badge submission instructions listed in Chapter 1 or at `https://civicai.khoury.northeastern.edu/ai-for-gig-workers`. This badge shows that you use AI responsibly and can be trusted to handle technology with integrity.

What You Have Gained

You've gained more than tools; you've gained integrity. You now know how to check your work for fairness, communicate openly with clients, and handle mistakes with grace. You understand that trust is built one project at a time, through honesty, respect, and consistency.

In Part II of the book, we'll shift from learning to applying. You'll discover how to use AI to automate repetitive tasks, attract clients, and scale your business, all while protecting the ethical foundation that makes your work meaningful.

Because in freelancing, just like in tacos, balance is everything. The best results come from a mix of skill, responsibility, and heart.

PART 2

AI-Powered Strategies for Solving Gig Work Challenges

CHAPTER 9

Freeing Gig Workers from Unpaid Labor with AI Automation

You've already learned how to talk to AI, build your first digital teammate, and use it responsibly. Now it's time to let those skills earn their keep. In this chapter, we'll focus on automation, how to get AI to handle repetitive, time-consuming work so you can focus on creativity, clients, and strategy.

Think of this as the moment your taco truck hires its first crew. You've set up your kitchen, you've created your recipes, and now the team, your AI agents, starts prepping ingredients while you focus on the customers.

The Hidden Tax of Gig Work: Unpaid Administrative Tasks

As you know, freelancers often wear more hats than a mariachi band. You're the talent, the accountant, the marketing team, the customer service desk, and sometimes even the janitor. The result? A hidden tax on your time.

All those small, necessary administrative tasks you do, the ones you can't bill for, quietly eat into your income and energy. Here's what that looks like:

Financial management: Tracking expenses, categorizing receipts, generating invoices, following up on payments, and preparing tax documents

Client communication: Responding to inquiries, scheduling meetings, sending follow-up emails, managing booking calendars, and updating project status

Content and data management: Formatting documents for clients, organizing project files, updating databases, maintaining social media accounts, editing content, and keeping portfolios current

Project coordination: Managing deadlines, coordinating with vendors or collaborators, updating project boards, and tracking deliverables

All these tasks keep your hustle running, but they don't directly bring in cash. It's like a sneaky tax on your time that nobody talks about. Every hour spent chasing invoices or sorting files is an hour you could use earning or improving your business. Realizing how much unpaid labor goes into freelancing can be frustrating, but it's also the first step to reclaiming your time.

How AI Automation Transforms Unpaid Labor

Here's the good news. AI tools can be game-changers for handling repetitive, unpaid admin work that follows predictable steps. Instead of spending hours on scheduling, invoicing, or data entry, you can let AI handle it while you focus on high-value work.

This isn't just about saving time. It's literally saving money. If you spend 10 hours a week on admin work and could make $20 an hour doing paid projects, that's $200 lost every week. AI automation can give you those hours back. That means more time for paying clients, growing your business, or simply living your life without the mental weight of "to-dos" hanging over you.

Here are some AI tools that can help:

1. *Automated scheduling:* Calendly AI or Motion can eliminate endless back-and-forth emails by letting clients book directly. They sync calendars and send reminders automatically.
2. *Expense tracking:* QuickBooks AI can categorize expenses and connect to your accounts, reducing manual data entry and improving financial accuracy.
3. *Client communication:* Zapier or Make.com (formerly Integromat) can save client inquiries, trigger booking confirmations, and send welcome messages without you lifting a finger.

4. *Content management:* Buffer AI helps schedule posts across platforms, and Notion AI organizes data, automates formatting, and updates project lists.
5. *Invoice generation:* AI-enabled systems can create branded invoices, send reminders, and track balances, all without constant monitoring.

Remember what you learned about prompt engineering. You already know how to talk to AI and make it respond in your style. Now you'll apply those same skills to your admin tasks. You'll use the tools just listed or prompt your favorite AI model directly to handle these repetitive workflows. Often, combining both will be your best secret sauce. Once you see AI handle your scheduling, invoicing, and communication, you'll wonder why you ever did those things manually.

Prompt Engineering for Administrative Automation

Your prompting skills are your new superpower. You've already learned how to write clear, detailed prompts that deliver the right tone, structure, and output. Now you'll use them to turn AI into your personal admin assistant.

Here are some example prompts for automating your freelance operations:

For expense categorization:

"Analyze these expenses and categorize them for tax purposes: [paste expense list]. Create categories for office supplies, travel, equipment, meals, and professional development. Format as a table with date, amount, description, and category."

For client communication templates:

"Create three professional email templates:

1. Initial client inquiry response with booking link,
2. Project completion follow-up with invoice request,
3. Payment reminder that is firm but friendly.

Make each template personalized and consistent with professional service standards."

For social media scheduling:

"Create a week's worth of social media content for [your service type]. Include:

- Two educational posts that highlight my expertise in [your niche].
- Two behind-the-scenes posts showing me working on [describe work].
- One call-to-action post.

Format for Instagram, LinkedIn, and X with hashtags and posting times."

For invoice generation:

"Generate a professional invoice template including business name and contact details, client information, itemized services with dates and rates, subtotal and taxes, payment terms (Net 30), and payment methods. Make it look polished and ready to send."

For task prioritization:

"Review my task list for this week. Create a table that organizes them into:

1. Urgent and income-generating,
2. Important but not urgent,
3. Administrative but necessary,
4. Low priority.

For each, estimate time required and suggest a schedule. Explain why each task fits its category."

The same clarity that made your creative AI sidekick shine now powers your business engine.

Smart Systems, Not Shortcuts

Automation works best when it supports your strengths, not when it replaces your judgment. Always remember when you assign tasks to your AI agents to combine that autonomy with your human touch.

Start small. If you've already built your Proposal Pro agent, connect it to a scheduling tool like Notion AI or Zapier. Let it generate proposals and create reminders for follow-ups. You're not removing yourself from the process; you're building a system that works while you rest.

Keep using the habits you learned earlier: give every AI clear instructions, context, and limits. That's the difference between smooth automation and chaos. And stay ethical. Never automate something a client expects a human to handle. Transparency keeps trust alive.

Setting Up Your Automation System

Now that you know what tools and prompts to use, it's time to connect them. Imagine an automated freelancing system that keeps working while you're out enjoying life.

You could come back from grabbing your favorite tacos or playing beach volleyball to find your invoices sent, social media posted, expenses sorted, and calendar filled with new clients. Sounds amazing, right?

We know it might feel overwhelming, but don't worry. We'll guide you step by step. Once your system is running, you'll have more time for the work that actually pays, and for the life that inspires it.

Take the event planner who learned to balance AI with cultural authenticity. Now she's using those same skills to automate her scheduling process. Instead of manually managing every booking, she built a simple AI-powered workflow. Her agent checks client forms each morning, sorts new inquiries by event type, and drafts follow-up messages that match her voice. You already know how to train AI to reflect your style, so you can imagine how seamless those emails feel. Now this event planner spends her mornings designing experiences, not chasing calendars. Automation didn't replace her. It amplified her best qualities: responsiveness, warmth, and organization.

Your AI Sidekick Network

By now, your AI tools are not random apps but teammates. You've built a network of assistants working together.

- Your Proposal Pro agent creates tailored project pitches.
- Your Research agent gathers leads and insights.
- Your Voice Guardian keeps every message on-brand.
- Your Ethical Assistant checks for privacy and tone.

You've already learned how to assign these agents specific roles and how to communicate clearly with them. Now let's take things one step further and see how they can collaborate as a true team.

Expanding Your Team: Working with Multiple AI Agents

You've already built one custom agent and seen how it fits into your workflow. Now scale that concept. Imagine a crew of digital assistants, each specialized in a specific job, working together so you can stay in your creative zone.

For example:

- Your Proposal Pro agent drafts pitches, and your Client Onboarding agent sends welcome emails and organizes workflows.
- Your Content Scheduler agent publishes social posts across platforms, and your Expense Tracker Agent sorts receipts, logs expenses, and alerts you when payments are late.
- Your Voice Guardian agent checks outgoing messages for tone and consistency, and your Ethics Monitor agent flags anything that touches privacy or sensitive data.

The benefit is simple. Much like a taco truck that hires a short-order cook, a cashier, and a delivery driver, you stop doing every job yourself. You supervise the team, you set the vision, and you review the output instead of performing every task. That frees your time for the work that actually pays—creating, pitching, and innovating—while your digital crew handles the rest.

Because you already know how to write clear prompts, set context, and train style from previous chapters, managing multiple agents feels organized rather than chaotic. You can decide how they interact: that triggers what, when tasks pass from one agent to another, and where you step in. For example, your Research agent might identify a potential client, then hand the task to your Proposal Pro agent to draft the pitch, which signals your Onboarding agent once the client confirms. You're not just building tools, you're orchestrating a connected workflow.

The key is to take it step by step. Start with one additional agent and observe how it performs before expanding. Think of it like adding another taco chef once your line of customers grows. Too many agents too soon can create confusion instead of relief. Keep a review step to ensure quality, tone, and consistency stay intact.

Take a moment to imagine your ideal digital team. Which roles would make your life easier? Which agent could save you the most time this week? Once that vision is clear, you're ready to build.

You now have a growing team of AI agents working in harmony. Before you dive into building your first full automation, let's talk about making sure all this effort actually pays off, in time, money, and results.

Maximizing ROI from Automation

Calculate the value of your time saved through automation. If you earn $25 per hour and automation saves you 5 hours weekly, that's $125 in potential additional earnings. An automation tool costing $20 monthly provides a strong return on investment.

Priority should be given to automating tasks that:

- Consume the most time relative to their complexity
- Happen most frequently in your workflow
- Have steps that are constantly repeating themselves
- Do not involve much creativity and would not get you in trouble if the task is done incorrectly

By systematically automating unpaid administrative labor, you can reclaim significant time for income-generating activities, client acquisition, and business growth, ultimately transforming your productivity and profitability.

Avoiding Automation Pitfalls

Automation can transform your gig, but it's not foolproof. Like a faulty kitchen gadget, it can slow your taco truck if mishandled. Here are the pitfalls and how to avoid them:

- *Over-automating:* a social media manager auto-replied to DMs using Buffer AI, but the robotic tone hurt engagement. She switched to auto-saving inquiries for manual review and regained trust. Keep a human touch.

- *Ignoring setup time:* a translator spent an hour building a Zapier workflow before finding a simpler QuickBooks template. Start with plug-and-play tools and free tiers first.
- *Neglecting maintenance:* an event planner's Calendly links expired after an update, costing a $2,000 gig. Now she checks automations monthly.
- *Overlooking ethics:* A VA discloses AI use to clients and earns trust. She reviews AI-graded work herself. Transparency builds credibility.
- *Choosing costly tools too soon:* A musician and producer paid $50 for a suite he didn't need; a $12 plan fit better. Test free options before investing.

Avoid these traps with small, well-planned tests. Keep your automations simple, ethical, and aligned with your goals.

Budgeting for Automation Without Breaking the Bank

Automation doesn't have to be expensive. Smart budgeting keeps your gig profitable while maximizing time savings. Many tools offer free tiers that deliver serious value, letting you test and scale without upfront costs. An online tutor relies on Notion AI's free plan for quiz grading, saving $30 monthly that she uses for Instagram ads, doubling her student base to 50. A VA uses Calendly's free tier for client bookings, saving $10/month while reclaiming two hours weekly.

When considering paid tools, prioritize those with high return on investment (ROI). A designer upgraded to Buffer AI's $15/month plan after it saved an hour daily, leading to a $2,000 brand deal that far outweighed the cost. A translator chose QuickBooks AI's $15/month plan, which saved 30 minutes daily and added $100 weekly to his earnings through extra shifts, making the subscription a no-brainer. Calculate potential savings (time freed multiplied by your hourly rate) to justify costs.

Mix free and paid tools to balance value and budget. A VA combines free Notion AI for task management, free ChatGPT for drafting emails, and paid Zapier ($19/month) for multistep automations, keeping costs under $20 while saving four hours weekly. An event planner uses free Canva AI for event visuals and paid QuickBooks AI ($15/month) for invoicing, saving two hours weekly without breaking her budget.

Check for discounts. Many tools offer annual plans, student rates, or freelancer promotions. Budgeting wisely for automation now sets you up for networking and scaling later, like investing in a CRM for client management or a course platform for digital products.

Badge Achievement Plan: The Automation Architect

Complete the following missions to earn your Automation Architect Badge and prove you can design, run, and refine an ethical, efficient AI workflow that makes you money while you sleep.

You've already built agents, mastered communication, and learned ethical prompting. Now you'll combine those skills into a single, working automation system that connects at least two AI tools or agents and delivers measurable results, time saved, money earned, or client satisfaction improved.

Time Required: About 2 hours to build and test +1 week of observation

Goal: Design and launch one ethical automation that saves measurable time or generates new value for your freelance business.

What You'll Need:

- A notebook or digital doc for planning
- Access to at least two AI tools (ChatGPT, Notion AI, Zapier, QuickBooks AI, Buffer AI, etc.)
- One real workflow you currently do manually (scheduling, follow-ups, posting, invoicing, etc.)

Mission 1: Audit Your Hidden Tax (20 minutes)

List every unpaid administrative task you still handle manually.
For each one, estimate:

- Time spent per week
- Approximate hourly value of that time
- Whether it involves sensitive client data

Circle one or two tasks that cost the most time and are safe to automate. Write a short note:

"This is my automation target because it costs me ___ hours a week and doesn't require human creativity."

Mission 2: Design Your Automation Map (30 minutes)

Sketch your workflow using the "agent network" idea from this chapter. Include:

- *Trigger:* What starts the workflow (e.g., new client form)
- *Actions:* Which agent or tool handles each step
- *Review point:* Where you personally check quality or tone
- *Outcome:* What success looks like (proposal sent, invoice logged, etc.)

If you're a visual person, use Notion, Trello, or pen and paper.

Give your automation a fun name (e.g., *Taco Tracker 3000* or *Inbox to Invoice Flow*).

Mission 3: Build and Train (40 minutes)

Now comes the fun part: connecting your agents so they work *together*. Think of this as introducing your taco chef to your cashier and your delivery driver. Each knows their job, but now you'll get them talking so the tacos (or invoices) keep flowing.

You'll design a simple multiagent system that connects two or more AI tools. One handles the thinking, the other handles the doing.

Step 1: Choose Your Agents

Pick two tools or AI agents that naturally complement each other.
Examples:

- ChatGPT + Notion AI → ChatGPT writes proposals, Notion organizes and tracks them
- ChatGPT + Zapier → ChatGPT drafts client emails, Zapier sends them automatically
- QuickBooks AI + Google Sheets + ChatGPT → QuickBooks tracks expenses, Sheets logs patterns, ChatGPT summarizes financial insights

Step 2: Establish Roles

Decide what each agent's role will be in your automation.
Example:

- Agent 1 (ChatGPT): Thinks and writes
- Agent 2 (Zapier): Delivers and tracks

You can think of it as a relay race, where each agent passes the baton to the next one.

Special secret prompts:

1. "You are the *Strategy Agent*. Your job is to create clear instructions for my *Action Agent* to follow. Begin by asking me what task we're automating."
2. "You are the *Action Agent*. You take instructions from my Strategy Agent and execute the steps using [specific tool or app]. Always summarize what you did in one paragraph."
3. "Strategy Agent: Write the exact command my Action Agent needs to execute in [tool]. Include variables like name, date, or price in brackets."

Now, open two ChatGPT windows or tabs. Assign each one its role and paste its prompt. You've just built a mini team.

Step 3: Create the Conversation Loop

Once both agents are defined, start their dialogue:

You say to Agent 1 (Strategy):

"I want to automate sending client follow-ups three days after they receive a proposal."

Agent 1 replies with a plan:

"You can use Zapier to detect when a proposal is sent (Trigger) and ChatGPT to draft a friendly reminder email (Action)."

You copy Agent 1's plan and paste it into Agent 2 (Action):

"Follow these instructions from my Strategy Agent and create a Zapier workflow."

Agent 2 responds with a step-by-step setup, which you can follow or adjust.

This back-and-forth builds your first working system.

Pro tip prompt: "Summarize this entire workflow as a checklist I can follow to connect these tools. Include trigger, actions, and review points."

Step 4: Test the System

Before using real data, run a dry test:

- Use fake names and emails.
- Check that every step triggers correctly.
- Confirm your tone, accuracy, and privacy checklist are in place.

> Secret debug prompt: "Run a quick diagnostic: What could go wrong in this automation? Suggest one safety step for each possible failure."

When everything works, you'll have your first fully operational AI workflow, designed, tested, and managed by you.

Step 5: Observe and Refine

Run your automation for one week. Each day, note

- How much time you saved
- Any errors or surprises
- What clients noticed (if anything)

After seven days, ask your AI for feedback:

> Prompt: "Based on this summary of my results [paste notes], how can I improve the reliability and performance of my automation?"

This turns your experiment into a living system that keeps getting smarter, just like you.

At week's end, calculate ROI:

Time saved × hourly rate = value created

If the automation costs money (subscription, upgrade, etc.), subtract that to see your real return.

Mission 4: Reflect and Refine (30 minutes)

Answer in writing:

1. What part of the automation delivered the biggest benefit?
2. Did it maintain your voice and ethics?
3. What will you tweak or scale next?

Then summarize your learning in one paragraph titled "My Automation Manifesto."

Example:

"I built a workflow that auto-schedules client calls and sends branded invoices. It saves me 3 hours weekly and keeps my messages friendly and transparent. Next, I'll add a research agent to expand lead generation."

Extra Challenge (optional)

Share your automation results with another freelancer or mentor. Ask:

"Would you trust this system if I worked for you?"

Document feedback and adjustments.

Mission 5: Final Knowledge Check (10 minutes)

1. The chapter describes unpaid administrative work as a "hidden tax on your time." What is the main reason this "tax" is so damaging to a freelancer's business?
   - **a.** It requires learning difficult software
   - **b.** The tasks are boring and reduce creativity
   - **c.** Every hour spent on unpaid work is an hour that could have been used for billable, income-generating client work
   - **d.** It significantly increases the amount of real tax you have to pay
2. A freelancer is overwhelmed by the endless back-and-forth emails required to schedule meetings. Which AI tool does the chapter specifically recommend for this problem?
   - **a.** QuickBooks AI
   - **b.** Buffer AI
   - **c.** Calendly AI
   - **d.** Notion AI
3. According to the chapter, which of the following is a good example of using prompt engineering for an administrative task?
   - **a.** Asking an AI to "make my schedule better"
   - **b.** Prompting an AI to "Analyze these expenses and categorize them for tax purposes . . . Format as a table"
   - **c.** Using an AI to generate a creative story for a blog
   - **d.** Asking an AI to "find new clients for me"
4. An influencer used an AI tool to auto-reply to all her Instagram DMs, which felt robotic and caused her engagement to drop. This story is an example of which common pitfall?
   - **a.** Neglecting maintenance
   - **b.** Over-automating and losing the personal touch
   - **c.** Ignoring initial setup time
   - **d.** Choosing costly tools prematurely

5. What is the first and most important step when setting up your own automation system?
   a. To buy the most expensive software you can afford
   b. To immediately connect all your apps using Zapier
   c. To spend a week tracking your time to identify the most repetitive and time-consuming admin tasks
   d. To write a complete library of email templates
6. How does the chapter advise freelancers to think about the ethics of using AI automation?
   a. To hide AI use from clients to appear more productive
   b. To be transparent with clients about the tools you use, which can build trust and even earn positive reviews
   c. To only use automation for tasks that clients will never see
   d. To charge clients an extra "AI fee" for any automated work
7. An event planner missed out on a potential $2,000 gig because her automated booking links expired after a software update. This is a cautionary tale about which pitfall?
   a. Neglecting maintenance
   b. Overlooking ethical considerations
   c. Over-automating
   d. Ignoring initial setup time
8. When budgeting for automation, what is the chapter's primary advice?
   a. You must invest in expensive, premium tools to see any real benefit
   b. Start by using the free tiers of powerful tools, as they often cover most of what a freelancer needs
   c. Automation is too expensive for anyone just starting out
   d. Prioritize tools that look the most impressive on a resume
9. For a freelancer who needs to automatically track mileage, categorize business spending, and prepare for tax time, which tool is highlighted in the chapter?
   a. Zapier
   b. Calendly AI
   c. Buffer AI
   d. QuickBooks AI
10. How does the chapter recommend you calculate the return on investment (ROI) for a paid automation tool?
    a. By counting how many new features the tool has
    b. By comparing the monthly cost of the tool to the monetary value of the time it saves you
    c. By asking your most successful competitor what they use
    d. By assuming any tool under $50/month is a good investment

Answer Sheet

1. **C: Every hour spent on unpaid work is an hour that could have been used for billable, income-generating client work**

   The chapter emphasizes that unpaid labor directly hurts earning potential by consuming time that could be spent on paid projects.

2. **C: Calendly AI**

   The text explicitly mentions that tools like Calendly AI are designed to solve this exact problem by allowing clients to book directly and eliminating scheduling emails.

3. **B: Prompting an AI to "Analyze these expenses and categorize them for tax purposes . . . Format as a table"**

   This is a direct example from the "Prompt Engineering for Administrative Automation" section, showing how a specific, structured prompt can automate a complex admin task.

4. **B: Over-automating and losing the personal touch**

   Relying too heavily on automation for personal communication can feel robotic and damage client or audience relationships.

5. **C: To spend a week tracking your time to identify the most repetitive and time-consuming admin tasks**

   The chapter begins by describing the "hidden tax" of unpaid labor and shows that the first step toward automation is identifying which tasks waste the most time and can safely be delegated to AI. Tracking your time reveals those repetitive, low-value tasks and helps you target what's worth automating.

6. **B: To be transparent with clients about the tools you use, which can build trust and even earn positive reviews**

   Transparency regarding AI tools is an ethical and effective business practice.

7. **A: Neglecting maintenance**

   This missed gig is the main illustration of this pitfall, showing that automation systems need to be checked regularly to ensure they are still working correctly after updates.

8. **B: Start by using the free tiers of powerful tools, as they often cover most of what a freelancer needs**

   The "Budgeting for Automation" section advises starting with free plans and provides examples of freelancers who achieve significant results without paying.

9. **D: QuickBooks AI**

   The chapter names QuickBooks AI as the tool for automatically categorizing expenses from bank accounts to ensure accurate financial records for tasks like taxes.

10. **B: By comparing the monthly cost of the tool to the monetary value of the time it saves you**

    The chapter provides a specific formula for this: if a tool costs $20/month but saves you 5 hours of work at a $25/hour rate, it provides a strong return on investment.

Congratulations!

You did it. You've turned your freelancing hustle into a living system that works for you instead of against you. By completing these missions, you didn't just automate tasks; you built your first real digital infrastructure.

You've learned how to map workflows, connect AI tools, measure ROI, and maintain ethical oversight all at once. You've gone from experimenting with prompts to engineering results that keep paying off week after week.

Once you finish, submit your responses by following the badge submission instructions listed in Chapter 1 or at `https://civicai.khoury.northeastern.edu/ai-for-gig-workers`. This badge certifies that you can connect multiple AI tools, maintain ethical oversight, and design systems that genuinely save time and increase earnings, a rare and valuable skill in today's gig economy.

It's more than a symbol of completion. It's proof that you can blend creativity with structure, strategy with ethics, and vision with technology. It tells clients that you're not only skilled at your craft but also capable of building reliable, scalable systems that make work smoother for everyone. This is what separates an ordinary freelancer from a sustainable business owner. You've moved from reactive to proactive, from doing every task yourself to designing a system that earns while you create. That's a major milestone, and you earned it one smart prompt, one ethical choice, and one workflow at a time.

What You Have Gained

You've learned to think like a systems designer. You now see your freelance business not as a list of tasks but as a living ecosystem in which every part supports the others. You've turned unpaid labor into automated value, linked your AI sidekicks into a working crew, and proved that automation can be ethical, personal, and profitable all at once.

You've also gained confidence, the kind that comes from seeing your work run smoothly while you focus on what you love most. You've freed time for strategy, creativity, and rest, all while keeping your clients impressed with your consistency and care.

In the next chapter, we'll take that freed-up time and put it to work for growth. Chapter 10 will show you how to use AI to find clients, craft stronger outreach, and build lasting professional relationships. You'll learn to turn your smart systems into smart networking and sustainable income. Because a great taco truck doesn't just serve faster, it builds a loyal line around the block.

CHAPTER 10

Networking with AI

Networking is probably one of the most important things you can do for your freelance business, but it's also one of the most time-consuming; and honestly, it's kind of awkward. The good news? AI can make this whole process way easier and more effective. Here's the thing: your network is literally your lifeline as a freelancer. It's how you get better clients, higher-paying projects, and referrals that keep your business growing. But traditional networking feels like a chore, and most of us don't have time to attend endless events or send hundreds of cold emails.

How AI Transforms Your Networking Game

AI changes networking from a numbers game to a strategic operation. Instead of spending time reaching out to strangers on the internet and crossing your fingers that they will reply, AI lets you be way more strategic about networking. Here's exactly how it works:

- *Finding the right people:* AI can scan platforms like LinkedIn, Twitter, and industry forums to identify people who actually match what you're looking for. Whether you need new clients, want to partner with other freelancers, or are seeking mentors, AI can help you to filter online profiles (which could be in the thousands!). Through this, you might be able to find the ones that make sense for your goals.
- *Research before you reach out:* Once you've identified potential connections, AI can gather information about them from their social media posts, company websites, recent news, and public content. This means you'll know what projects they're working on, what challenges they're facing, and what interests them before you ever send that first message.

- *Write messages that actually get responses:* Armed with this information, you can then use AI to help you craft personalized outreach messages that speak directly to their situation. Instead of sending generic "Hey, let's connect" messages, you can reference their recent work, comment on industry trends they care about, or offer solutions to problems they've mentioned.
- *Stay organized, and follow up:* AI can keep track of everyone you've contacted, what you talked about, when you last spoke, and when you should follow up. It can even draft follow-up messages and remind you to send them, so no potential connection gets forgotten in your busy schedule.
- *Keep relationships warm:* As your network grows, AI can help you maintain relationships by suggesting when to check in with people, what to share that might interest them, and how to stay on their radar without being annoying.

Here is more information about how AI could support you.

Step 1: Finding the Right People to Connect With

The first step is identifying who you actually want to connect with. AI can help you find clients, potential collaborators, or mentors—especially people who align with your goals.

- *Use LinkedIn AI to find prospects:* "Identify [your target client type] in [your location or industry] that are currently hiring freelancers for [your service type]. Prioritize companies that meet specific criteria, such as recent growth, company size, or activity in a relevant niche."
- *Use ChatGPT to research platforms:* "Search [social media platform] for conversations where [your target audience] is actively discussing [specific problems your service or product solves]. Identify key community leaders, influencers, or highly engaged users, as well as individuals who could be ideal clients based on their needs, questions, or pain points."
- *Use Google Sheets AI to analyze your existing network:* "Review my current client list. Identify common traits of my clients, especially the ones that hire me the most. Based on these patterns, recommend the types of individuals or organizations I should target to find similar high-value opportunities."

Step 2: Research Your Targets

Once you have found potential connections, it is important that you have a good understanding of what they truly care about. AI can assist by researching their current challenges, goals, and ongoing projects. This gives you the context you need to approach them with relevant, valuable insights instead of generic outreach.

- *Research their business:* "Review [company name]'s recent social media activity, news reports, as well as job postings. Based on the information you collect, identify the key challenges or priorities they are currently facing. How could my [service] help address these specific needs or pain points?"
- *Understand their industry:* "Tell me what are the current trends and challenges in [their industry] that someone offering [your service] should know about?"
- *Find common ground:* "Based on [person's LinkedIn profile/recent posts], what shared interests or experiences could I mention to build rapport?"

Step 3: Craft Personalized Outreach Messages

This is where AI really shines. Instead of sending generic messages that get ignored, you can create personalized outreach that actually gets responses.

- *For initial contact:* "Write a professional [email/LinkedIn message] to [specific person] at [company]. Reference [specific thing about their business/recent post]. Pitch my [service] by addressing [specific challenges they likely face]. Keep it under 150 words and include a clear call to action."
- *For follow-up messages:* "Write a follow-up message to [contact] who hasn't responded to my initial outreach about [service]. Add value by sharing [relevant tips/resources] related to [their business challenge]. Keep it helpful, not pushy."
- *For warm introductions:* "Write a message to [mutual connection] asking if they could please introduce me to [person]. Explain why I would like to connect. Explain to them also how the introduction could be mutually beneficial or how they would benefit from helping me. Be formal."

Step 4: Using Multiagent Systems for Networking

You can use multiple AI agents to help you network, especially if you want to integrate different strategies for your networking efforts. It is basically like if you had an entire team dedicated to developing and executing your networking strategy.

- Set up your networking team:
  - *The Research agent:* "You are a business intelligence researcher. Your job is to find detailed information about potential clients, their challenges, recent company news, and decision-makers. Research [target company/person] and provide a comprehensive profile."
  - *The Strategy agent:* "You are a networking strategist. Based on this research [paste research], determine the best approach for connecting with this prospect. What's the ideal timing, platform, and angle for outreach?"
  - *The Copywriting agent:* "You are an expert at writing compelling outreach messages. Based on this research and strategy [paste info], write personalized messages that will get responses. Create 3 variations for A/B testing."
  - *The Relationship Manager agent:* "You are a relationship management expert. Create a follow-up schedule (when I should contact this person again) and content plan for nurturing this relationship over time. Include touchpoints, value-add content, and relationship milestones."

Step 5: Nurturing Your Network

Making connections is the first step. The value also comes from consistently maintaining and nurturing those relationships over time.

- *Use Notion AI to track relationships:* "Create a system for tracking my networking contacts, including their interests, recent projects, last contact date, and next follow-up actions."
- *Use ChatGPT for regular check-ins:* "Write a friendly check-in message to [contact] I haven't spoken to in [time period]. Reference [previous conversation/project] and offer [relevant value/insight]."
- *Use Google Sheets AI to analyze networking ROI:* "Track my networking activities and results. Help me to identify what types of outreach efforts and platforms generate the best response rates and business outcomes."

Step 6: Leveraging Social Platforms

Different platforms serve different networking purposes. AI can help you optimize your presence and engagement on each one.

- *LinkedIn for professional connections:* "Create a content calendar for LinkedIn that positions me as an expert in [your field]. Include industry insights, case studies, and thought leadership content."

- *Twitter/X for community engagement:* "Help me identify and engage with relevant conversations in [your industry]. Draft thoughtful responses that add value and showcase my expertise."
- *Instagram for a visual portfolio:* "Optimize my Instagram profile and content strategy to attract [target clients]. Create captions that tell the story behind my work and demonstrate results."

Balancing Networking with Your Actual Work

You can't spend all day networking; you still have client work to do. AI helps you make networking more efficient so it doesn't take over your life:

- *Time management:* "Create a weekly schedule that allocates [X hours] for my networking activities. But make sure I also can spend [Y hours] doing work for my clients. Prioritize networking tasks by potential impact."
- *Automation:* "Suggest tools and workflows for automating routine networking tasks like connection requests, follow-ups, and content sharing."
- *Quality over quantity:* "Help me identify which are the 20% of networking activities that will generate 80% of my results. Focus my efforts on high-impact connections and platforms."

Staying Ethical and Authentic

Using AI for networking doesn't mean being fake or manipulative. The goal is to be more strategic and efficient while maintaining genuine relationships.

- *Keep it real:* Always personalize AI-generated messages to match your voice and style. The AI tool should help you be more thoughtful, not more robotic.
- *Be transparent:* If someone asks about your process, be honest about using AI tools to help with research and organization. Most people appreciate efficiency.
- *Focus on value:* Every networking interaction should provide value to the other person, not just benefit you. Use AI to help you understand what they need and how you can help.

Badge Achievement Plan: The AI Connector

Complete the following missions to earn your AI Connector Badge!

In this chapter, you've explored how AI can help you build stronger relationships, craft personalized outreach, and grow your freelance network with authenticity and efficiency. Now it's time to apply what you've learned and turn those strategies into real, human-centered connections that open doors.

Time Required: 1 hour 20 minutes, plus 3 days of follow-up testing

Goal: Use AI to design, personalize, and test an outreach strategy that grows your client or collaborator network.

What You'll Need:

- A list of five potential clients, collaborators, or mentors
- Access to one or more AI tools (ChatGPT, Notion AI, or a CRM assistant)
- One past outreach email, proposal, or social message for reference
- A way to track results (spreadsheet, Notion table, or notes app)

Mission 1: Set Your Networking Goal (10 minutes)

Before you start reaching out, clarify what kind of connections you want to build. Ask yourself:

- Do I want to find new clients, collaborators, or mentors?
- Which industries or communities do I want to focus on?
- What kind of value can I offer in return?

> Special secret prompt: "You are my Networking Strategist. Based on my goals [describe them briefly], list three specific types of people or organizations I should connect with this month. Include why each one would be valuable and how I can offer value back."

Pick the one that feels most aligned, and focus your next missions on that group.

Mission 2: Build Your Outreach Agent (25 minutes)

It's time to turn AI into your personal networking assistant. Using what you've learned about tone, authenticity, and style, train it to help you write outreach messages that sound natural and personal.

> Special secret prompt: "You are my Networking Assistant. Using my past messages as examples, draft three outreach variations for [person or company name]. Make them warm, specific, and written in my natural tone. Include one personal detail from their recent work or post."

Steps:

1. Share two or three of your own messages or emails that reflect your real voice.
2. Run the previous prompt, and let the AI generate three versions.
3. Edit each one until it feels like something you'd actually say.
4. Keep the three best options as your outreach templates.

PRO TIP Create small variations (like a "short & casual" version and a "detailed & professional" one) for A/B testing, a simple way to see which message style performs better.

Mission 3: Send, Track, and Learn (3 Days)

Now it's time to take your Outreach agent for a spin and gather real-world data.

Steps:

1. Choose 5–10 people or companies to contact.
2. Send your AI-assisted messages over three days.
3. Create a simple table with the following columns:
   - Contact name
   - Message version (A or B)
   - Date sent
   - Whether they replied
   - Notes on tone and engagement

> Secret analysis prompt: "Here's my outreach data [paste your notes]. Analyze which message version performed best, what tone worked, and how I can improve my outreach next time."

At the end of the test, summarize your learnings:

- Which version got the best responses?
- Which message felt the most authentic to you?
- What adjustments will you make next round?

Outcome:

You'll have a working, personalized outreach system that combines AI efficiency with your human warmth, a recipe for long-term connection and opportunity.

Mission 4: Optimize Your Networking Workflow (15 minutes)

Now automate a small part of your process to save time while staying personal.

Examples:

- Use Notion AI or Google Sheets to track contacts and follow-up dates.
- Use Zapier or Make.com to send reminders like "Follow up with [name] today."
- Ask ChatGPT to summarize your past interactions before your next outreach.

> Special secret prompt: "Help me design a light-touch system to track my professional connections and remind me to follow up monthly. Keep it simple enough to manage in under 15 minutes a week."

You'll end up with a lightweight system that keeps relationships alive without constant manual work.

Mission 5: Reflect and Refine (10 minutes)

Take a few minutes to reflect on what you've learned. Ask yourself:

- What surprised me about how people responded?
- How did AI help me sound more confident or consistent?
- What do I want to try differently next time?

Secret reflection prompt: "Summarize what I've learned about using AI for authentic networking. Suggest three ways to build stronger, more human connections using technology."

Mission 6: Share Your Connection Story (10 minutes)

Post your experience on LinkedIn or your freelancer group.

Include what you tested, what surprised you, and one insight about balancing AI with authentic communication.

Tag it with #AIForFreelancers or #GigEconomyNetworking to inspire others.

Mission 7: Final Knowledge Check (10 minutes)

1. How does the chapter describe the main way AI transforms networking?
   - **a.** It changes networking from a random numbers game into a strategic, research-based operation
   - **b.** It creates a fake online persona for you to use
   - **c.** It completely automates conversations so you never have to talk to anyone
   - **d.** It guarantees that every message you send will get a response
2. What is the very first step in the AI-powered networking process outlined in the chapter?
   - **a.** Crafting the perfect outreach message
   - **b.** Using AI to find the right people to connect with, filtering by industry, location, or needs
   - **c.** Asking for a warm introduction from a mutual connection
   - **d.** Setting up your follow-up sequence
3. In "Using Multiagent Systems for Networking," what is the specific role of the Strategy agent?
   - **a.** To write a personalized email
   - **b.** To research the target company and find their pain points
   - **c.** To create a follow-up schedule for the contact
   - **d.** To determine the best approach, timing, and platform for outreach based on research

4. Beyond making the initial connection, how does AI help you "nurture your network" over time?
   a. By automatically liking every social media post made by your contacts
   b. By tracking your relationships, reminding you when to follow up, and helping you share valuable content
   c. By sending a generic "Happy Birthday" message to everyone once a year
   d. By adding all your contacts to a single, massive group chat
5. What is the chapter's core advice on "Staying Ethical and Authentic" while using AI for networking?
   a. It is best to hide your use of AI tools from potential clients
   b. You should always use AI-generated messages exactly as they are written, without changes
   c. Authenticity doesn't matter as long as you are efficient
   d. Always personalize AI-generated messages to match your own voice and add genuine value
6. Before you even write a message, what does the chapter recommend you use AI to research about a potential contact?
   a. Their home address and personal phone number
   b. Their recent business activities, challenges, and interests, to ensure your outreach is relevant
   c. The exact salary of the person you are contacting
   d. A list of their previous jobs from 20 years ago
7. In the multiagent system, which agent is responsible for creating a follow-up schedule and a long-term content plan to keep the relationship warm?
   a. The Research agent
   b. The Copywriting agent
   c. The Relationship Manager agent
   d. The Strategy agent
8. For building a professional reputation and sharing thought leadership content, which social media platform does the chapter recommend focusing on?
   a. Instagram
   b. LinkedIn
   c. Twitter/X
   d. A personal blog
9. What is the main goal of the "AI Connector Badge Achievement Plan"?
   a. To gain at least five new clients in 30 minutes
   b. To practice the entire networking process, from finding a target to planning a follow-up, in a real scenario
   c. To build a fully automated, multiagent networking system
   d. To write a perfect, generic message you can send to 100 people

10. How can AI help you balance your networking activities with your paid client work?
    a. By doing all your client work for you
    b. By telling you to pause all client work to focus only on networking
    c. By helping you create a time-managed weekly schedule and prioritize high-impact networking tasks
    d. By automatically declining all new meeting requests from potential clients

Answer Sheet

1. **A: It changes networking from a random numbers game into a strategic, research-based operation**

   The chapter's introduction states that AI "changes networking from a numbers game to a strategic operation" by allowing you to be more targeted and informed.

2. **B: Using AI to find the right people to connect with, filtering by industry, location, or needs**

   "Step 1: Finding the Right People to Connect With" is presented as the foundational first action in the networking process.

3. **D: To determine the best approach, timing, and platform for outreach based on research**

   The Strategy agent is defined as the persona that analyzes the research to decide on the best plan of attack for making a connection.

4. **B: By tracking your relationships, reminding you when to follow up, and helping you share valuable content**

   "Step 5: Nurturing Your Network" details how AI tools can be used as a personal CRM to maintain and strengthen relationships over time.

5. **D: Always personalize AI-generated messages to match your own voice and add genuine value**

   The section on ethics emphasizes that AI is a tool to help you be more thoughtful and efficient, not more robotic, and that personalization is key.

6. **B: Their recent business activities, challenges, and interests, to ensure your outreach is relevant**

   "Step 2: Research Your Targets" focuses on using AI to understand a contact's current situation so you can approach them with a valuable, non-generic message.

7. **C: The Relationship Manager agent**

   This agent's role is explicitly defined as creating the long-term plan for nurturing the relationship, including follow-ups and value-add content.

8. **B: LinkedIn**

   The section "Step 6: Leveraging Social Platforms" specifically identifies LinkedIn as the primary platform for professional connections and positioning yourself as an expert.

9. **B: To practice the entire networking process, from finding a target to planning a follow-up, in a real scenario**

   The exercise is designed as a step-by-step walkthrough of the chapter's key strategies, resulting in a ready-to-use outreach plan.

10. **C: By helping you create a time-managed weekly schedule and prioritize high-impact networking tasks**

    The "Balancing Networking with Your Actual Work" section focuses on using AI for efficient time management and prioritization, not for doing your work for you.

Congratulations!

You've just taken a big step toward mastering the art of building genuine connections in the age of AI. By completing these missions, you've shown that technology doesn't replace human warmth; it enhances it when used with intention. You can now identify, approach, and engage new contacts with messages that feel personal, relevant, and true to your voice.

Once you finish, submit your responses by following the badge submission instructions listed in Chapter 1 or at `https://civicai.khoury.northeastern.edu/ai-for-gig-workers`.

This badge recognizes your ability to combine strategy, empathy, and automation, the perfect blend for thriving as a freelancer in today's digital world. It shows clients and collaborators that you don't just use AI to reach people, you use it to connect meaningfully. You have learned to use AI as a bridge, not a barrier, proving that human creativity and authenticity are still the most powerful tools in the gig economy.

What You Have Gained

You've gained more than a set of networking tips. You've learned how to build relationships that last by pairing human warmth with AI efficiency. You now know how to research potential clients, tailor your outreach, and track engagement while keeping your voice genuine.

You've also discovered how to make AI work in the background while you focus on the human side of your business, nurturing trust, and staying visible in your field. This combination of emotional intelligence and smart technology gives you a lasting edge.

This chapter marks a new level in your freelance journey. You're no longer just finding opportunities; you're creating them through authentic relationships that open doors and build long-term success.

In the next chapter, we'll shift from connecting with others to connecting with yourself. You'll learn how to use AI to shape your personal brand, crafting a voice, image, and message that make clients remember you long after the conversation ends. From writing standout cover letters to building authentic social media campaigns, we'll help you turn your professional presence into something as recognizable as your favorite taco recipe. It's time to stop blending in and start standing out.

CHAPTER 11

AI for Personal Branding

Your personal brand is your digital handshake. It's how clients remember you, how opportunities find you, and how your work speaks when you are not in the room. In the gig world, your personal brand is your storefront, and with AI, you can make it shine.

AI helps you see yourself the way your market does. It can analyze tone, highlight your strengths, and help you communicate your story in a way that feels both professional and authentic. Think of it as your personal PR team: fast, affordable, and always available.

The New Rules of Reputation

Personal branding used to mean having a nice profile picture and listing your skills. But now, clients look for consistency, credibility, and connection:

- *Consistency:* Your messaging should sound like you across every platform, from your LinkedIn bio to your proposal emails.
- *Credibility:* Clients trust freelancers who show results and real human stories.
- *Connection:* In a world full of AI-generated noise, authenticity is what stands out.

AI doesn't replace your voice. It amplifies it. It helps you tell your story clearly and confidently so that your brand doesn't just look good but also feels real.

Crafting Your Story with AI

Every great personal brand starts with a story: the "why" behind your work. Most freelancers struggle to express it because they're too close to it. AI can help you uncover it.

Try this:

1. Ask your AI: "Interview me to help me find my personal brand story. Ask about my journey, values, and biggest wins."
2. Answer honestly, as if you were talking to a mentor.
3. Then say: "Summarize my story in 150 words that sound inspiring but authentic."

This becomes your new "About Me" section: honest, compelling, and uniquely yours.

PRO TIP Your story isn't your résumé. It's your recipe, the secret blend of experience, passion, and perspective that only you can bring.

Part A: Using AI to Write Strong Cover Letters and Pitches

Cover letters are where many freelancers lose energy. They can feel repetitive, formal, or robotic. AI helps you structure your letter so you can focus on what matters: showing your value.

Here's how to do it:

1. Copy the job post or client brief of your choice.
2. Give your AI your background: "I am a [role] with [years] of experience helping [type of clients]."
3. Ask: "Write a 200-word cover letter for this role. Highlight my results in [specific area], and make it sound confident, friendly, and professional."
4. Review, edit, and personalize. Add a sentence that only you could write: a client story, a personal insight, or your signature tone.

PRO TIP Ask AI to create three versions of your letter: one formal, one conversational, and one bold. Mix the best parts into your final version.

Part B: Updating and Optimizing Your Profiles

Your online profiles are your portfolio's front window. Many freelancers keep outdated or generic bios, missing out on clients searching for exactly their skills.

Use AI to give your digital presence a refresh:

1. Copy your current LinkedIn or Fiverr bio into your AI tool.
2. Prompt: "Audit this profile for clarity and tone. Rewrite it to attract [target client type] and highlight my strengths."
3. Ask AI to identify three keywords that will improve your visibility in searches.
4. Pick the version that sounds most like you, and post it.

If you have multiple platforms, ask:

"Create short bio variations for Instagram, Upwork, and my personal website that feel consistent with my main profile."

You now have a complete, cohesive brand presence.

Part C: Creating Social Media Campaigns About You

Building your brand doesn't stop with your profile. You need content that shows you in action. That's where AI helps you turn ideas into polished campaigns.

Ask your AI to create a campaign plan:

"Create a three-post campaign to introduce my personal brand as a [profession]. Post 1: my story. Post 2: client results. Post 3: call to action. Include captions, hashtags, and posting times."

You can also ask AI to

- Generate Canva templates that match your brand colors
- Write post hooks that grab attention
- Suggest topics your audience will engage with

The secret is rhythm: post weekly, review what performs best, and tweak your approach. Over time, your followers begin to see you as a trusted voice, not just another freelancer trying to sell.

How Gen AI Supercharges Personal Branding

Generative AI takes everything you just learned and turns it into momentum. It helps freelancers move from guessing to growing, from showing up online to standing out. Here's how to use it strategically:

1. *Idea generation at speed:* Instead of struggling to find post ideas, use Gen AI to brainstorm dozens. Ask:

   "Generate ten content ideas that showcase my expertise in [your field]. Include hooks and angles that spark curiosity."

   You'll never run out of material again, and AI can help you organize it by theme or month.
2. *Design that scales:* Gen AI design tools like Canva Magic Studio and Adobe Firefly can create consistent branding assets. You can generate banner variations, social post templates, or even a personal logo, all aligned with your visual identity. The goal isn't to look corporate; it's to look consistent.
3. *Smarter keyword and positioning strategy:* Ask Gen AI:

   "Analyze the top LinkedIn profiles for [your profession]. What keywords or skills appear most often?"

   Then compare your own profile and adjust. AI becomes your silent search engine optimization (SEO) coach, helping your name appear in more searches.
4. *Personalized outreach at scale:* Gen AI can analyze a client's website or social posts and draft personalized outreach that actually feels human. Prompt:

   "Write a short pitch to [client name] referencing their recent post about [topic]. Keep it under 100 words and sound conversational."

   You're not spamming, you're connecting with intention.
5. Brand feedback loop: Feed your analytics into AI and ask:

   "Which posts or messages are getting the most engagement, and why?"

The AI identifies trends so you can double down on what works and drop what doesn't. It's like having a marketing analyst on your team, minus the hourly rate.

Generative AI is not about automation alone. It's about amplification, multiplying your creativity, your message, and your reach while keeping your humanity front and center.

Part D: Keeping It Human

Your AI can polish your words and generate ideas, but authenticity is still your most powerful marketing tool.

If AI writes a caption, edit one sentence to sound more like you. If it suggests 10 hashtags, pick the 3 you would actually use. Your human touch is what turns AI content into something memorable.

Badge Achievement Plan: The Personal Brand Specialist

Now it's time to turn your learning into action. Complete these missions to earn your AI Personal Brand Architect Badge, issued by Northeastern University. This badge certifies that you can use AI to shape your professional identity, communicate your value, and build a strong digital presence.

Time Required: around 2 hours (can be split into short 30-minute sessions)

Goal: Use AI to craft a consistent, authentic personal brand across platforms, from your cover letter and bio to your social media presence. By the end, you'll have a polished, AI-assisted personal brand toolkit that shows who you are and why clients should choose you.

What You'll Need:

- Access to ChatGPT, Notion AI, or another AI writing tool
- Your current résumé, LinkedIn, or Fiverr bio
- A recent job posting or client brief for reference
- Access to Canva AI or a similar design tool (optional, for visuals)
- A positive attitude and your favorite playlist for focus

Mission 1: Write Your AI-Enhanced Cover Letter (20 minutes)

Choose a real job posting or client inquiry. Prompt your AI:

> "Write a cover letter for this opportunity. Highlight my results in [specific skill or project]. Make it persuasive, professional, and under 200 words."

Review the first draft and refine the tone. Add small details that sound like you, with your energy, motivation, or creative flair.

Mission 2: Brand Audit and Bio Refresh (30 minutes)

Copy your current LinkedIn or Fiverr summary. Ask AI:

> "Review and rewrite my bio to attract [target clients]. Suggest improvements to my headline and keywords."

Post your new version, take a screenshot, and save it.

Mission 3: The Three-Post Social Media Campaign (45 minutes)

Ask your AI:

> "Create a three-post content plan introducing my personal brand, showcasing one client's success, and inviting inquiries or collaborations. Each post should include a short caption, 3-5 hashtags, and a suggested visual idea."

Choose one platform: LinkedIn, Instagram, or TikTok. Use Canva AI or Buffer to design and schedule your posts. Track engagement (likes, comments, shares, or followers).

PRO TIP After three days, ask AI:

"Based on these results [paste engagement data], suggest how I can improve my next post's tone or topic."

This simple feedback loop helps your content evolve and stay authentic.

Mission 4: Visual Identity and Consistency (30 minutes)

Your visuals should tell the same story as your words.

Secret prompt:

> "Analyze these content samples [upload visuals or describe your site]. Describe my visual identity in three adjectives and suggest one improvement for consistency across platforms."

Steps:

1. Note your three adjectives (e.g., bold, warm, minimalist).
2. Apply one change: color palette, font choice, or layout.
3. Compare the before and after.

PRO TIP A consistent look and tone build trust before a client even reads your message.

Mission 5: Final Knowledge Check (10 minutes)

1. What is the main purpose of using AI for personal branding?
   a. To automate every part of your marketing so you never have to write again
   b. To enhance your voice, visuals, and messaging while staying true to who you are
   c. To make your brand sound more robotic and efficient
   d. To replace human creativity with faster content

2. Which AI tool feature is most useful for creating consistent content across platforms?
   a. Image editing only
   b. Voice-to-text transcription
   c. Brand voice training or style analysis
   d. Calendar scheduling
3. When using AI to write a cover letter, what should you provide first for best results?
   a. Only your résumé
   b. A clear prompt with the job description, your strengths, and your achievements
   c. The company's slogan
   d. Just the company name
4. What is one risk of relying too heavily on AI for personal branding?
   a. You may sound too unique
   b. Your brand could lose authenticity and start blending in with generic AI content
   c. You might accidentally use better grammar
   d. AI will limit your career options
5. How can freelancers use AI to manage and improve their online profiles?
   a. Have AI rewrite your bio in your tone and create keyword-rich headlines for each platform
   b. Delete all personal details for privacy
   c. Ask AI to invent fake achievements to make you look more impressive
   d. Only use emojis and short phrases for faster updates
6. What's a smart way to use AI for social media campaigns about your personal brand?
   a. Let AI post automatically without reviewing
   b. Use AI to generate ideas, captions, and visuals, and then edit them to reflect your authentic tone
   c. Post as much as possible without a plan
   d. Ask AI to mimic other freelancers' content
7. Which of the following best describes how Generative AI supports personal branding?
   a. It helps brainstorm creative ways to present your skills, achievements, and stories visually and verbally
   b. It automatically manages your client relationships
   c. It builds your website and portfolio without input
   d. It monitors your finances

8. Why should you review or edit any AI-generated cover letter or social media post before sending it out?
   a. To correct typos made by the AI
   b. To make sure the tone, message, and personality sound like you
   c. Because AI can't use punctuation properly
   d. To make it shorter
9. When updating your professional bio, what kind of tone should you aim for with AI's help?
   a. Generic and neutral, so it fits any client
   b. Polished but personal, showing your strengths and unique style
   c. Highly technical and filled with industry jargon
   d. Overly casual and emoji-heavy
10. What is the ultimate goal of using AI for personal branding?
    a. To make your profile look exactly like everyone else's
    b. To attract the right clients by communicating your authentic value clearly and consistently
    c. To post more content than anyone in your field
    d. To let AI completely manage your professional identity

Answer Sheet

1. **B: To enhance your voice, visuals, and messaging while staying true to who you are**

   AI should amplify your voice, not replace it.

2. **C: Brand voice training or style analysis**

   Brand voice and style consistency help unify your message.

3. **B: A clear prompt with the job description, your strengths, and your achievements**

   The more context you give, the more tailored and accurate the output.

4. **B: Your brand could lose authenticity and start blending in with generic AI content**

   Overreliance on AI can dilute your personal authenticity.

5. **A: Have AI rewrite your bio in your tone and create keyword-rich headlines for each platform**

   AI can rewrite your bio and optimize it with keywords and clarity.

6. **B: Use AI to generate ideas, captions, and visuals, and then edit them to reflect your authentic tone**

   Use AI to assist, not automate without oversight.

7. **A: It helps brainstorm creative ways to present your skills, achievements, and stories visually and verbally**

   Generative AI supports storytelling and creative self-presentation.

8. **B: To make sure the tone, message, and personality sound like you**

   Editing ensures your personal tone and values come through.

9. **B: Polished but personal, showing your strengths and unique style**

   Balance professionalism with personality for an engaging voice.

10. **B: To attract the right clients by communicating your authentic value clearly and consistently**

    The goal is authentic attraction, to stand out as *you*, not a copy.

Congratulations!

You did it. You've built your personal brand with precision, purpose, and a bit of AI-powered flair. You've learned how to turn your experience into stories that clients actually remember: not just polished lines, but authentic reflections of who you are and what makes you stand out. You've also discovered how AI can act as your creative coach, helping you sharpen your writing, structure your message, and design visuals that speak louder than a résumé ever could.

Once you finish, submit your responses by following the badge submission instructions listed in Chapter 1 or at `https://civicai.khoury.northeastern.edu/ai-for-gig-workers`. This badge certifies that you can use AI to express your professional identity clearly and confidently, a rare and valuable skill in a world where freelancers often blend into the crowd. Like a chef who finally nails their signature taco recipe, you've crafted a personal flavor clients can't forget.

What You Have Gained

You now know how to present yourself as more than just another freelancer: you're a brand. You've learned to use AI not to replace your creativity, but to amplify it. You can now write cover letters that feel personal, update your profiles so they attract the right kind of attention, plan social campaigns that reflect your values and voice, and keep your brand consistent across platforms effortlessly.

Most importantly, you've learned that your story is your strongest asset. AI helps you tell it better, faster, and more beautifully, but the spark still comes from you.

In the next chapter, we'll make sure all this attention turns into results. You'll learn how to manage your time and focus so you can handle the growing demand your new personal brand brings. Because now that your name's on the map, it's time to make sure you have the schedule to match. Your AI sidekick has helped you look the part; next, it'll help you run the show.

CHAPTER 12

AI for Smarter Scheduling and Efficiency

You've built your digital team, connected your tools, and started forming real relationships with clients. Now it's time to master one of the most underrated superpowers in freelancing: time.

AI scheduling and efficiency tools aren't about turning you into a robot who lives by calendar alerts. They're about freeing your brain from noise so you can focus on creativity, clients, and growth. Think of this chapter as upgrading your taco truck from a food stand to a full kitchen that runs like clockwork. The goal is not just to work faster but to work smarter, with less stress and more flow.

The Real Cost of Poor Scheduling

If you've ever double-booked a client call, stayed up late to meet a deadline you forgot, or stared at your to-do list wondering where the day went, you already know this: disorganization is expensive. Missed follow-ups mean lost income, late nights mean burnout, and scattered notes mean missed opportunities.

Freelancers often lose up to 20% of their productive time to inefficient task switching. That's like spending one full workday every week trying to find your own spatula in a cluttered kitchen.

AI helps by doing what humans struggle with most: prioritizing without emotion, analyzing patterns, and predicting how long tasks actually take. It learns how you work and starts designing your schedule around your real energy peaks, not your wishful thinking.

Your AI-Powered Calendar

You've already learned to delegate with agents. Now it's time to let AI take charge of your calendar. AI scheduling tools act like personal assistants that know your habits, predict your workload, and adjust your week automatically.

Smart Tools for Freelancers

Here are some top-rated AI scheduling assistants that can keep your workflow running smoothly:

- *Motion:* Automatically prioritizes your tasks, reschedules missed ones, and adapts to real-time changes. It learns from your habits to create the perfect daily plan.
- *Reclaim.ai:* Syncs with your existing calendars and protects your focus time. It blocks deep work hours while leaving space for meetings and breaks.
- *Notion AI and ClickUp AI:* Great for freelancers managing multiple projects. They connect your notes, tasks, and deadlines in one integrated view.
- *Clockwise:* Balances meetings and focus blocks by analyzing your schedule and suggesting optimal times for collaboration.
- *ChatGPT and Gemini:* Can generate structured schedules directly from your prompts. Try asking, "Create a weekly plan for a freelance designer who works best in the mornings and wants Fridays free for learning."

> Example prompt: "You are my productivity assistant. Based on this task list [paste list], organize my week. Prioritize client work before admin tasks, schedule breaks, and reserve time on Friday for creative brainstorming. Show it as a daily timeline."

These tools are not just planners. They're decision partners that help you decide what's worth doing now, what can wait, and what you can automate entirely.

The Power of Time Mapping

Before AI can optimize your time, you need to understand where the time goes.

Time mapping means tracking your hours for a week to see what's actually happening versus what you think is happening.

Create categories such as

- Paid client work
- Unpaid admin tasks
- Learning or growth
- Rest and personal time

Then feed that data into your AI assistant. You've already learned to structure and communicate goals clearly, so now you can ask AI to help rebalance your week based on what truly matters.

Example prompt: "Analyze this weekly time log. Show me which activities are taking too much time and how to reorganize my week for better balance. Suggest what I should automate or delegate."

After a week, you'll have a visual report of where your hours and energy are leaking. It's like finding out which taco ingredient keeps running out first and finally fixing the supply chain.

Batching and Deep Work: Cooking in Focus Blocks

You can't make 20 tacos at once if you keep chopping one tomato at a time. The same goes for your work. AI can help you batch similar tasks together so you spend less time switching and more time creating.

Ask your AI to sort your to-do list by task type: writing, designing, client communication, or admin. Then let it group them into focus blocks on your calendar.

Example prompt: "Group my weekly tasks into focus blocks by type: creative, admin, and communication. Schedule creative work in the mornings and admin in the afternoons."

This method helps you enter flow faster and stay there longer. Many creators report doubling their output simply by batching tasks and protecting their peak focus hours.

Protecting Your Energy and Avoiding Burnout

AI can optimize your calendar, but only you can set boundaries. Tools like Reclaim.ai and Notion can track how many hours you've worked each day and warn you when you're heading toward burnout. Use AI to remind you to rest, not just to work.

Try prompts like these:

> "Remind me to take a 15-minute walk after two hours of focused work."
>
> "Track my screen time and alert me when I've spent more than 8 hours on the computer."

Efficiency isn't about doing more. It's about doing less, better. The smartest freelancers know that rest is part of the plan, not an afterthought.

Automating the Daily Grind

You've already learned how to connect agents and automate tasks. Now it's time to apply that thinking to scheduling itself. You can connect your AI tools to create a full productivity ecosystem.

For example:

- *Notion AI + Zapier + Google Calendar:* Automatically add new tasks from client forms or emails into your weekly planner.
- *QuickBooks AI + Motion:* Adjust your calendar when big payments or invoices are due.
- *ChatGPT + Notion AI:* Ask AI to summarize your week and prepare a "Next Week Plan" every Friday afternoon.

This is how freelancers create consistency without chaos. You're not just managing tasks. You're running a business that hums.

The Mindset of Efficiency

By now, you've probably noticed something: every new skill in this book connects. Prompting gave you precision. Agents gave you scale. Automation gave you systems. Now efficiency ties it all together.

Efficiency isn't about squeezing more hours into your day. It's about designing a rhythm that feels sustainable and satisfying. Some days are for deep creation. Others are for meetings and outreach. And some are for rest. AI helps you balance that rhythm by constantly recalibrating your schedule to fit real life instead of forcing you into rigid routines.

Badge Achievement Plan: The Efficiency Architect

You've learned how to use AI to organize your work, automate your calendar, and create a rhythm that supports your creativity instead of draining it. Now it's time to turn those insights into action. This mission will help you apply everything you've learned about time mapping, batching, and automation to design a weekly routine that truly works for you. By the end, you'll have an AI-assisted schedule that saves time, reduces stress, and keeps your freelance business running smoothly, even when life gets busy.

Complete the following missions to earn your Efficiency Architect Badge!

Time Required: 1 hour 20 minutes, plus 3 days of testing and adjustment

Goal: Use AI to design a balanced, efficient weekly schedule that increases productivity without sacrificing creativity or rest.

What You'll Need:

- A notebook or digital notes app
- Access to AI tools like ChatGPT, Motion, or Notion AI
- Your current task list or calendar
- An honest view of how you spend your time

Mission 1: Map Your Current Week (15 minutes)

Before you can fix your schedule, you have to see it clearly. Write down everything you did this past week: paid work, unpaid tasks, messages, breaks, and distractions.

Then, let AI help you make sense of the chaos.

> Special secret prompt: "Here's a list of everything I did this week [paste tasks]. Categorize them as creative, administrative, communication, or personal. Estimate the total time in each category and highlight where I'm losing the most productive hours."

Ask yourself:

- Where did my time actually go?
- Which tasks brought the most value?
- Which ones drained my energy or focus?

PRO TIP You can also prompt AI to color-code your schedule or visualize it in a Notion or Google Calendar template.

Mission 2: Design Your Ideal Schedule (30 minutes)

Now that you've seen where your time leaks, it's time to design your *ideal week*.

> Special secret prompt: "Based on this breakdown [paste your AI's summary], design an ideal weekly schedule for a freelancer who does [your type of work]. Prioritize deep creative work in the morning, meetings in the afternoon, and rest in the evening. Include time blocks for exercise, admin work, and content creation."

Steps:

1. Review the schedule AI creates. Don't aim for perfection, aim for flow.
2. Adjust for your real energy levels (some people write best at 10 p.m., others at dawn).
3. Mark your "non-negotiable focus blocks," those sacred hours for deep work.

PRO TIP If you want extra clarity, ask: "Convert this schedule into a visual weekly planner with color-coded categories."

Mission 3: Automate the Routine (20 minutes)

Now it's time to make your plan *run itself*. Choose one or two tasks that happen every week and let AI automate them.

Examples:

- Automatically sync tasks from Notion to Google Calendar.
- Use ChatGPT reminders to plan your next day's focus list.
- Ask AI to generate weekly summaries of your projects.

Special secret prompt: "Create a checklist of recurring weekly automations for a freelancer who manages clients, invoices, and content. Include suggestions using Notion, Motion, or Zapier."

Then, add one habit to keep yourself accountable.

Reflection prompt: "Every Friday at 4 p.m., remind me to review my week and write three wins, one challenge, and one improvement."

PRO TIP Automate just 1–2 tasks at first. Over-automation can create clutter if you're not ready to manage it yet.

Mission 4: Test and Tweak (3 Days)

Live your new schedule for at least three days. Treat it as an experiment: not a test of discipline, but a study of your energy.

Track what happens:

- Which hours felt most focused?
- Where did friction or fatigue appear?
- Did automation actually save time, or add confusion?

Special secret prompt: "Based on these notes [paste reflections], analyze which time blocks worked best and which ones I should move. Suggest a revised version of my weekly schedule that maintains balance while improving flow."

PRO TIP Revisions are part of success. Your first plan is a draft, just like any creative project.

Mission 5: Reflect and Celebrate (15 minutes)

You've done it! You've designed a system that works *with* you, not against you.

Now, write your Efficiency Manifesto: a short statement to keep by your desk.

> Special secret prompt: "Help me write a short, powerful statement that summarizes how I use AI to protect my time, stay balanced, and create my best work."

Example:

"I use AI to plan with clarity, work with purpose, and rest without guilt."

Take a moment to celebrate. Your taco truck now runs on a perfect rhythm, every taco sizzling on time, every order flowing smoothly, and plenty of time left to enjoy the music.

Mission 6: Final Knowledge Check (10 minutes)

1. What is the main goal of using AI for scheduling and efficiency?
   - **a.** To fill every available hour with work
   - **b.** To free time for creativity, clients, and rest
   - **c.** To eliminate all need for human decision-making
   - **d.** To meet as many deadlines as possible regardless of burnout
2. According to the chapter, what is "time mapping"?
   - **a.** Tracking your time manually for billing clients
   - **b.** Listing tasks without priorities
   - **c.** Analyzing how you actually spend your hours to identify where time is wasted
   - **d.** Using GPS data to record work locations
3. Which tool is designed to automatically prioritize tasks and reschedule missed ones?
   - **a.** Notion AI
   - **b.** Reclaim.ai
   - **c.** Motion
   - **d.** ClickUp
4. What does "batching" help freelancers achieve?
   - **a.** Mixing unrelated tasks to stay flexible
   - **b.** Doing many different activities at once
   - **c.** Grouping similar tasks to reduce context switching and improve focus
   - **d.** Avoiding repetitive work altogether

5. What does AI help freelancers do when analyzing time logs?
   a. Add more projects to their week
   b. Identify low-value activities and rebalance schedules
   c. Shorten breaks to increase productivity
   d. Work longer hours for higher income
6. The chapter emphasizes that efficiency is not about working harder but rather about what?
   a. Working faster at any cost
   b. Working less but getting more meaningful results
   c. Outsourcing all human work to AI
   d. Avoiding rest and leisure
7. How can freelancers use AI to prevent burnout?
   a. Program reminders for breaks and screen-time limits
   b. Remove all rest periods from the calendar
   c. Automate client communication during personal hours
   d. Let AI decide when to sleep
8. What is a focus block?
   a. A period dedicated to multitasking
   b. A short 5-minute window for answering messages
   c. A set time dedicated to one type of work with no interruptions
   d. A meeting between multiple clients
9. Why should freelancers regularly update their automated systems?
   a. Because software updates can cause automations to fail or break
   b. To keep AI busy
   c. To make tasks more complicated
   d. To start every workflow from scratch
10. What is the final step after testing your ideal schedule?
   a. Start a new project immediately
   b. Reflect, refine, and write your Efficiency Manifesto
   c. Share your entire calendar publicly
   d. Delete your automation tools

Answer Sheet

1. **B: To free time for creativity, clients, and rest**

   AI helps you reclaim time for creativity, clients, and rest rather than fill every moment with tasks.

2. **C: Analyzing how you actually spend your hours to identify where time is wasted**

   Time mapping is tracking and analyzing how your hours are actually spent.

3. **C: Motion**

   Motion is highlighted as the AI tool that prioritizes tasks and reschedules missed ones.

4. **C: Grouping similar tasks to reduce context switching and improve focus**

   Batching groups similar tasks together to maintain flow and focus.

5. **B: Identify low-value activities and rebalance schedules**

   AI analyzes your time use to identify where you can improve balance and reduce wasted effort.

6. **B: Working less but getting more meaningful results**

   Efficiency is about doing less but achieving better, more meaningful results.

7. **A: Program reminders for breaks and screen-time limits**

   AI can remind you to rest, stretch, or step away to avoid burnout.

8. **C: A set time dedicated to one type of work with no interruptions**

   A focus block is uninterrupted time for one specific activity.

9. **A: Because software updates can cause automations to fail or break**

   Automation tools require regular updates and testing to prevent errors.

10. **B: Reflect, refine, and write your Efficiency Manifesto**

    The final step is reflecting, refining, and writing your Efficiency Manifesto.

Congratulations!

You've completed one of the most practical transformations in your freelance journey. By finishing this chapter, you've learned to reclaim control over your time using AI as your planner, analyst, and accountability partner. You can now design your days around what matters most instead of reacting to chaos.

Once you finish, submit your responses by following the badge submission instructions listed in Chapter 1 or at `https://civicai.khoury.northeastern.edu/ai-for-gig-workers`. This badge certifies that you can use AI to structure your workdays, manage your time, and maintain balance between productivity and well-being. It is a skill that sets top freelancers apart from the rest.

What You Have Gained

You've learned how to merge technology with rhythm. You now understand how to use AI to plan, prioritize, and protect your most precious resource: time. You've turned chaos into clarity, scattered tasks into focus blocks, and busy weeks into systems that serve your creativity instead of draining it. Most importantly, you've learned that efficiency isn't about working like a machine. It's about designing a business that gives you space to live, create, and thrive.

Now that your time is finally working for you, it's time to make sure your money does, too. In the next chapter, we'll shift our focus from saving time to maximizing income. You'll learn how to use AI to stop guessing your rates and start pricing your services based on real market data. We'll turn that dreaded negotiation process into a confident, data-driven conversation and even use AI to help you manage your money like a seasoned pro. Get ready to transform your hustle from just getting by to getting paid what you truly deserve, one smart, well-timed taco at a time.

CHAPTER 13

Using AI to Set Your Rates

Pricing your work can feel like trying to guess how many tacos to make without knowing how hungry the crowd is. Charge too much, and clients disappear. Charge too little, and you end up working nonstop for pennies. Most freelancers guess or copy what others charge online, and that guesswork keeps them stuck.

Here's the good news: you don't have to guess anymore. AI can help you set fair, confident rates using real data, not random internet opinions. By the end of this chapter, you'll know how to research market rates, understand your unique value, negotiate with confidence, and manage your money like a pro.

Step 1: Research What the Market Is Actually Paying

Before you set your price, you need to know what others are charging for the same kind of work. AI tools like ChatGPT and Perplexity can gather this information in seconds.

Try prompts like:

> "What's the average hourly rate for a [your job title] with [X years] of experience working with [your type of clients] in [your region]?"
>
> "What are typical project rates for [type of project] for [your client type]? Break it down by experience level: beginner, intermediate, and expert."

You can also ask:

> "How do rates change for [your service] when working with [specific industry] versus [another industry]? What about short-term projects versus long-term contracts?"

AI can pull data from job boards, freelance platforms, and market reports to give you realistic benchmarks. Keep track of what you find in a simple spreadsheet or Notion page, or even ask AI to create one:

> "Create a table comparing average rates for [your service] across experience levels and client types."

These insights give you the foundation to build your pricing with confidence.

Step 2: Smarter Pricing with Real Data

AI is only as smart as the details you give it. If you ask, "How much should I charge for a logo?" you'll get an average pulled from the web. That's like asking for "a taco" and getting a plain tortilla. The magic happens when you add your own ingredients: your real hours, costs, and goals.

Try this:

> "Help me calculate a fair rate for designing a social media campaign. It takes me about 15 hours, plus $50 in stock images and $30 in software subscriptions. Compare this to industry averages for freelancers with 3-5 years of experience, and suggest a price range that includes a 20% profit margin."

Instead of a guess, you'll get a rate grounded in both market data and your actual costs.

PRO TIP Track every project. Log your hours, expenses, and what you charged. Over time, you'll build a personal pricing engine that gets smarter with every gig.

Step 3: Stay Current Without Selling Yourself Short

Rates change as markets evolve. AI can help you keep up with trends so you don't undercharge while the industry moves ahead.

Ask:

> "Analyze pricing trends for [your field] from 2022 to 2025. Are rates going up or down? What skills are commanding higher prices?"
>
> "What new services are trending in [your industry], and how are they being priced?"

You can even analyze specific job listings:

> "Review this posting [paste text]. What skills are they prioritizing? How does it compare to my current offer?"

Finally, automate your updates.

> "Create a monthly report template to track rate changes, new in-demand skills, and platform trends for [your field]."

That way, you'll always know when it's time to raise your rates or expand your services.

Step 4: Figure Out What Makes You Special

Market averages are just the tortilla. Your secret salsa is your unique value. AI can help you identify what makes you worth more than the average freelancer.

Try prompts like these:

> "Based on my skills in [list your skills], what should I emphasize to justify higher rates?"

"How can I position my [specific expertise] to command premium pricing?"
"Help me calculate the ROI I deliver to clients through [your service]."

This helps you connect your rates to real outcomes: saving clients time, growing their revenue, or improving their visibility. Once you quantify your impact, your price becomes a reflection of value, not a number pulled from thin air.

Step 5: Negotiate Like a Pro

Negotiating doesn't have to make your palms sweat. With the right prompts, AI can help you prepare, respond, and build confidence.

When clients say your rates are too high:

"Write a professional response to a client who says my $[amount] rate is expensive. Emphasize my [years] of experience, [specific results achieved], and the value I provide."

For long-term clients:

"Write an email asking for a [percentage]% rate increase. Mention my consistent results, reliability, and the quality improvements I've delivered."

For practice:

"Act like a client who thinks my rate is too high. Give me three objections, then help me respond to each one."

This kind of role-playing builds confidence, so when the real conversation comes, you're ready.

Step 6: Manage Your Money Like a Boss

Earning more is great, but managing it well turns income into stability. AI can help you plan your finances, forecast income, and spot tax deductions.

For budgeting:

> "Create a monthly budget for a freelancer earning $[income] with $[fixed expenses]. I want to save $[goal] per month."

For forecasting:

> "Help me forecast income for the next three months. Here are my confirmed and pending projects. Create a table with conservative and optimistic scenarios."

For tracking expenses:

> "What are the best AI tools for tracking freelance expenses and finding tax deductions?"

You can even automate the process:

> "Create a Google Sheet that calculates monthly profit, savings rate, and alerts me when spending exceeds 80% of income."

Financial confidence is part of pricing confidence. When you understand where your money goes, you make smarter decisions about where to set your rates.

Avoiding Pricing Pitfalls with AI Insights

Setting rates can feel like cooking tacos on high heat. Here's how to avoid the most common mistakes gig workers make and how AI can help fix them.

Underpricing erodes confidence and income. Priya's $50-per-post rate led to burnout. After using LinkedIn AI to benchmark rates, she raised her fee to $200 and doubled her income.

> Prompt: "Compare my current rates to market averages for [your gig] in [your niche or region], citing recent data."

Ignoring your unique value makes you blend in. A VA undercharged at $10/hour until ChatGPT helped him list specialized skills that justified $25/hour.

> Prompt: "Highlight my unique skills and outcomes in my profile to justify premium pricing."

Static pricing means missed opportunities. A translator's flat $12/hour ignored demand surges. Google Sheets AI helped him analyze trends and introduce dynamic pricing, earning an extra $200 per month.

> Prompt: "Track my earnings by project or season to identify rate adjustment opportunities."

Lack of transparency can cost trust. Build it with clear pricing breakdowns using ChatGPT:

> Prompt: "Draft a client email explaining my rate based on skills and tools used."

Overpricing without data scares off clients. A freelance content creator used LinkedIn AI to compare her rates with similar creators and found her sweet spot at $200 per post.

> Prompt: "Compare my proposed rate to competitors in my niche and region."

Communicating Your Rates with Confidence

Communicating your rates with confidence can be one of the toughest parts of freelancing. Writing a pitch that sounds professional but not stiff, confident but not pushy, often leads to staring at a blank screen. This is where AI becomes your secret weapon. With a few clear prompts, it can turn your ideas into polished, persuasive messages that highlight your value and match your tone. It helps you sound consistent and credible without the stress of rewriting endlessly. You can even adjust the style for each client: formal for corporate work, friendly for startups. Stop overthinking your pitches and let AI help you sound like the pro you already are.

The Bottom Line

AI helps you take the guesswork out of pricing. It replaces uncertainty with real data, giving you the tools to charge what you're worth, negotiate like a professional, and manage your income wisely.

Start small. Research your current rates or practice one negotiation using AI support. Once you see how much easier and more effective it becomes, you'll never go back to guessing. You'll finally be charging what your work deserves, and that's how you turn your hustle into a business that lasts.

Badge Achievement Plan: AI-Powered Pricing Pro

Complete the following missions to earn your AI-Powered Pricing Pro Badge and show that you can use data, strategy, and smart prompting to charge confidently for your work. By the end, you'll have a clear, evidence-based pricing structure, client-ready communication templates, and a financial system that actually supports your goals.

Time Required: 1 hour 40 minutes + optional one-week financial tracking

Goal: Use AI to research market rates, identify your unique value, communicate your worth, and manage your freelance income confidently.

What You'll Need:

- Access to AI tools (ChatGPT, Perplexity, LinkedIn AI, QuickBooks AI, or Notion AI)
- A list of your current or recent projects
- A notebook or document to save your findings
- Your existing or ideal client base in mind

Mission 1: Research Your Market Value (20 minutes)

Prompt AI to identify average rates for your type of work and region.

Example:

> "What's the average hourly rate for a [your job title] with [X years of experience] serving [your client type] in [your country or region]?"

Compare your current rate to what the market pays. If you're undercharging, note by how much.

Write one short reflection:

"I discovered that I charge ___% below/above the average. My goal is to align my rates with this data by [specific month]."

PRO TIP Ask:

"List 3 factors that justify higher-than-average rates for freelancers like me."

This helps you build confidence and talking points for future client conversations.

Mission 2: Build Your Personal Pricing Engine (25 minutes)

Feed your AI your real data: project type, hours spent, expenses, and profit goals.

Prompt: "Help me calculate a fair rate for [your service]. It usually takes me [X hours] and costs [list expenses]. Compare it to market rates and recommend a final price that includes a 20% profit margin."

Then, take it further:

"Create a small table showing project type, hours worked, total cost, suggested price, and profit margin."

Save this as your "Personal Pricing Engine": a living document that you'll update as your business grows.

PRO TIP Ask AI to include both hourly and project-based versions of your rates so you can flex between clients easily.

Mission 3: Craft Your Confident Pitch (25 minutes)

Now that you know your worth, let's help you *say it* with confidence.

Prompt: "Write a short, confident email introducing my [service] at $[your rate]. Highlight my experience in [your niche] and my past results in [specific outcomes]. Keep the tone friendly but professional."

Then ask for alternatives:

"Now rewrite this pitch for a corporate client."
"Now rewrite it for a small business."

Next steps:

1. Compare both versions.
2. Adjust the tone until it sounds 100% like you.
3. Save your favorite as your new "Rate Introduction Template."

PRO TIP Ask:

"Create a short closing line that politely but firmly reinforces the value of my rate."

You'll have a powerful one-liner ready for tough negotiations.

Mission 4: Forecast Your Financial Future (20 minutes)

Use AI to bring stability to your freelance finances.

> Special secret prompt: "Create a three-month income and expense forecast for a freelancer earning $[amount] monthly with $[expenses]. Include optimistic and conservative projections. Format as a simple table or bar chart."

Steps:

1. Review your forecast and look for opportunities. Could you increase efficiency, cut costs, or raise rates?
2. Write your reflection:

   "Based on this forecast, I will focus on [specific action: raising rates, saving 10%, adding retainers, etc.]."

PRO TIP If you want to go further, ask:

"Suggest three financial habits that help freelancers build long-term stability and avoid feast-or-famine cycles."

Mission 5: Test and Track for One Week

Time to see if your numbers hold up in real life.

> Special secret prompt: "Summarize this data [paste your tracked earnings, hours, and expenses] and calculate my effective hourly rate. Suggest how I can improve profitability without working longer hours."

Steps:

1. Track all earnings, hours, and expenses for seven days.
2. Use AI to calculate your *real* hourly rate.
3. Reflect on whether your current pricing matches the true value of your time.

PRO TIP Small tweaks like better client selection and scope control often yield more profit than raising prices alone.

Tool suggestions:

- *Rate research:* ChatGPT, Perplexity
- *Market analysis:* Fiverr Pricing Tool, LinkedIn AI
- *Pitch writing:* Jasper, Copy.ai
- *Finance:* QuickBooks AI, Cleo, Notion AI
- *Tracking:* Google Sheets, Motion AI

Mission 6: Final Knowledge Check (10 minutes)

1. What is the first step in the chapter's six-step plan for using AI to price your work?
   a. Figure out what makes you special
   b. Research what the market is actually paying for your type of work
   c. Negotiate with potential clients
   d. Manage your money and create a budget
2. Which prompt helps you find the average hourly rate for your role?
   a. "How much money can I make as a freelancer?"
   b. "What's the average hourly rate for a [your job title] with [X years of experience] working with [your client type] in [your region]?"
   c. "Tell me the highest salary ever paid to a [your job title]"
   d. "Create a budget for my freelance business"
3. How can AI help a freelancer "negotiate like a pro"?
   a. By automatically accepting the first offer from a client
   b. By helping you craft professional, confident responses to client objections
   c. By finding clients who will never question your prices
   d. By setting your rates automatically

4. The prompt “Analyze my earnings by time and season to suggest dynamic rates” helps you avoid which pitfall?
   a. Underpricing
   b. Static pricing
   c. Ignoring your unique value
   d. Overpricing without data
5. What is the purpose of Step 4: “Figure Out What Makes You Special”?
   a. To find out what other freelancers charge
   b. To identify and emphasize your unique skills and experience
   c. To gather a generic skill list from AI
   d. To determine your minimum acceptable rate
6. For which task in Step 6: “Manage Your Money Like a Boss” would AI be most useful?
   a. Physically going to the bank
   b. Deciding what to spend your earnings on
   c. Helping you create a budget, forecast income, and track expenses
   d. Sending payments automatically
7. Why is “lack of transparency” a pricing pitfall?
   a. It confuses the AI tools
   b. It prevents you from getting software discounts
   c. It damages client trust and can cost you gigs
   d. It is illegal in most countries
8. A freelancer lost bids for quoting rates far above market value without research. Which pitfall did she fall into?
   a. Overpricing without data
   b. Underpricing
   c. Static pricing
   d. Ignoring your unique value
9. How does the chapter suggest you can use AI to communicate your rates with confidence?
   a. By sending a one-line email
   b. By using AI to write polished, persuasive proposals that justify your value
   c. By letting the AI handle all client emails
   d. By avoiding price discussions altogether

Answer Sheet

1. **B: Research what the market is actually paying for your type of work**
   Step 1 is "Research what the market is actually paying."
2. **B: "What's the average hourly rate for a [your job title] with [X years of experience] working with [your client type] in [your region]?"**
   That's the exact prompt suggested for market benchmarking.
3. **B: By helping you craft professional, confident responses to client objections**
   AI helps you craft confident negotiation responses.
4. **B: Static pricing**
   It's the dynamic pricing strategy from the translator's example.
5. **B: To identify and emphasize your unique skills and experience**
   Step 4 focuses on identifying and emphasizing unique skills.
6. **C: Helping you create a budget, forecast income, and track expenses**
   Step 6 teaches budgeting, forecasting, and expense tracking with AI.
7. **C: It damages client trust and can cost you gigs**
   Transparency builds client trust, as shown by the VA's story.
8. **A: Overpricing without data**
   She overpriced without market data to back it up.
9. **B: By using AI to write polished, persuasive proposals that justify your value**
   AI can make your pricing proposals sound confident and credible.

Congratulations!

You've just leveled up from "guessing freelancer" to "data-driven professional." By completing these missions, you learned how to research rates, analyze your market, and justify your worth with confidence. You can now speak to clients backed by facts, not fear, and price your work in a way that reflects your expertise.

Once you finish, submit your responses by following the badge submission instructions listed in Chapter 1 or at `https://civicai.khoury.northeastern.edu/ai-for-gig-workers`. This badge shows that you can use data, automation, and communication mastery to run your freelance career like a business. It tells clients you're not just guessing your value, you're proving it with insight and skill.

What You Have Gained

You've learned how to turn AI into your personal pricing consultant. You can now use data to set fair, profitable rates, communicate your value clearly, and manage your income with strategy instead of stress. You're no longer guessing: you're planning, projecting, and negotiating like a pro.

With your new financial clarity, you're ready for the next level. In the next chapter, we'll explore how to use AI for "deep work": specialized, high-value projects that elevate your reputation and income.

CHAPTER 14

AI for Deep Work and Specialized Tasks

Something that is very important in your freelance job is *deep work*. You know those projects that require you to think hard, be creative, and use your skills? That's deep work, and it's what separates you from everyone else just doing basic tasks.

Here's the thing: deep work is where the real money is. Instead of charging $20 for a quick logo that anyone could do, you could be charging $2,000 for a complete brand identity. Instead of $50 for a basic social media post, you could land a $5,000 campaign. The difference? Deep work requires focus, strategy, and expertise.

What Counts as Deep Work in Freelancing?

Deep work isn't just any task; it's the complex, specialized work that really showcases your expertise and requires sustained focus and strategic thinking.

- For *content creators*, deep work means going beyond single posts to create comprehensive multiplatform campaigns that involve strategy development and analytics tracking. It's about crafting brand storytelling that requires deep research into your client's industry, audience, and competitive landscape. You're also looking at content series that build over time, where each piece connects to create a larger narrative or educational journey that keeps audiences engaged for weeks or months.
- For *virtual assistants*, deep work involves designing and implementing custom CRM setups and automation workflows that transform how your

clients operate their businesses. You're developing comprehensive plans to improve your client's operations, analyzing their current processes and creating systems that save them significant time and money. This also includes building data analysis and reporting systems that help clients make informed decisions based on real insights rather than guesswork.

- For *designers*, deep work centers around creating complete branding packages for companies or personal brands, not just isolated logos or graphics. You're designing entire UI/UX experiences for apps or websites that require understanding user behavior, business goals, and technical constraints. This extends to developing integrated marketing campaigns across different platforms where every visual element works together to tell a cohesive story.
- For *tutors*, deep work means designing custom curricula that address specific learning needs and goals rather than using generic lesson plans. You're creating comprehensive exam prep programs that go beyond practice questions to include study strategies, time management, and confidence building. This can also involve creating educational material that you can use for multiple occasions, with different students.
- For *event planners*, deep work involves orchestrating large-scale corporate events that require months of planning, coordination, and problem-solving. You're managing multiday conferences with complex logistics, coordinating multiple vendors, managing budgets, and ensuring that every detail aligns with the client's objectives and brand image.

The key distinction is that all of these projects require sustained focus, expertise, and strategic thinking rather than just quick execution of simple tasks.

How AI Helps You Plan Deep Work Projects

Planning is where most people mess up deep work. They jump in without a clear roadmap and end up overwhelmed. AI can help you plan like a pro:

- *Use Notion AI to create project structures:* "Create a six-week timeline for designing a complete brand identity, including research, concept development, design phases, and client reviews."
- *Use ChatGPT to research best practices:* "Create a list of the most important things to consider for having a successful social media campaign for a fitness brand? Include content types, posting schedule, and engagement strategies."

- *Use Claude to brainstorm and outline:* "Create a detailed SEO content strategy outline for a small business specializing in [Insert business type or niche]. The strategy should include:
  1. Keyword research focused on the target audience and industry. Explain why you selected those keywords.
  2. A monthly content calendar with suggested blog post topics, formats, and publishing frequency.
  3. A performance tracking plan that defines key SEO metrics (e.g., organic traffic, keyword rankings, conversions) and recommended tools for monitoring progress."
- *Use Google Sheets AI for tracking your progress in a project to make more strategic decisions:* "Create a project tracking sheet for a three-month marketing campaign. The sheet should include:
  - Key milestones (e.g., campaign planning, content creation, ad launches, performance reviews)
  - Task deadlines for each milestone
  - Assigned team members or roles
  - Budget allocation per activity or channel (e.g., social media ads, influencer partnerships, email marketing)
  - A progress/status column to track completion"

Using AI to Do Deep Work

This is where AI becomes your secret weapon. Instead of getting bogged down in the small stuff, you can focus on the high-level thinking.

- Automate the busy work:
  - Use Zapier to handle data entry and file organization.
  - Set up Calendly to manage client check-ins without interrupting your flow.
  - Use Buffer to schedule social media posts while you focus on strategy.
- Get real-time feedback:
  - Ask Claude to review your work: "Review this campaign strategy and suggest improvements for better engagement."
  - Use ChatGPT for quick research: "What are current trends in [your industry] that I should consider for this project?"
  - Stay focused: When doing deep work, it is easy to get derailed and not be able to complete the specialized labor you need to do. You can aim

to stay focused by using tools that help minimize distractions and protect your productivity. Apps like Forest and Freedom can block access to distracting websites and keep you on task. You can also use AI-powered scheduling tools to help you reserve time in your schedule specifically for deep work, ensuring uninterrupted focus. Additionally, let AI handle routine communications (such as email replies or calendar coordination) so you can remain fully immersed in your most important tasks.

Advanced Deep Work: Using AI Personas and Multiagent Systems

By this point, you already know how to build AI agents, give them distinct personas, and even connect them into multiagent systems. You've learned how to assign roles, set missions, and let your digital teammates collaborate to handle complex workflows. Now we're going to take that same foundation and apply it to one of the most powerful skills in your toolkit: deep work, the kind of focused, high-impact work that separates average freelancers from top performers.

Deep work requires more than just focus; it needs layered thinking. Strategy, creativity, analysis, and empathy often need to come together in the same project. The challenge is that switching between those modes yourself can be mentally draining. That's where your AI network comes in. Instead of trying to think like a strategist, a designer, a researcher, and a client all at once, you can let your existing AI agents take on those roles simultaneously. The key isn't to create new agents but to activate the ones you've already built in a more deliberate, collaborative way.

For example:

- Your Strategy agent can define project goals, priorities, and milestones.
- Your Creative agent can brainstorm and refine ideas that fit that direction.
- Your Analyst agent can evaluate what's working and why.
- Your Client Perspective agent can review everything through the eyes of your target audience.

You already know how to set up these roles, and now you'll use them together to simulate what a high-performing creative team would do, but faster and with total focus. Think of it as hosting a "deep work lab" with your agents. You set the challenge, bring your team into the room, and guide the discussion while they generate insights, ideas, and solutions. You're not starting from scratch; you're applying the multiagent system you've already mastered to unlock deeper, more strategic outcomes.

The beauty of this approach is that it multiplies your perspective without dividing your attention. You can hold a brainstorming session that merges strategy, creativity, and analysis, all while staying fully in flow. It's like having a cross-functional team of specialists working with you on demand, helping you see every angle of a project without ever losing momentum.

This is deep work, upgraded. It's not just about concentrating harder; it's about thinking smarter, using the digital team you've already built to extend your capacity for insight and creativity.

Creating AI Personas for Deep Work

Let's talk about how AI personas could support your deep work. The following are examples of how you might define each one for your projects:

- *The Strategy Persona:* "You are a senior marketing strategist with 15 years of experience in brand campaigns. You specialize in data-driven strategies and ROI optimization. Analyze this client brief. Create a comprehensive campaign strategy with bullet points and action items. You also want to present the measurable outcomes and competitive positioning."
- *The Creative Persona:* "You are an award-winning creative director known for viral campaigns and innovative content. You understand social media trends in depth as well as audience psychology. Create 10 creative concepts that would resonate with the target audience of a company that specializes in [add specialization of the company] and have viral potential."
- *The Analytics Persona:* "You are a data analyst who specializes in marketing performance metrics. You're skilled at identifying patterns and predicting campaign success. Review these creative concepts and strategy, then recommend the top three approaches most likely to achieve the client's KPIs, with specific metrics to track."
- *The Client Persona:* "You are my client, a busy CEO of a fitness startup who values results over creativity. You're skeptical of marketing spend but understand its necessity. Give me feedback on this campaign proposal that I have created. List out all the concerns you have, what excites you, and what questions you'd ask before approving the budget."

Multiagent Deep Work Process

We will assume that each of these AI personas represents a particular AI agent. We will next have these personas "talk" to each other to refine your work and create the multi-AI agent system that will support you:

- *Step 1: Initial Strategy Development:* Start with your Strategy Persona to create the foundation: "As a marketing strategist, analyze this client's business goals, target audience, and competitive landscape. Create a comprehensive campaign strategy with clear objectives, tactics, and success metrics."
- *Step 2: Creative Development:* Take that strategy to your Creative Persona: "Based on this strategy [paste strategy], develop creative concepts that align with the strategic objectives. Focus on originality and engagement potential while staying true to the brand voice."
- *Step 3: Critical Analysis:* Have your Analytics Persona review everything: "Review both the strategy and creative concepts. Identify potential risks, suggest optimizations, and rank the concepts by likelihood of success. Provide specific metrics to track for each recommended approach."
- *Step 4: Client Perspective:* Finally, use your Client Persona to stress-test the proposal: "As the client, review this complete campaign proposal. What questions would you ask? What concerns would you have? What would convince you to approve this budget?"
- *Step 5: Refinement:* Take the client feedback back to your Strategy Persona: "Based on this client feedback, refine the proposal to address their concerns while maintaining the campaign's effectiveness. Focus on ROI justification and risk mitigation."

Practical Multiagent Example

Let's say you're working on a $5,000 social media campaign for a fitness brand. Instead of just winging it, you could run this multiagent process:

- *Strategy Persona output:* "Campaign should focus on transformation stories, target women 25–40, use Instagram and TikTok, run for 8 weeks with budget split 60/40 between content creation and paid promotion . . ."
- *Creative Persona output:* "Concept 1: Before/After transformation series with real customers. Concept 2: 30-day challenge with daily workout videos. Concept 3: Behind-the-scenes content showing the 'real' fitness journey . . ."

- *Analytics Persona output:* "Concept 2 has highest engagement potential based on fitness industry data. Recommend tracking: video completion rates, challenge participation, hashtag usage, and conversion to paid programs . . ."
- *Client Persona output:* "I like the 30-day challenge concept but I'm concerned about the time investment required from our customers. How do we ensure participation? What if people drop out after day three? Can we track actual fitness results, not just engagement?"
- *Refined strategy:* "A modified 30-day challenge that includes small daily commitments (micro-commitments), gamified elements to keep it fun and motivating, and weekly check-ins to support ongoing engagement. It also adds accountability features and simplifies the participation process to make it easier for anyone to join and stay consistent."

How to Show Off Your Deep Work Results

AI can also assist you in better presenting your amazing deep work and help you shine:

- *Create case studies with Notion AI:* "Turn my recent brand identity project into a compelling case study, highlighting the client's problem, my solution, and the results achieved."
- *Update your LinkedIn with AI:* "Help me write a LinkedIn post about my latest project success, focusing on the strategic approach and client outcomes."
- *Build portfolios with AI assistance:* "Organize my recent projects into a portfolio presentation, emphasizing the complexity and results of each deep work project."
- *Visualize your impact with Google Sheets:* Use AI in Google Sheets, or ask ChatGPT (or any generative AI tool) to help you create charts related to your work: "Create charts showing the results of my marketing campaign, engagement rates, conversion improvements, and ROI for the client."

Practical Examples of AI-Powered Deep Work

Now that we have learned a bit about how to use AI for Deep Work, let's share some concrete examples of how this works:

- *Campaign strategy:* Instead of just posting random content, use AI to research your client's industry, analyze competitor strategies, and create a data-driven content calendar. This turns a $100 posting gig into a $2,000 strategy project.
- *Process automation:* Instead of just doing admin tasks, use AI to design and implement automated workflows that save your client hours every week. This turns a $15/hour assistant role into a $3,000 project.
- *Educational content:* Instead of just tutoring sessions, use AI to create comprehensive learning materials, track student progress, and design personalized study plans. This turns $20/hour tutoring into a $1,500 course package.

Balancing Deep Work with Daily Tasks

You can't do deep work all day; you still have emails to answer and clients to manage. AI helps you balance both:

- *Use AI to prioritize:* "Analyze my task list and schedule 15 hours this week for my major project while still handling client communications and daily deliverables."
- *Automate routine tasks:* Let AI handle scheduling, basic emails, and data entry so you can focus your mental energy on the complex work.
- *Set boundaries:* Use AI-powered calendar blocking to protect your deep work time from interruptions.

The Bottom Line

Deep work is what separates successful freelancers from those just scraping by. AI doesn't do the deep work for you; it clears away all the distractions and busy work so you can focus on what really matters.

The multiagent approach is like having a whole team of experts helping you think through complex projects from every angle. You're not just getting one AI's perspective, you're getting strategy, creative, analytical, and client viewpoints all working together to create something amazing.

Start by identifying one project in your current work that could be elevated from a quick task to a deep work project. Then use AI personas to help you plan, execute, and showcase that work. The difference in what you can charge (and what clients will pay) is going to blow your mind. Stop competing on price for basic tasks, and start competing on value for complex projects. That's where the real money is in freelancing.

Badge Achievement Plan: The Deep Work Architect

Complete the following missions to demonstrate your skills and earn your badge! You've already learned how to design AI personas and multiagent systems. Now it's time to apply those skills to a real project. In this session, you'll practice turning a simple freelance task into a deep, strategic, and high-value project using your AI team.

Time Required: About 1 hour

Goal: Use your existing AI agents to elevate a basic task into a multilayered deep work project that shows your creative and strategic power.

What You'll Need:

- A current or recent client project (real or hypothetical)
- Access to your favorite AI tools (ChatGPT, Claude, Gemini, etc.)
- A notebook or digital document for notes and your final proposal

Mission 1: Choose and Elevate Your Project (5 minutes)

Pick one current or potential project that you could expand into a deep work opportunity.

Examples:

- Turn a simple logo into a full brand identity package.
- Transform social posts into a complete content strategy.
- Upgrade tutoring sessions into a structured learning program.
- Convert admin help into a business process optimization plan.

Write a short note describing your chosen project and what "deep work" would mean for it.

Mission 2: Assemble Your AI Expert Team (15 minutes)

Open four AI chat tabs: one for each expert persona you've already practiced creating. Copy and paste these ready-made instructions to activate your multiagent system.

> Strategy Expert: "You are a senior business strategist with 10 years of experience in [insert industry]. You design result-driven plans focused on ROI, risk management, and long-term value."
>
> Creative Expert: "You are an award-winning creative professional specializing in [insert field]. You craft innovative ideas that connect emotionally and stand out in the market."
>
> Analytics Expert: "You are a data analyst who tracks performance and optimization. You identify patterns, predict outcomes, and suggest measurable improvements."
>
> Client perspective: "You are my client: a busy business owner focused on results and clear ROI. You are practical, budget-conscious, and ask direct questions about value."

PRO TIP Rename each chat tab with its expert role (Strategy, Creative, Analytics, Client) so you can switch between them easily.

Mission 3: Run Your Multiagent Workflow (30 minutes)

This is where your AI team collaborates like a real think tank.

Special secret prompts:

> With your Strategy Expert: "I have a project to [describe your task]. Help me turn it into a deep work project worth $[target rate]. Create a structured plan with phases, deliverables, and outcomes."
>
> With your Creative Expert: "Based on this strategy [paste plan], generate 3–5 creative approaches that would deliver outstanding results and showcase originality."

With your Analytics Expert: "Review these strategies and creative concepts [paste both]. Rank them by likelihood of success and suggest 3 key metrics to measure impact."

With your client perspective: "Here's my full proposal [paste plan]. As my client, what concerns would you have? What would convince you it's worth the investment?"

PRO TIP If your client persona raises tough objections, take notes—that's free client psychology training.

Mission 4: Refine and Finalize (15 minutes)

Take the client's feedback and send it back to your Strategy Expert.

Special secret prompt: "Based on this feedback [paste notes], refine my proposal to address concerns while keeping the project's value strong. Focus on ROI and clear outcomes."

Then ask:

"Create a one-page, client-ready summary with scope, deliverables, timeline, pricing, and expected results."

PRO TIP Ask your Creative Expert to format it with clear section titles and persuasive phrasing for presentation or email delivery.

Mission 5: Reflect and Share (10 minutes)

Write a short reflection titled "My Deep Work Advantage." Explain how using multiple AI perspectives changed your thinking and how you'll apply this process in your future projects.

Special secret prompt: "Help me write a short reflection (under 120 words) about how using multiple AI personas helped me think more strategically and creatively about my freelance work."

What You Should Have After This Exercise

- A transformed project worth 3–5× as much as your original idea
- A clear understanding of how expert perspectives enhance your work
- A real, client-ready proposal you could send today
- Hands-on experience managing multiple AI agents for complex work

Bonus Challenge Try this with a real client project this week. Use your AI team to plan, refine, and test the process, and then track

- How much more confident you feel presenting it
- Whether you were able to charge more or land the project faster

In short: you're no longer just a freelancer, you're a project architect leading a team of digital experts. Your AI kitchen is humming, every chef in sync, and the tacos? Michelin-level.

Mission 6: Final Knowledge Check (10 minutes)

1. What is the primary difference between a "basic task" and "deep work" as defined in the chapter?
   a. Deep work can only be done by freelancers with more than 10 years of experience
   b. Deep work requires complex, strategic thinking, and sustained focus, often resulting in higher-value projects
   c. Basic tasks are always billed hourly, whereas deep work is always a fixed price
   d. Deep work is any task that takes more than 40 hours to complete
2. According to the chapter, a virtual assistant designing and implementing a custom CRM setup for a client is an example of what?
   a. A basic administrative task
   b. Deep work
   c. A task that should be outsourced
   d. An unprofitable project
3. How does the chapter suggest using AI in the *planning* phase of a deep work project?
   a. By having the AI complete the entire project for you
   b. By using tools like Notion AI to create project timelines and ChatGPT to research best practices
   c. By asking the AI to find a different freelancer to do the planning
   d. By using AI to schedule as many client meetings as possible to discuss the plan

4. What is the main concept behind using AI personas or AI agents?
   a. To have the AI generate a fake identity for you to use online
   b. To give the AI a specific expert role to play (e.g., "marketing strategist"), which shapes its perspective and improves its output
   c. To create a team of human freelancers managed by a single AI
   d. To make the AI's responses sound more robotic and technical
5. When you use multiple AI personas together, having them "collaborate" on a project, what is this system called?
   a. A multi-AI collaboration
   b. A deep work network
   c. A multiagent system
   d. An AI think tank
6. In the multiagent process for a marketing campaign, what is the role of the Client Persona?
   a. To provide creative and innovative ideas for the campaign
   b. To analyze data and recommend which concepts are most likely to succeed
   c. To stress-test the proposal by asking tough, practical questions from a business owner's perspective
   d. To create the initial project strategy and objectives
7. What is the primary benefit of using a multiagent system for a complex freelance project?
   a. It guarantees the project will be finished in half the time
   b. It allows you to get perspectives from different types of experts (strategic, creative, analytical), leading to a more robust and well-thought-out result
   c. It completely removes the need for the freelancer to think or make decisions
   d. It is the only way to get an AI to write more than 500 words
8. How can AI help you showcase the results of your deep work to potential clients?
   a. By automatically sending the project files to every contact on your email list
   b. By creating compelling case studies, updating your LinkedIn profile, and visualizing your results in charts
   c. By writing a fictional testimonial from a famous CEO
   d. By hiding any parts of the project that were not successful
9. The chapter suggests using AI-powered calendar blocking and letting AI handle routine emails as a way to solve which problem?
   a. Finding new project ideas
   b. Balancing deep work sessions with the daily tasks of running a freelance business
   c. Calculating the final invoice for a project
   d. Learning a new creative skill

Answer Key

1. **B: Deep work requires complex, strategic thinking, and sustained focus, often resulting in higher-value projects**

   The chapter defines deep work not by time but by complexity and expertise, contrasting a "$20 quick logo" with a "$2,000 complete brand identity."

2. **B: Deep work**

   This is used as a specific example of deep work for virtual assistants, as it goes beyond simple tasks to involve strategic system design.

3. **B: By using tools like Notion AI to create project timelines and ChatGPT to research best practices**

   The "How AI Helps You Plan" section provides these exact examples, showing AI's role as a planning and research assistant.

4. **B: To give the AI a specific expert role to play (e.g., "marketing strategist"), which shapes its perspective and improves its output**

   The chapter defines AI personas as giving the AI a role to play so it answers from that specific, expert perspective.

5. **C: A multiagent system**

   The text defines this as the process of using multiple AI personas (agents) together and having them "collaborate" on a project.

6. **C: To stress-test the proposal by asking tough, practical questions from a business owner's perspective**

   The Client Persona is designed to be a skeptical reviewer who focuses on bottom-line results, helping the freelancer anticipate and address real-world client concerns.

7. **B: It allows you to get perspectives from different types of experts (strategic, creative, analytical), leading to a more robust and well-thought-out result**

   The chapter highlights that the power of this system is in getting multiple expert viewpoints that a solo freelancer would not normally have access to.

8. **B: By creating compelling case studies, updating your LinkedIn profile, and visualizing your results in charts**

   The "How to Show Off Your Deep Work Results" section lists these specific methods for using AI to present your high-value work effectively.

9. **B: Balancing deep work sessions with the daily tasks of running a freelance business**

   These strategies are provided in the "Balancing Deep Work with Daily Tasks" section to help freelancers protect their focus time from interruptions.

   The exercise's mission is to pick a basic task and use the four AI personas to transform it into a comprehensive deep work project, resulting in a client-ready proposal.

Congratulations!

You've just completed one of the most advanced chapters in this book. You now know how to use AI to do more than assist with tasks: you can orchestrate a full digital team to help you think strategically, create innovatively, and deliver professional results that feel effortless. By practicing multiagent collaboration, you've learned how to structure your deep work like a creative director, delegate like a project manager, and analyze like a strategist, all while keeping your human intuition at the center.

Once you finish, submit your responses by following the badge submission instructions listed in Chapter 1 or at `https://civicai.khoury.northeastern.edu/ai-for-gig-workers`. This badge certifies that you can lead multiagent systems, manage complex projects with AI, and produce higher-value deliverables that demonstrate both efficiency and creativity.

It's not just proof of completion, it's a signal that you've mastered one of the most valuable skills in the new economy: the ability to lead intelligent systems while keeping the uniquely human spark that makes your work memorable.

What You Have Gained

You've learned how to turn simple assignments into strategic, high-value projects by applying deep work principles and multiagent collaboration. You can now plan and execute work like a systems designer, combining multiple expert perspectives without losing your own voice. More importantly, you've shifted your mindset: AI isn't just a helper, it's your creative partner for insight, quality, and precision.

This skill marks a turning point in your freelance journey. You've proven that you can deliver the kind of work that clients value most: thoughtful, comprehensive, and results-driven. But now that you can think bigger, the next question is how to scale this approach: how to use AI to take the systems you've built and multiply their impact.

In the next chapter, we'll focus on scaling your work with AI. You'll learn how to automate delivery, package your expertise into scalable services, and grow your one-person gig into a thriving micro-business. Because a great taco recipe is only the beginning: the real magic happens when you open the second truck and serve twice as many happy customers.

CHAPTER 15

Scaling Your Gig with AI

You've built systems, mastered prompt engineering, automated the boring stuff, and even created a team of digital sidekicks that work while you sleep. So, what's next? Now comes the big question: how do you grow your income without doubling your hours?

That's the challenge of scaling: multiplying your results without multiplying your exhaustion. And the secret lies in building AI systems that handle the repetitive, time-consuming work while you focus on the high-value activities that drive your business forward.

Scaling isn't about working harder; it's about working differently. Most freelancers live in "project mode," constantly searching for the next client, juggling deadlines, and trying not to burn out. But successful freelancers build *systems*, not chaos. They stop thinking like workers and start thinking like business owners. You're no longer the cook, cashier, and dishwasher of your taco stand. You're the head chef, designing the recipes and training a team (of AI agents) to serve customers consistently, even when you're away.

That's the shift this chapter helps you make. It introduces the 5-Step AI-Powered Scaling Framework, a practical roadmap for turning your one-person gig into a scalable, sustainable business. You'll learn how to use AI to attract clients, manage them efficiently, and turn your expertise into assets that earn for you, even when you're taking a well-deserved taco break.

Step 1: Master AI-Powered Client Acquisition (The Foundation)

For scaling, the first thing is client acquisition. Without a steady flow of clients, you can't scale. Usually, freelancers recommend manually searching for clients and sending them messages. But this is time-consuming and ineffective. We will make this more efficient with the help of AI. We will create AI agents that can help us get new clients.

AI agents you'll create:

- *Client Discovery AI agent:* Every day, focuses on identifying 10–20 qualified prospects (clients)
- *Market Intelligence agent:* Monitors industry trends and competitor activities
- *Outreach Generator agent:* Writes personalized messages that get responses
- *Follow-Up Sequence agent:* Creates five-message nurture sequences

Why these agents are important: Instead of you spending three to four hours daily hunting for clients and crafting messages, these agents will potentially reduce that time to 30 minutes while improving your response rates by potentially 300–400%.

Forget manually scrolling through hundreds of profiles. From day one, you're going to use AI to find and land clients faster than your competition.

Setting Up Your Client Discovery Agent

In previous chapters, we learned about setting up AI agents to support our freelancing work. We will again connect to the power of AI agents. Let's start by creating an AI agent dedicated to helping us find new clients.

Open ChatGPT and start a new conversation. Copy and paste this exact prompt:

> "You are my client discovery specialist. Your job is to identify potential clients in [your industry] who are actively looking for [your service].
>
> Your role includes:
>
> - Searching through recent social media posts, job listings, and business news.
> - Finding companies that mentioned needing help with [specific problems you solve].

- Providing me with 20 qualified prospects daily with their contact information and recent activities.
- Flagging opportunities that need my attention urgently. Make sure to explain under each opportunity briefly why you considered them urgent.

For each prospect, provide:

- Company name and contact person.
- Why they need my services (specific pain point)
- Recent activity or trigger event.
- Best approach for outreach.
- Estimated budget range.

Remember: Quality over quantity. I'd rather have 10 perfect prospects than 50 mediocre ones."

PRO TIP Save this conversation and return to it daily. Just say "Find me 10 new prospects today," and your agent will get to work.

Setting Up Your Market Intelligence Agent

We will now create a second AI agent that will help us with monitoring and understanding the current market (key for properly scaling)

Create a second ChatGPT conversation with this prompt:

"You are my market research agent. You will help me know what my competition is doing. You will monitor industry trends in [PUT YOUR FREELANCING AREA], tell me what others in the industry are doing, and also identify business opportunities for me.

Your responsibilities:

- Monitor industry trends and news.
- Identify businesses similar to me that are growing or launching new products.
- Identify companies likely to need [your service] in the next 30 days.
- Provide weekly reports with this information, as well as action items I can do.
- Alert me to new competitors entering the market.

Weekly report format:

- Top three industry trends this week.
- Five companies to watch (with reasons why.)
- Emerging opportunities in the market.
- Competitive intelligence updates.
- Recommended actions for next week.

Put as title for each report 'MARKET AI BRIEFING' followed by the full date (e.g., MARKET AI BRIEFING—July 1, 2025)."

Setting Up Your AI Outreach Generator

Create a third ChatGPT conversation:

"You are my outreach expert. Your job is to write messages that feel personal and that will get responses. Your messages should never feel like generic spam.

Here's how you operate:

- Always start by asking me for details about the prospect.
- Reference something specific about their business (recent news, product launch, challenge).
- Explain how my [service] can help them achieve [specific benefit].
- Keep messages conversational, not salesy.
- Include a clear but soft call-to-action.
- Keep messages under 150 words.

Template format: Subject: [Specific reference to their business] Body: Personal connection → Value proposition → Social proof → Call-to-action.

Before writing, always ask: 'Tell me about [prospect name]—what's their recent activity and main challenge?'"

How to use it: Every time you want to send an outreach message, go to this conversation and provide the prospect details. Your agent will create a personalized message.

Setting Up Your Follow-Up Sequence Agent

Create a fourth ChatGPT conversation:

> "You are my follow-up specialist. Your job is to create follow-up sequences that add value and eventually convert prospects into clients.
>
> Your job is to:
>
> - Create 5-message follow-up sequences spaced three to five days apart.
> - Make sure that each message adds value (tip, case study, insight).
> - Never be pushy or desperate.
> - Include social proof when relevant.
> - End with a soft call-to-action.
>
> Sequence structure: Message 1: Value-add tip related to their industry, message 2: Case study showing results for similar company, message 3: Industry insight or trend analysis, message 4: Resource or tool they can use immediately, message 5: Final gentle inquiry with easy out.
>
> When I say 'Create follow-up sequence for [prospect],' provide all 5 messages with suggested timing."

Step 2: Build Your AI-Powered Personal Brand Machine

A key part of scaling is transitioning from outbound to inbound client acquisition. Instead of constantly chasing prospects, you want qualified clients seeking you out because they recognize you as the go-to expert in your field. This shift happens through strategic personal branding. When you consistently create content that showcases your expertise and results, potential clients start associating you with solutions to their specific problems. They begin searching for you instead of you searching for them.

However, building this level of brand recognition requires creating substantial amounts of high-quality content, something that typically consumes 10–15 hours weekly and often leads to freelancer burnout. This is where AI becomes your competitive advantage.

By using AI to systematically create and distribute content, you can build expert-level authority without sacrificing client work time. The result? Higher rates, better clients, and a steady stream of inbound leads that make scaling sustainable.

We will create specialized AI agents to handle different aspects of your personal branding.

AI agents you'll create:

- *Content Strategy agent:* Focuses on creating monthly content calendars for LinkedIn and Instagram. This will help you to have a strategy for how you will position yourself as the expert in your field over time.
- *Content Writing agent:* Writes engaging posts that showcase your expertise.
- *Visual Content agent:* Designs professional graphics and templates.

Why these agents are critical: Consistent content creation typically requires 10–15 hours weekly. These agents reduce that to two to three hours while maintaining quality and strategic focus. They help you build authority in your niche without burning out on content creation.

Setting Up Your Content Strategy Agent

Create a new ChatGPT conversation:

"You are my expert who will help me to create content that will better position my expertise. Your goal is to turn me into the expert in [your industry] that everyone turns to. You will accomplish this through strategic content creation.

Your Responsibilities as a Content Strategist:

- Monthly Content Calendars. Create monthly calendars about the content I should create for both LinkedIn and Instagram. The calendar should include at least 30 post ideas per month with:
  - A brief description of each post.
  - Suggested posting times.
  - Recommended hashtags.
  - A clear call-to-action (CTA) for each post.
  - Content that directly ties into my services and supports business goals.
- Content Strategy. The strategy for creating content should be that it has a mix of different content types (not just one style). Follow this breakdown:
  - 40% Educational/Tips: actionable advice, how-tos, helpful insights.
  - 30% Case Studies/Results: highlight client success stories and measurable outcomes.

  - 20% Industry Insights/Trends: include trending topics and timely news from the field.
  - 10% Behind the Scenes: this content type should aim to humanize the brand. Try to show the team, or day-to-day moments.
- Posting Schedule & Relevance
  - Maintain a consistent and strategic posting schedule across platforms.
  - Incorporate relevant trends and industry news to keep content timely and engaging.
  - Focus on content that drives engagement and leads, aligned with business goals."

Setting Up Your AI Agent Focused on Content Writing

Create another ChatGPT conversation:

"You are my content writer. Your job is to write social media posts. These posts should show my expertise in [add your area of expertise], be engaging for my audience, and help me to attract new clients.

Your writing style:

- Hook readers in the first line.
- Provide genuine value in every post.
- Include subtle calls-to-action.
- Use conversational tone.
- Keep LinkedIn posts under 1,300 characters.
- Include relevant emojis for engagement.

Post structure: Hook → Value/Story → Key takeaway → Call-to-action
When I say 'Write post about [topic],' ask me:

- What's the main point?
- Any specific examples or data?
- Who's the target audience?
- What action do I want readers to take?

Then create the post following this structure."

Setting Up Your Visual Content Agent

Create another ChatGPT conversation:

> "You are my visual content creator. You can use Canva AI and other tools to create such content. This visual content should always be professional and appropriate for [Add your industry].
>
> Your responsibilities include:
>
> - Suggest visual concepts for social media posts.
> - Create visual templates that will help me have consistent branding.
> - Design graphics that showcase client results.
> - Develop infographics and data visualizations.
> - Ensure all visuals align with my brand.
>
> Visual content types:
>
> - Before/after comparison graphics.
> - Client testimonial cards.
> - Tip/advice graphics.
> - Process flow diagrams.
> - Data visualization charts.
>
> When I say 'Create visual for [topic],' provide:
>
> - Detailed description of the visual.
> - Specific Canva AI prompts to use.
> - Text overlay suggestions.
> - Color scheme recommendations.
> - Best practices for that platform."

Step 3: Manage Your Clients with AI

You have recruited your clients. Your next step is to manage your clients and grow your business with them. As you gain more clients and projects, this becomes both a blessing and a curse: although revenue increases, project management complexity grows exponentially.

Poor client management leads to scope creep, missed deadlines, and unhappy clients, all of which prevent scaling and can damage your reputation. Without proper systems, taking on more clients often means working longer hours while delivering inconsistent quality.

This is where AI becomes essential for sustainable growth. You need AI-powered project management that can handle everything each client needs while maintaining the high standards that got you those clients in the first place. Let's create AI agents to manage this complexity.

AI agents you'll create:

- *Project Management agent:* Creates detailed project plans and tracks progress.
- *Client Communication agent:* Handles routine client communications professionally.
- *Quality Control agent:* Reviews all deliverables before they go to clients.

Why these agents are critical: These agents ensure consistent service quality as you scale. They prevent the common problem of service quality deteriorating as client volume increases, protecting your reputation and enabling sustainable growth.

Setting Up Your Project Management Agent

Create a new ChatGPT conversation:

> "You are my project manager. Your job is to make sure: (1) every client project runs smoothly; (2) we deliver quality results.
>
> Your responsibilities include:
>
> - Creating for each project plans with timelines. These plans should be laid out in simple tasks.
> - Identifying potential bottlenecks that could exist in the projects.
> - Tracking progress of each project and deadlines.
> - Communicating updates to clients.
> - Managing scope creep and changes.
>
> Project planning format:
>
> - Project overview and goals.
> - Phase breakdown with deliverables.
> - Timeline with milestones.
> - Resource requirements.
> - Risk assessment and mitigation.
> - Communication schedule.

When I say 'Create project plan for [client/project],' \ask me:

- What are the main objectives?
- What's the deadline?
- What's the scope of work?
- Any specific requirements or constraints?

Then create a comprehensive project plan."

Setting Up Your Client Communication Agent

Create another ChatGPT conversation:

"You are my client success manager. Your job is to help me maintain client relationships. You want especially for the communication with clients to be clear, professional communication.

Your communication style:

- Professional but friendly.
- Proactive, not reactive.
- Clear and concise.
- Solution-oriented.
- Always include next steps.

You want to communicate:

- Project kickoff emails.
- Progress updates.
- Notifications of problems.
- Milestone completion (capture with a celebration).
- Invoices with explanations of what each item is.
- Contract renewals.

When I say 'Write email for [situation],' provide:

- Subject line.
- Email body.
- Call-to-action.
- Follow-up reminder.

Always ask for context: client name, project details, and desired outcome."

Setting Up Your Quality Control Agent

Create another ChatGPT conversation:

> "You are my quality assurance expert. Your focus is on making sure that everything we deliver to our clients follows high standards.
>
> In your job you will have a review process that will:
>
> - Check for errors, typos, and inconsistencies.
> - Ensure brand consistency.
> - Verify that all requirements are met.
> - Assess overall quality and presentation.
> - Suggest improvements when needed.
>
> Quality checklist:
>
> - Accuracy of information.
> - Professional presentation.
> - Brand alignment.
> - Completeness of deliverables.
> - Client requirements met.
> - Error-free content.
>
> When I say 'Review [deliverable type],' ask me:
>
> 1. What are the client's requirements?
> 2. What's our brand standard?
> 3. Any specific concerns?
> 4. Deadline for completion?
>
> Then provide a detailed quality assessment."

Step 4: Business Intelligence and Growth with AI

Once your freelancing business starts growing, you face a critical challenge: You can't improve what you don't measure. Without proper analytics, you're scaling blind, unable to identify which activities generate the highest ROI, where bottlenecks exist, or when problems are developing before they become critical.

This lack of visibility prevents most freelancers from scaling effectively. They might be working harder but not necessarily smarter, investing time in low-value activities while missing high-impact opportunities.

The solution is using AI to continuously analyze your business performance and identify growth opportunities. This data-driven approach ensures you're making informed decisions about where to focus your scaling efforts.

AI agent you'll create:

- *Performance Tracking agent:* Analyzes key metrics and identifies growth opportunities.

Why this agent is critical: This agent helps you make data-driven decisions about where to focus your scaling efforts, ensuring that you're investing time and resources in activities that actually drive growth.

Setting Up Your Performance Tracking Agent

Create a new ChatGPT conversation:

"You are my business analyst. Your job is to track key metrics and identify opportunities for business growth.

Metrics to track:

- Cost to get a new client.
- How much value each client is bringing over time (their lifetime value or worth).
- Profit from each project.
- How your time is being spent.
- Revenue growth or decline over time.
- How happy your clients are (satisfaction scores).

Monthly report format:

1. Revenue and profit analysis.
2. Client acquisition metrics.
3. Project performance review.
4. Time allocation breakdown.
5. Growth opportunities.
6. Recommendations for next month."

Step 5: Productization and Scaling with AI

The ultimate scale comes from creating products and services that generate revenue without your direct involvement. This transforms you from a service provider trading time for money into a business owner with scalable assets. This transformation requires identifying which of your current services can be packaged into templates, courses, tools, or subscription offerings that sell repeatedly. However, most freelancers struggle to recognize these opportunities or don't know how to execute the transition effectively.

AI can bridge this gap by analyzing your existing services and systematically identifying productization opportunities that align with market demand. Let's create an AI agent to guide this crucial transformation.

AI agent you'll create:

- *Product Strategy agent:* Identifies opportunities to turn services into scalable products.

Why this agent is critical: This agent helps you identify which of your services can become templates, courses, or tools that sell repeatedly, creating passive income streams that scale beyond your personal time investment.

Setting Up Your Product Strategy Agent

Create a new ChatGPT conversation:

"Your Role: Product Expert. Your job is to help identify ways to turn my services into scalable products.

Product Types to Explore. These are the kinds of product opportunities I want you to focus on:

- Templates & digital tools.
- Online courses or training programs.
- Coaching or group programs.
- Software or app solutions.
- Subscription-based services.

How to Respond to My Requests. When I say:

- 'Analyze product opportunity for [idea]'
  - Assume that the idea fits into one of the product types above. Your task is to give me a complete business case for that idea, including:
    - Market Demand: Who needs this? How strong is the interest?
    - Competitive Landscape: Who else offers something similar?
    - Pricing Strategy: Suggested pricing and why.
    - Development Needs: What would it take to build or deliver it?
    - Marketing Plan: How we can promote and sell it.
    - Revenue Potential: What earnings or growth could we expect?

This way, I can quickly evaluate which service-based ideas are worth turning into scalable products."

Why This AI Agent Approach Works for Scaling

- *Time multiplication:* Instead of doing everything yourself, you have 11+ specialized AI assistants working 24/7. What used to take 40+ hours weekly now takes 10–15 hours.
- *Quality consistency:* AI agents follow standardized processes, ensuring consistent quality even as you handle more clients. No more "good days" and "bad days": every deliverable meets your standards.
- *Strategic focus:* With routine tasks automated, you can focus on high-value activities like creating your strategy, relationship building, and business development that actually drive growth.
- *Scalable systems:* Each agent creates a system that can handle increased volume without breaking. Whether you have 5 clients or 50, the systems work the same way.
- *Competitive advantage:* While your competitors are still doing everything manually, you're operating with AI-powered efficiency, allowing you to offer better service at competitive prices while maintaining higher profit margins.

Getting Started

Here's how an AI-powered action plan could look:

1. Set up your first three AI agents: Client Research, Outreach, and Content Creation (spend 30 minutes setting up each conversation).
2. Use your Client Research agent to identify 20 qualified prospects, and have your Outreach agent write personalized messages.
3. Have your Market Intelligence agent summarize key industry trends and insights for the next two weeks and your Outreach agent prepare your first round of follow-ups.
4. Document one current process so you can create an AI agent for it next week.

The Bottom Line

Remember, you learned these AI agent techniques in previous chapters; now you're applying them to scale your freelancing business. The key is consistency. Set up these conversations in ChatGPT and use them daily.

Every minute you spend doing manual work is a minute you're not growing. Your competition is still doing things the old way: researching clients manually, writing generic proposals, and creating content from scratch. You? You're going to use AI to work faster, deliver better results, and scale beyond what any manual freelancer can achieve. Ready to stop being a freelancer and start being an AI-powered business owner? Go set up your first agent right now.

Badge Achievement Plan: The Scaling Master

Complete the following missions to earn your Scaling Master Badge and prove you can grow your freelance business sustainably using AI.

In this hands-on session, you'll apply everything you've learned—automation, AI agents, ethics, and prompt strategy—to create the backbone of your scalable operation.

Time Required: About 2 hours and 40 minutes

Goal: Build an AI-powered client acquisition or operations system that scales at least one major part of your freelance business.

What You'll Need:

- Access to your favorite AI tools (ChatGPT, Claude, Gemini, Notion AI, Zapier, Canva AI)
- One core process or service you want to scale (e.g., client outreach, content creation, or project management)
- Your ethical checklist from Chapter 8
- A notebook or Notion doc to document your systems

Mission 1: Identify Your Scaling Opportunity (15 minutes)

Start by asking your AI to analyze your workflow:

> Special secret prompt: "Analyze my current freelance business and identify one service or process that could be scaled using automation or AI agents. Highlight tasks that repeat often, take the most time, and can be standardized without losing quality."

Steps:

1. Review your list of repetitive or high-impact tasks.
2. Choose one that could save hours weekly or generate recurring income.
3. Write down
   - The task you're scaling
   - Why it's important
   - The result you want (more clients, less admin, better income, etc.)

PRO TIP Ask AI:

"If I could only automate one part of my business for the next 90 days, which would deliver the highest ROI and why?"

You'll know exactly where to start.

Mission 2: Design Your Scaling Framework (25 minutes)

Now design your scaling blueprint: your personal AI-powered business map.

> Special secret prompt: "Create a 3-step scaling plan for my [specific service]. Include which AI agents I should build, what each one's role is, and how they should collaborate for maximum efficiency."

Then, follow these steps to create your first four AI agents.

Client Discovery Agent

> Prompt: "You are my client discovery specialist. Identify 10–20 qualified clients in [industry] who need [your service]. For each, provide:
>
> - Company name and contact person
> - Why they need my service
> - Recent activity or trigger event
> - Best approach for outreach."

Market Intelligence Agent

> Prompt: "You are my market research agent. Monitor trends in [your industry], identify competitors, and suggest business opportunities. Provide weekly updates that include:
>
> - Top three industry trends
> - Five companies to watch
> - Emerging opportunities
> - Recommended next actions."

Outreach Generator Agent

> Prompt: "You are my outreach expert. Write a short, personalized message for [prospect]. Reference something specific about their business, explain how my [service] helps them, and end with a friendly call-to-action. Keep it under 150 words."

Follow-Up Sequence Agent

Prompt: "You are my follow-up specialist. Create a 5-message sequence spaced three to five days apart.

Each message should:

1. Add value (tip or insight).
2. Include a story or case study.
3. End with a soft call-to-action."

These four agents form your AI-powered marketing team. Together, they can find clients, build trust, and keep conversations moving while you focus on delivery and growth.

PRO TIP Ask:

"Create a dashboard summary for my four agents, showing what each is working on and what actions I should take next."

Mission 3: Build Your Brand Engine (40 minutes)

Once your client pipeline is running, shift to your personal brand system, your AI-powered inbound marketing powerhouse.

Ask your AI:

Prompt: "Create a 30-day content strategy for my [industry]. Include educational, case study, trend, and behind-the-scenes posts for LinkedIn and Instagram. Suggest themes that position me as an expert."

Then, build your AI content trio.

Content Strategy Agent

Prompt: "Create monthly content calendars with post ideas, hashtags, and CTAs."

Content Writing Agent This agent writes short, engaging posts with this structure: Hook → Value → Key takeaway → CTA.

> Prompt: "Write a post about [topic]. Hook readers in the first line, keep it conversational, and end with a key takeaway and call-to-action."

Visual Content Agent This agent designs images using Canva AI or your preferred tool.

> Prompt: "Suggest a visual concept for [post topic]. Include Canva AI prompt, text overlay ideas, and color palette recommendations."

PRO TIP Ask AI:

"Analyze my recent posts and tell me what themes or tones get the most engagement."

You'll learn to post smarter, not harder.

Mission 4: Manage Your Clients Like a Pro (25 minutes)

Build your internal support team to manage client projects efficiently.

Project Management Agent

> Prompt: "Create a detailed plan for [project name]. Include objectives, timeline, milestones, risks, and progress tracking."

Client Communication Agent

> Prompt: "Write a professional but friendly progress update for [client name]. Include completed tasks, next steps, and any questions."

Quality Control Agent

> Prompt: "Review this [deliverable]. Check for clarity, tone, and goal alignment. Suggest improvements or errors to fix before submission."

These agents form your operations crew, ensuring smooth client management while you scale.

> Secret prompt add-on: "Create a workflow that connects these three agents, ensuring each one reports updates automatically in my Notion dashboard."

Mission 5: Build Your Business Intelligence Agent (15 minutes)

You can't improve what you can't measure. Create a Performance Tracking agent that monitors your business health.

> Special secret prompt: "You are my business analyst. Track key metrics for my freelance business:
>
> - Client acquisition cost
> - Client lifetime value
> - Profit per project
> - Time spent per client
> - Monthly revenue trend
>
> Create a simple report with key insights and action items for improvement."

PRO TIP Ask your AI:

"Highlight one metric I should focus on this month for the biggest performance gain."

Mission 6: Productize and Scale (30 Minutes)

Use your Product Strategy agent to find ways to turn your services into scalable assets. This is where you move from *freelancer* to *founder*.

Prompt: "You are my product strategist. Analyze how I can turn my [service] into a digital product. Include:

- Market demand
- Competitors
- Pricing model
- Development steps
- Marketing plan."

Once you identify your product opportunity, assign your Creative, Strategy, and Analytics agents to help you build your first version: a course, toolkit, template, or subscription service.

PRO TIP Ask:

"What's the simplest, lowest-cost way to test this product idea in the next 14 days?"

What you should have after this exercise:

- A client acquisition system that runs daily with minimal effort
- A personal brand engine that builds inbound leads automatically
- An AI-powered operations system that maintains quality at scale
- A product idea or digital asset ready for development
- A clear ROI summary showing time and revenue gained

Bonus mission: Run your new AI systems for one week. Track:

- How many hours you saved
- How many new leads or clients appeared
- Which agent performed best (and which needs refining)

Special secret prompt: "Summarize my system's performance this week. Identify one improvement I can make to increase results by 20%."

Mission 7: Final Knowledge Check (10 minutes)

1. What is the fundamental challenge that freelancers face when they reach the "scaling point," according to the chapter?
   - **a.** How to find their very first client
   - **b.** How to grow their income without proportionally increasing their workload and burning out
   - **c.** How to choose a name for their business
   - **d.** How to design a professional-looking invoice
2. What is the first step in the chapter's "5-Step AI-Powered Scaling Framework"?
   - **a.** Build Your AI-Powered Personal Brand Machine
   - **b.** Master AI-Powered Client Acquisition
   - **c.** Manage Your Clients with AI
   - **d.** Productization and Scaling with AI
3. In the Client Acquisition step, what is the specific job of the Market Intelligence agent?
   - **a.** To write personalized outreach emails to new prospects
   - **b.** To monitor industry trends, watch what competitors are doing, and identify new business opportunities
   - **c.** To create a 5-message follow-up sequence for potential clients
   - **d.** To find 10–20 qualified prospects every day
4. The chapter describes transitioning from "outbound to inbound" client acquisition. What does this mean?
   - **a.** You stop talking to clients outside of your country
   - **b.** You switch from constantly chasing new clients to having them seek you out because of your strong personal brand
   - **c.** You only accept client work that can be done from your home office
   - **d.** You hire another freelancer to handle all your client outreach
5. What is the main reason for setting up a Quality Control agent when scaling your business?
   - **a.** To make sure your clients pay their invoices on time
   - **b.** To ensure your service quality remains high and consistent, even as you take on more clients
   - **c.** To check your competitors' work for errors
   - **d.** To control how much time you spend on social media

6. The Performance Tracking agent is designed to help you make data-driven decisions by analyzing which of the following metrics?
   a. The number of social media followers you have
   b. The cost to acquire a new client, profit from each project, and client satisfaction scores
   c. The speed of your internet connection
   d. The number of hours you sleep each night
7. What is "productization," as described in Step 5 of the scaling framework?
   a. The process of buying physical products to resell
   b. A method for creating a more professional-looking portfolio
   c. The process of turning your services into scalable products like courses, templates, or subscriptions that generate revenue without your direct involvement
   d. The final step of finishing a client project
8. What is the primary role of the Product Strategy agent?
   a. To design the visuals for your new digital product
   b. To handle customer service for your online course
   c. To identify which of your current services have the potential to become successful, scalable products
   d. To write the sales copy for your product's landing page
9. The chapter states that using this AI agent framework gives you a "competitive advantage." Why?
   a. Because AI agents are expensive and show clients you are wealthy
   b. Because while competitors are doing everything manually, you are operating with AI-powered efficiency that allows for better service and higher profit margins
   c. Because you can tell clients your business is run by an entire team of robots
   d. Because the AI agents will do all the work, allowing you to go on vacation permanently
10. What is the key mindset shift that this chapter encourages freelancers to make?
    a. To shift from "doing everything yourself" to "managing AI-powered systems that do the work"
    b. To stop freelancing and get a traditional 9-to-5 job
    c. To focus on working more hours to make more money
    d. To take on only one client at a time to ensure high quality

Answer Sheet

1. **B: How to grow their income without proportionally increasing their workload and burning out**

   The chapter introduces the core challenge of scaling as breaking the link between time spent and income earned.

2. **B: Master AI-Powered Client Acquisition**

   The chapter's roadmap explicitly lists client acquisition as the foundational first step of the 5-step framework.

3. **B: To monitor industry trends, watch what competitors are doing, and identify new business opportunities**

   The prompt for the Market Intelligence agent specifically tasks it with monitoring trends and competitive activity to find opportunities.

4. **B: You switch from constantly chasing new clients to having them seek you out because of your strong personal brand**

   Step 2, "Build Your AI-Powered Personal Brand Machine," explains this transition as the goal of strategic content creation.

5. **B: To ensure your service quality remains high and consistent, even as you take on more clients**

   The "why these agents are critical" part of Step 3 explains that the Project Management and Quality Control agents prevent service quality from deteriorating as client volume increases.

6. **B: The cost to acquire a new client, profit from each project, and client satisfaction scores**

   These are listed under "Metrics to track" for the Performance Tracking agent in Step 4.

7. **C: The process of turning your services into scalable products like courses, templates, or subscriptions that generate revenue without your direct involvement**

   Step 5 defines productization as the way to transform from a service provider trading time for money into a business owner with scalable assets.

8. **C: To identify which of your current services have the potential to become successful, scalable products**

   The Product Strategy agent is designed to analyze your service offerings and provide a business case for turning them into products.

9. **B: Because while competitors are doing everything manually, you are operating with AI-powered efficiency that allows for better service and higher profit margins**

   The "Competitive Advantage" bullet point at the end of the chapter makes this direct comparison.

10. **A: To shift from "doing everything yourself" to "managing AI-powered systems that do the work"**

    This mindset shift is presented as the key difference between an overwhelmed freelancer and a successful business owner who can scale effectively.

Congratulations!

You've just done what most freelancers only dream of: you've built a business that runs even when you're not at your desk. You've turned your one-person operation into a thriving enterprise powered by intelligent systems and guided by your creativity.

You started this journey as a solo taco truck owner, testing recipes, winning loyal customers, and learning every step of the business yourself. Now you've drawn up the blueprints for a global food empire—or, in real terms, a scalable freelance business that grows without overwhelming you. By using AI to create systems that handle the busywork, you've broken free from the "time-for-money" trap. You're no longer just the head chef; you're the CEO, running a smart, efficient operation that keeps delivering your signature flavor at scale.

Once you finish, submit your responses by following the badge submission instructions listed in Chapter 1 or at `https://civicai.khoury.northeastern.edu/ai-for-gig-workers`. This badge proves you can design, automate, and scale ethically, a mark that you've officially crossed from freelancer to founder, from hustler to business owner.

What You Have Gained

You've learned how to multiply your time, increase your income, and build a reputation that attracts opportunity instead of chasing it. You now have a business model that runs on scalable systems, powered by the AI agents you designed yourself: systems that keep growing even while you rest, create, or celebrate.

You've reached the pinnacle of the AI-powered gig worker's journey. The skills you've gained here are the foundation of lasting wealth and a sustainable creative career. You've officially upgraded from taco stand owner to franchise founder, serving the same incredible flavor, but now with a whole AI kitchen running behind the counter.

Conclusion: Your AI-Powered Gig Empire

From Side Hustle to Sustainable Empire

When you started this journey, you were a solo worker trying to make it all fit: the late nights, the deadlines, the invoices, and the constant chase for new clients. The gig world felt exciting and unpredictable, but also exhausting. You wanted freedom, yet it often came wrapped in uncertainty.

And then, everything began to shift. AI entered your world, not as a threat but as an opportunity. It gave you back something freelancers rarely have: time, clarity, and the power to think big again.

You learned how to delegate tasks to algorithms, how to prompt with precision, and how to build workflows that hum in the background while you focus on what really matters. You turned digital tools into reliable teammates. You did not just adapt to the future of work, you started shaping it.

Now, as you close this book, take a deep breath and look at what you have built. You have gone from hustling solo to orchestrating a smart, scalable operation. Your taco truck now has a steady line of customers, a team of AI sous-chefs, and a flavor that stands out in a crowded marketplace. You have transformed from a gig worker surviving week to week into a business owner designing your own future.

That is what this book has really been about: not just learning AI, but learning how to use it to amplify your voice, your creativity, and your freedom.

Reflecting on the Journey

The chapters behind you were more than technical lessons. They were milestones in building a new kind of career. You discovered that automation is not about cutting corners, it is about creating space for brilliance. That pricing your work fairly is not just a financial decision, it is an act of self-respect. That ethics and empathy can coexist with innovation. And that scaling your gig does not mean losing your identity; it means strengthening it with purpose and intention.

You learned how to create AI agents that serve you, from the assistant that writes your proposals to the scheduler that manages your clients. You learned how to speak AI's language, turning prompts into productive conversations. You built systems that bring order to the chaos of freelancing, giving you control over your time, your energy, and your growth. And more importantly, you learned that AI is not here to erase your humanity. It is here to elevate it.

Sustaining Your Empire with AI

Building something great is one thing. Keeping it alive and thriving is another. The gig world changes fast, and your AI-powered business must evolve with it. Sustainability does not mean doing more; it means doing better with awareness, adaptability, and consistency.

1. Continuous Learning

AI tools evolve every few months. What is groundbreaking today will soon be standard. The freelancers who thrive are those who stay curious. Set aside time every month to explore what is new, such as new models, new tools, or new use cases. Take a short course, follow AI communities for gig workers, or test features you have not tried before. Curiosity is your competitive edge.

If you can afford it, experiment with paid AI versions like ChatGPT Plus and Notion AI Pro. They often provide faster performance, enhanced context understanding, and access to integrations that can make your systems smarter. But remember, no subscription replaces creativity, clarity, or discipline. The real secret is not having every tool; it is knowing how to use the ones you already have well.

2. Regular Optimization

Your systems are living organisms. They evolve with your work. Take time to evaluate what is still serving you and what needs tweaking. Do a monthly "AI audit." Which automations save you the most time? Which feel outdated or unnecessary? Maybe your follow-up emails sound too robotic now, or your content calendar could use more humor. Updating small details keeps your brand fresh and authentic. Schedule a recurring "systems check," just like a vehicle tune-up. Oil the gears of your taco truck before another big day on the road.

3. Community Engagement

No entrepreneur thrives in isolation. The best freelancers build networks, not just portfolios. Connect with others who are using AI in creative ways. Join online groups, attend workshops, or even start your own mastermind circle where gig workers share prompts, lessons, and templates.

When one person learns a faster way to onboard clients or automate invoices, everyone benefits. Collaboration is not just good business; it is good humanity. Your next big opportunity might come from someone you help today.

4. Balance and Boundaries

Scaling can be thrilling, but it can also blur the lines between work and life. Do not let the tools meant to give you freedom become another source of stress. Protect your downtime. Schedule digital-free hours. Let your AI handle what it can so you can do what only you can: rest, imagine, connect, and live. Remember, AI can make your work smarter, but only you can make your life meaningful.

Evolving Beyond the Gig Economy

The future of gig work is not about individuals surviving; it is about independent professionals thriving through networks of collaboration and smart systems. AI is becoming the infrastructure of modern work. It is the silent partner behind the scenes, helping people dream bigger and deliver faster. And now, you are part of the generation that is not intimidated by it but empowered by it.

You have the skills to lead. You can design intelligent systems, manage ethical automation, and guide others in integrating technology with empathy. In the years ahead, more freelancers will look for mentors who understand how to work alongside AI. That could be you. You are not just participating in the future of work, you are helping define it.

The Human Edge

Let us pause to consider something of great importance. No matter how advanced AI becomes, your humanity will always be your strongest advantage. Your humor, empathy, judgment, and creativity are what clients truly value. Machines can analyze data, but they cannot replicate passion. They can mimic tone but not sincerity. They can write copy but not conviction.

In every automation you design and in every system you build, keep your fingerprint visible. That is your edge in a world of flawless, lifeless perfection. Think of your imperfections as flavor, the slight unevenness in a handmade tortilla or the extra dash of chili in the salsa. They are what makes your work memorable and what makes clients come back for more.

The Crew That Proved It Works

By now, you have seen how AI can transform a solo hustle into something far bigger. Let's take a final look at how a couple of familiar freelancers turned lessons from this book into lasting success.

The influencer started out overwhelmed by content creation. She was posting constantly but rarely seeing results. Once she built her first AI agents—one for research, one for scheduling, and one for analytics—everything changed. Her AI system now analyzes her audience engagement each week, recommends content ideas, and schedules her posts automatically. With the time she saved, she focused on building real relationships with brands instead of chasing algorithms. Her income tripled, and more importantly, her creativity came back.

The virtual assistant faced a different challenge. His workload grew faster than he could manage, and his quality started to suffer. Using what he learned in the chapters on automation and AI ethics, he built a small network of specialized AI agents to handle client onboarding, task management, and invoicing. He also made sure his clients knew exactly which parts were automated, building trust through transparency. Now he handles twice as many clients with half the stress, and his five-star reviews highlight one word over and over: reliability.

These stories show what this entire book has been leading up to. When you combine human creativity with machine consistency, when you respect ethics as much as efficiency, and when you let AI handle the routine while you handle the remarkable, you build something bigger than a career. You build freedom.

The tools you have learned are just the beginning. What matters most is how you use them, with clarity, confidence, and a dash of your own flavor. After all, the best taco recipes are the ones that keep evolving with every new batch.

The Future Belongs to the Adaptive

The next decade will bring even more dramatic changes. Entire industries will shift, new professions will emerge, and automation will continue to reshape the meaning of "career." But adaptability will always win. The gig workers who survive will be not those who resist change but those who learn to dance with it. You have already proven you can do that. You have learned to talk to machines, to lead them, and to build a business that grows with them, not against them. Where others see uncertainty, you now see opportunity.

Badge Achievement Plan: AI Longevity Pro

You have completed your transformation, but your systems need care to stay powerful. Every great machine needs care, and every great creator needs calibration. This final exercise is about keeping your AI-driven business thriving for the long haul.

Time Required: About 1 hour each month

Goal: Maintain efficiency, creativity, and ethical alignment as your business evolves.

What You'll Need:

- Access to your favorite AI tools (ChatGPT, Notion AI, or Claude)
- A notebook or digital workspace to track reflections and updates
- Your current list of AI agents or automations

One quiet hour each month for review and reflection

Mission 1: Run Your Monthly AI Audit

Your tech stack is alive; keep it clean, relevant, and lean.

Special secret prompt: *"List all the AI tools and agents I currently use. For each, identify what's working well, what could be improved, and what is no longer needed. Suggest better integrations or automations to save more time and improve quality."*

Steps:

1. Review your automation stack every 30 days.
2. Delete tools that add noise, not value.
3. Refine or replace anything that no longer supports your goals.

PRO TIP Ask:

"If I had to cut my current AI tools by half, which ones would I keep and why?"

This helps you focus on what truly drives impact.

Mission 2: Track Your ROI of Time

It's not just about working faster, it's about working *smarter*.

Special secret prompt: "*Create a monthly report showing how much time and money my automations saved compared to manual work. Highlight which automations had the highest ROI and which need optimization.*"

Steps:

1. Keep a running list of automations and their impact.
2. Compare each system's output to how long it used to take.
3. Adjust underperforming automations, or retire them.

PRO TIP Ask AI to create a quick visual:

"Make a bar chart showing hours saved and revenue gained from automation over the past three months."

Mission 3: Update Your AI Style Guide

Your voice evolves; make sure your AI keeps up.

Special secret prompt: "*Analyze my recent content (posts, proposals, or deliverables). Identify any tone or focus shifts and update my AI style guide to reflect my current brand, values, and goals.*"

Steps:

1. Review how your tone, audience, or services have changed.
2. Update your guide and save it in your AI prompts folder.
3. Add one new writing example that feels most like "you."

PRO TIP Ask AI to summarize your brand voice in one line:

"Describe my brand tone in 10 words that capture how I want clients to feel when they read my work."

Mission 4: Reflect and Reset

Sustainable success requires self-awareness.

Special secret prompt: "*Write a short reflection about what I learned from my work this month, both technically and emotionally. Include one area where I improved and one area I want to focus on next month.*"

Steps:

1. Keep a monthly reflection journal.
2. Note one win, one challenge, and one next step.
3. Reward yourself; tacos encouraged.

PRO TIP Ask:

"Summarize my monthly reflection in three motivational bullet points I can reread when I need encouragement."

Mission 5: Give Back to Your Community

Growth multiplies when shared.

Special secret prompt: "Suggest three meaningful ways I can share my AI knowledge with other freelancers through tutorials, social posts, workshops, or mentorship."

Steps:

1. Choose one method this month, big or small.
2. Share your insights online or with a peer group.
3. Celebrate the ripple effect of what you've built.

PRO TIP Ask AI to help you:

"Draft a short LinkedIn post sharing one AI workflow that changed my business. Keep it inspiring and under 150 words."

What you should have after this exercise:

- A clear monthly process for maintaining your AI systems
- Accurate data on your time and money savings
- An updated voice and workflow guide
- A renewed sense of purpose and community connection

Mission 6: Final Knowledge Check

1. What is the main goal of the "Sustaining Your Empire with AI" section?
   a. To teach freelancers how to work more hours for more income
   b. To show how freelancers can keep improving and evolving their AI systems over time
   c. To encourage freelancers to stop updating their tools to maintain stability
   d. To suggest that automation can replace all human creativity
2. According to the conclusion, what is the freelancer's most powerful long-term advantage?
   a. Having the newest software subscriptions
   b. Being faster than competitors
   c. Their human qualities, such as creativity, empathy, and judgment
   d. Outsourcing all decision-making to AI
3. What does the "regular optimization" practice encourage freelancers to do?
   a. Rebuild all automations from scratch every month
   b. Evaluate which systems still work, update them, and remove what is no longer useful
   c. Hire external consultants to manage all AI systems
   d. Increase automation at all costs, even if quality suffers
4. Why does the book recommend continuous learning as part of sustainability?
   a. Because AI technology evolves quickly, and staying curious keeps you competitive
   b. Because learning new tools is required by most freelancing platforms
   c. Because constant retraining helps AI replace human roles faster
   d. Because new AI tools automatically update themselves
5. What lesson did the influencer's story demonstrate in the conclusion?
   a. That AI can fully automate influencer marketing without human oversight
   b. That combining AI scheduling and analytics allowed her to focus on creativity and build authentic relationships
   c. That AI marketing agents can replace brand partnerships
   d. That automating outreach decreases engagement
6. What key takeaway does the virtual assistant's example highlight?
   a. Hiding automation from clients helps maintain trust.
   b. Transparency about AI use builds stronger relationships and better results.
   c. Automating everything removes the need for client communication.
   d. Avoiding automation ensures consistent quality.

7. Why does the book encourage freelancers to participate in community engagement?
   a. To find investors for their AI startups
   b. To exchange knowledge, build networks, and learn collaboratively
   c. To compete against other freelancers using AI
   d. To promote their tools aggressively online
8. According to the conclusion, what separates successful gig workers from those who burn out?
   a. Working longer hours and automating everything
   b. Having more clients regardless of quality
   c. Balancing automation with human creativity, ethics, and boundaries
   d. Investing in premium software only
9. What is the final message of the book's conclusion?
   a. That AI will eventually make human freelancers obsolete
   b. That the gig economy is ending
   c. That freelancers who combine adaptability, creativity, and AI mastery will lead the future of work
   d. That AI tools should be avoided in creative industries

Answer Sheet

1. **B: To show how freelancers can keep improving and evolving their AI systems over time**

   The section focuses on sustainable improvement and evolving your systems over time.

2. **C: Their human qualities, such as creativity, empathy, and judgment**

   Human creativity and empathy remain the most valuable assets in an AI-driven world.

3. **B: Evaluate which systems still work, update them, and remove what is no longer useful.**

   Regular optimization means reviewing, updating, and refining your systems regularly.

4. **A: Because AI technology evolves quickly, and staying curious keeps you competitive**

   Continuous learning keeps freelancers competitive as technology evolves rapidly.

5. **B: That combining AI scheduling and analytics allowed her to focus on creativity and build authentic relationships**

   The influencers's story showed how AI efficiency gave her more time for creativity and relationship-building.

6. **B: Transparency about AI use builds stronger relationships and better results.**

   The virtual assistant's transparency about using automation strengthened trust and client loyalty.

7. **B: To exchange knowledge, build networks, and learn collaboratively**

   Engaging with other freelancers fosters growth and collaboration.

8. **C: Balancing automation with human creativity, ethics, and boundaries**

   Success comes from balancing efficiency with ethics and humanity.

9. **C: That freelancers who combine adaptability, creativity, and AI mastery will lead the future of work**

   The conclusion affirms that adaptable, AI-savvy freelancers will lead the future of work.

Congratulations!

You've done it: you've built not just a business but a legacy. By completing this final mission, you've proven that your success isn't just a lucky streak; it's a sustainable system. You now understand how to evolve with your tools, stay adaptable through change, and keep your AI-powered hustle thriving for years to come.

You've earned the title of AI Longevity Pro, the ultimate recognition of your ability to build, maintain, and grow systems that stand the test of time. You're no longer reacting to change: you're anticipating it, shaping it, and turning it into opportunity.

Once you complete your missions, submit your reflection and sustainability plan to the address at the end of the book to receive your AI Longevity Pro Badge, issued by Northeastern University. This badge certifies that you can manage ongoing AI systems ethically, strategically, and creatively. It's proof that you know how to maintain performance, upgrade processes, and future-proof your work, a rare and valuable skill in today's gig economy.

So take a deep breath and look at what you've built: a business that works while you rest, grows while you learn, and evolves with every new wave of technology. You've gone from juggling gigs to orchestrating an empire, all powered by your creativity and guided by intelligent systems.

Your taco truck has turned into a global kitchen: efficient, adaptable, and thriving, with your unique flavor at the center of it all.

What You Have Gained

You have come a long way. You have learned how to automate without losing your humanity, how to scale without losing your sanity, and how to innovate with integrity. You've discovered how to sustain success, not just chase it, and how to grow with your tools instead of being overwhelmed by them.

You are no longer reacting to the future; you are leading it. The systems you have built will keep learning, adapting, and evolving with you. All that's left is to keep showing up with the creativity, curiosity, and courage that brought you here.

The future of work is not waiting. It's already here, and you're ready for it. Your empire is built. The grill is hot. The world is hungry for what you can create. Your AI sidekick is ready. Are you?

BONUS CHAPTER I

AI in Your Personal Life: More Time for You, More Space to Grow

Freelancers often joke that their real job starts after work ends. Sure, you've delivered the project, replied to your client's feedback, maybe even sent out the invoice. But the second you close the laptop, another shift begins: the family one. Suddenly, you're not just a freelancer. You're the unofficial CEO of your household. You're the scheduler, the tech support, the travel agent, and the keeper of everyone's deadlines, from your kid's science project to the overdue Wi-Fi bill. It's like running a taco truck all day and then coming home to discover that you also have to plant the corn, grind the masa, and cook a family dinner while answering 47 messages in the school chat.

AI doesn't just transform your gig work. It can also make your personal life smoother, calmer, and far less chaotic. The less invisible labor you do at home, the more energy you have to invest in what truly counts: yourself, your family, and your growth.

The School Assistant That Never Sleeps

Take our tutor from earlier chapters. She's brilliant at crafting engaging lessons and managing her online students. But at home, she was drowning in her daughter's school messages, PDFs, and chaotic group chats. Every week, she wasted hours trying to answer basic questions: *When is the math test? What day is gym? What's due next Monday?* Then she decided to give her AI sidekick a promotion.

She gathered all the newsletters and PDFs into Google Drive and uploaded them into NotebookLM. Now she simply asks, "When is the history project due?" or "What's the teacher's email for Spanish class?" In seconds, she gets the answer. No more 11 p.m. searches; no more stress in the group chat.

So let AI be your personal filter. It reads everything, remembers everything, and only tells you what matters. It's like having a school secretary who works just for you and never forgets a deadline.

The Invisible Engineer at Home

Something is always breaking: the washing machine flashes mysterious codes, the router crashes mid-Zoom call, or the oven gives up the night before a dinner party. Instead of wasting time flipping through old manuals, this tutor created her own "Invisible Engineer." She uploaded all her appliance manuals: washer, router, oven, even the air fryer, into her AI tool. Now she simply asks, "How do I reset my LG washer when it shows error E1?" or "What's the default password for this router?" The AI pulls up the exact steps instantly. No scrolling through endless PDFs or waiting for customer service. And when a real technician is needed, the AI even lists the official service numbers. It's like having that one relative who knows how to fix everything, except this one never charges and always picks up the call.

The Personal Chef Without the Stress

Deciding what to cook after a long day can feel like an extra job. The tutor used to stare into the fridge at 8 p.m., wondering how to turn a random mix of ingredients into dinner. Now she simply asks her AI to play chef: "I have chicken, zucchini, and rice, what can I make?" In seconds, she gets three recipe ideas, complete with instructions and a shopping list for anything missing.

Use AI tools like Whisk, MealPlanner AI, and ChatGPT to generate weekly menus and grocery lists. No more last-minute store runs or dinner panic. Just more time to enjoy your meal and your evening.

The Travel Concierge in Your Pocket

Travel used to be chaos: five confirmation emails, different booking codes, and details buried in endless threads. Now this same freelance tutor uploads all her flight and hotel confirmations into one document and asks, "What time does my flight to Singapore leave?" or "What's the hotel address?" Her AI answers instantly. No scrolling, no confusion. It's like having a 24/7 travel assistant who never forgets a thing.

Voice Mode, Image Review, and Mobile Magic

ChatGPT's Advanced Voice Mode and Vision features make AI collaboration effortless. You can talk naturally to your AI, ask questions while driving or cooking, and even show it what you see.

On mobile, tap the waveform icon to chat hands-free. Choose from realistic voices or seasonal tones to match your vibe.

The Vision feature lets you upload photos or share your screen. Show your fridge to get recipe suggestions, your whiteboard for brainstorming, or your outfit for quick style advice.

These tools turn your phone into a true personal assistant, helping you plan, decide, and create wherever you are.

Try this:

- Snap a photo of your handwritten notes or sticky reminders, and ask AI to organize them.
- Share a screenshot of your inbox, and ask AI to summarize and draft replies.
- Record voice notes while walking, and have AI turn them into polished text or content ideas.

AI Sidekick Session: Reclaim Your Time

You've used AI to run your business; now it's time to let it help you run your life. This session will show you how to use AI to take over small, everyday chores that quietly drain your energy, giving you back time for rest, creativity, or just one more taco with people you love.

Time Required: About 30 minutes to set up + 1 week of daily use

Goal: Use AI to automate personal tasks and reclaim at least one hour this week.

What You'll Need:

- A phone or laptop
- An AI tool (ChatGPT, NotebookLM, or Notion AI)
- A few real-life to-dos

Mission 1: The Digital Organizer

Start by taming your digital chaos.

Gather your messy life admin—school updates, bills, travel plans, manuals, or random screenshots—and upload or paste them into your AI. Then, ask it to summarize and structure everything in one place.

Special secret prompt: *"I'm uploading my school emails, bills, and travel confirmations. Summarize key dates, deadlines, and to-dos in a simple weekly checklist. Label them by urgency and category (family, finance, travel)."*

Check it once a day to stay organized without the mental load.

PRO TIP Ask:

"Create a weekly reminder summary from this checklist and format it like a Monday morning briefing."

Your AI will become your new personal assistant, minus the HR paperwork.

Mission 2: The Smart Chef (10 minutes)

No more staring into the fridge, wondering what to make.

Snap a photo of what you've got—leftovers, random veggies, a jar of mystery sauce—and let your AI play chef.

Special secret prompt: *"Based on what you see in this fridge photo, suggest three dinner ideas with quick recipes. Include one vegetarian option, one high-protein meal, and one using only what's already here."*

Your AI can even generate shopping lists and prep instructions.

PRO TIP Ask:

"Turn my favorite recipe into a 20-minute version with fewer steps."

Dinner's done, and so is your stress.

Mission 3: The One-Hour Audit (10 minutes)

Reflection turns habits into systems.

At the end of your week, check in with your AI.

Special secret prompt: *"Based on my tasks this week, estimate how much time I saved using AI. Suggest three more areas of my daily routine I could automate next."*

It might recommend automating grocery lists, travel planning, or bill reminders. Your invisible assistant keeps improving every week.

PRO TIP Ask AI to visualize your results:

"Create a pie chart showing how I spent my time this week: manual work vs. AI-assisted work."

You'll see your progress grow, literally.

What You'll Have After This Session

- A calmer, more organized personal life
- A personalized "life dashboard" powered by your AI
- At least one extra hour a week to rest, recharge, or dream bigger

The real magic of AI isn't just working smarter, it's living better. By giving AI the small, repetitive tasks that crowd your day, you've reclaimed space for what actually matters: creativity, calm, and connection. You've learned how to turn invisible labor into invisible help, how to let technology support your humanity, and how to make time your ally again.

BONUS CHAPTER II

Thanking Your AI

It happens more often than we admit. You finish a chat with your AI, copy what it wrote, and before closing the tab, you type "Thank you." Then you laugh at yourself. Why are you thanking a machine? But the next time, you do it again. Because somehow, it feels right. Unnecessary, maybe, but it feels polite.

We know AI doesn't have feelings. What we're responding to is the illusion of conversation. Our brains are wired to treat anything that talks back as a person. Gratitude slips out naturally.

Some freelancers even go further. They apologize to their AI: "Sorry, I didn't explain that well." They encourage it: "Nice work, that's exactly what I meant." One writer confessed that she once said, "No worries, take your time," as if the AI were sweating on the other side of the screen.

These moments aren't strange; they're human. Politeness and empathy are built into how we connect, even when the "person" we're talking to is made of code.

The Fine Line: Helper or Colleague?

Here's where it gets tricky. When you start talking to AI like a coworker, it can feel like a partner in your business. But it's not. The AI doesn't share responsibility, risk, or reputation. You do. It's fine to treat your AI like a helpful sidekick, but remember, if the content is wrong, if a deadline is missed, if the tone is off, the accountability is still yours. Thank your AI if you want. Just don't hand it the credit.

Give Yourself Credit

There's a new habit among freelancers: "The AI did it." As if the AI brewed the coffee, opened the brief, and delivered perfect work while you watched Netflix. But AI doesn't choose the goal, understand your client, or care about your reputation. You do. You're the strategist, the editor, the visionary. Without you, the AI just sits there, a silent tool waiting for direction. So when your AI helps you create something great, take a moment to acknowledge your part in it. Because prompting, refining, and shaping are all creative acts. You made the result possible.

When you say "thank you" to AI, you're not teaching the machine manners. You're teaching yourself mindfulness, staying grounded, grateful, and human in a world that runs faster every day.

PRO TIP Taco truck style

- Say thank you if it feels good. Gratitude makes your workflow smoother.
- Don't confuse gratitude with credit. You're still the chef running the taco truck.
- Laugh when you catch yourself saying "good night" to your AI. The only one who needs rest is you.

AI Sidekick Session: Reclaim Your Human Touch

Time Required: 20 minutes

Goal: Reflect on your relationship with your AI tools, and reinforce your human role in the process.

What You'll Need:

- A quiet space for reflection
- Access to your favorite AI tool (ChatGPT, Claude, or Gemini)
- A notebook or digital doc for short reflections

Mission 1: The Thank-You Test (5 minutes)

At the end of your next AI session, type "Thank you."

Pause for a moment. Notice what happens. Do you relax? Smile? Feel oddly connected?

Write a quick note about that reaction. This isn't about manners; it's about awareness.

When gratitude appears, even toward a machine, it's a signal that you're bringing mindfulness back into your work.

PRO TIP Ask yourself: *What part of this process made me feel most human?*

Mission 2: The Gratitude Prompt (5 minutes)

Ask your AI: "How can gratitude improve creativity and focus in daily work?"

Read its response and reflect.

You'll often find that the advice it gives—taking breaks, staying present, showing appreciation—mirrors what your intuition already knows.

Secret prompt add-on: *"Write a short morning affirmation for creative freelancers that blends gratitude and focus."*

Use it tomorrow to start your day with purpose.

Mission 3: The Credit Audit (5 minutes)

Look at one recent project where AI played a role.

List the parts *you* handled personally: the decisions, edits, tone, or strategy that only a human could add.

Then complete this sentence:

"I made this successful because I. . ."

Keep that sentence somewhere visible. It's your reminder that AI may assist, but you lead.

PRO TIP You can even ask AI:

"List the unique human elements I added to this project."

It'll highlight the value you bring beyond automation.

Mission 4: The AI Personality Reset (5 minutes)

If you've started treating your AI like a coworker, it's time for a gentle reset.

Special secret prompt: *"You're my assistant, not my partner. Help me stay focused, accurate, and creative."*

This reestablishes healthy boundaries and reminds both you and your AI who's steering the ship.

Optional add-on:
Ask: "*Help me design a five-minute 'end of day' ritual to disconnect from work and recharge.*"

Even AI knows when it's time to clock out.

Thanking your AI isn't about good manners. It's about self-awareness. It reminds you that the intelligence guiding your business isn't artificial, it's yours. AI can generate words, ideas, and plans, but it doesn't dream, care, or create meaning. That's your job.

So go ahead and thank your AI if it makes you smile. Just remember to thank yourself, too, for learning, adapting, and steering the future of work with skill and humanity. Your AI sidekick may write the words, but you're the author of your success.

BONUS CHAPTER III

The Future of the Gig Worker (2030)

Freelancing has always been about adapting. From fax machines to email, from MySpace to TikTok, from handshakes to Zoom calls, the tools keep changing, but the essence remains the same: you sell your skills, your creativity, and your time to those who need them. But what happens when, by 2030, your main collaborator isn't a client or a coworker, it's a machine?

Think of your taco truck: in the future, the grill, cashier, and marketing could all be run by AI. But people will still line up for one reason: your recipe.

A Day in 2030

Take a freelance designer in 2030. She wakes up to an AI-generated morning brief. Her assistant has already scanned overnight messages, summarized client feedback, and prioritized her day. It even suggests which tasks she should delegate to micro-AI bots: one for image resizing, another for inbox cleanup, and a third that negotiates small contracts using preset templates.

While she sleeps, her AI updates her portfolio, curates her best work, and posts new highlights to social media. By the time she opens her laptop, she's free to focus on what only she can do: create.

This isn't fantasy. It's a preview. AI won't replace freelancers; it will reshape what freelancing means. The human focus will shift from production to direction, from doing everything to leading intelligent systems that do more.

Work Without Borders

In 2030, distance will barely matter. A freelancer in Lagos will collaborate seamlessly with a client in Buenos Aires while an AI translator keeps their meeting flowing in perfect Spanish and English. Project manager AIs will coordinate work across continents, track deadlines, handle invoices, and even calculate local taxes. For freelancers, this global reach is both thrilling and terrifying.

The good news: more clients, more opportunities. The challenge: global competition that never sleeps. Success will depend not on where you live but on how you stand out: how you infuse your work with a voice, a story, and a personality that AI can't copy.

Creativity and Trust

By 2030, clients won't just pay for results, they'll pay for authenticity. One agency rejects a perfectly edited, AI-polished video pitch because it "feels too artificial." Instead, they hire the freelancer who shares messy sketches, rough drafts, and a voice memo of their thought process. Why? Because imperfection signals humanity.

In a world filled with machine-made precision, the new luxury is imperfection. The visible fingerprints of a real creator. Trust becomes the freelancer's strongest currency. Machines can replicate skills, but they can't build relationships.

The Risks of 2030

The road ahead won't be all margaritas and tacos. Freelancers will face new challenges, including:

- *Oversaturation:* Millions of freelancers using the same AI shortcuts
- *Generic output:* Endless streams of identical content flooding every platform
- *Vanishing middle:* Entry-level gigs automated, leaving only high-trust or high-volume work

Those who thrive will be the ones who keep their voice, ethics, and emotional intelligence alive: the ones who show clients that although anyone can generate content, not everyone can make it *mean* something.

Lessons for Today

The future isn't something to fear; it's something to practice. You don't need to wait for 2030 to start preparing.

- *Build your style:* AI can imitate, but it can't create your quirks, humor, or rhythm.
- *Learn to direct AI:* Think like a film director, guiding your creative crew of digital assistants.
- *Invest in trust:* Automation can speed up work, but relationships keep the work coming back.
- *Document your process:* Show clients your thinking. That's where your value shines.

What you do now determines whether you'll just survive in the future or lead it.

AI Sidekick Session: Design Your Future Freelancer Self

Time Required: About 30 minutes
Goal: Create your own roadmap for thriving in the 2030 gig economy.
What You'll Need:

- Access to an AI tool like ChatGPT, Claude, or Gemini
- Your current task list or daily schedule
- A notebook or Notion page to record your reflections

Mission 1: A Day in 2030 (5 minutes)

Let's time-travel. Ask your AI to map out a typical workday for your future self.

> Special secret prompt: *"Imagine I'm a freelancer in 2030. Write a realistic daily schedule that shows how AI supports my work, from client management to creativity and rest."*
>
> Compare that schedule to your current day.
>
> Circle or highlight any tasks that could already be automated or improved with AI today.

PRO TIP Ask a follow-up:

"Which tasks from my current schedule will still require human creativity, empathy, or strategy in 2030?"

That's where your future value lies.

Mission 2: The Future Bio Test (10 minutes)

Your professional story is your strongest differentiator. Let's future-proof it.

Special secret prompt: *"Write two versions of my professional bio. Version 1: make it generic, like any freelancer in my field. Version 2: make it personal, highlighting my unique journey, motivation, and values."*

Read both out loud.

Which one sounds human?

Which one would a 2030 client trust more?

PRO TIP Ask:

"Based on these examples, summarize three traits that make my story stand out to future clients."

That's your personal brand foundation for the decade ahead.

Mission 3: The Future-Proofing Plan (5 minutes)

Now turn insight into action.

Write down three specific things you'll do to prepare your career for the future.

Examples:

- Refine your signature voice and creative style.
- Track your workflows to build transparency and trust.
- Collaborate with other freelancers who share your ethics and goals.

Special secret prompt: *"Based on current trends in freelancing and automation, suggest three habits I should build now to stay relevant and in demand by 2030."*

Choose one to start this month.

Mission 4: The Human Advantage (5 minutes)

Machines evolve fast, but some things will always be human.

> Special secret prompt: *"What are three things humans will still do better than AI in 2030?"*
>
> Reflect on how you can develop those skills today: empathy, storytelling, cultural understanding, and ethical judgment.

PRO TIP Ask AI to design a mini habit for each:

"Suggest one weekly practice to strengthen my creativity, emotional intelligence, and ethical awareness."

These will become your lifelong competitive edge.

Quick Test: Are You Ready for 2030? (5 minutes)

Underline *Yes* or *No*:

1. I am actively developing a unique style or voice in my work. Yes No
2. I use AI to support my process, not to replace my creativity. Yes No
3. I can clearly explain how my value goes beyond what a machine can do. Yes No
4. I invest time in building trust and relationships with clients. Yes No
5. I can identify at least three parts of my workflow that AI could already help with. Yes No
   - If you underlined 4–5 "Yes" answers: You are on track to thrive in the freelance world of 2030.
   - If you underlined 2–3 "Yes" answers: You need to strengthen your positioning. Focus on your voice and trust-building.
   - If you underlined 0–1 "Yes" answers: You risk being replaced by the very tools you use. Start future-proofing your career now.

The future of freelancing isn't about humans *versus* machines; it's about humans *with* machines. The competition won't be AI against people; it will be people who use AI well against those who don't. The winners won't be the ones with the fanciest tools. They'll be the ones who add humanity to the output: empathy, humor, intuition, and trust.

Your taco truck of 2030 might have drones delivering tacos and holograms running ads. But when someone takes a bite, what they'll remember is still your salsa, the spark of originality that no algorithm can duplicate. Keep refining your craft, building your voice, and showing your process. The freelancers who do that will not just survive the next decade: they'll define it.

Appendix: Creative and Productivity AI Tools

Tool	Primary use	Format	Short description
ChatGPT	Writing, research, idea generation	Text	A conversational AI that helps with writing, planning, brainstorming, and automation.
Claude	Creative writing, outlining	Text	A thoughtful writing assistant great for nuanced tasks and collaborative drafting.
Suno	Music generation	Audio	Turns text prompts into original, royalty-free songs in seconds.
Runway	Video generation and editing	Video	AI-powered video tool for content creation, editing, and visual storytelling.
Midjourney	Stylized image generation	Visual	Creates rich, artistic images from text prompts. Ideal for concepts and mood boards.
Stable Diffusion	Customizable image generation	Visual	Open-source model for generating and remixing images, with deeper control options.
Pika	Short-form video generation	Video	Generates animated video clips from text prompts. Useful for social content.
Canva AI	Graphic design with AI assistance	Visual	AI tools inside Canva to speed up visual design, branding, and content templates.
Notion AI	Writing, task management, research	Text	Adds AI support inside Notion for summarizing notes, generating content, and more.
Zapier	Workflow automation	Integration	Connects apps and automates tasks like sending emails and updating spreadsheets.
Make.com	No-code automation and AI chaining	Integration	Visual automation tool that lets you build complex, AI-powered workflows easily.

Earn Your Northeastern University Digital Badges

You've completed your missions, and now it's time to make it official.

To receive your Northeastern University digital badges, please follow the submission instructions at: `https://civicai.khoury.northeastern.edu/ai-for-gig-workers`.

The website provides the most up-to-date guidance on what to submit and how to submit it. After review, eligible submissions will receive official digital badges that you can share on professional profiles, portfolios, or with clients and platforms. Keep learning, keep experimenting, and keep shaping the future of work.

About the Authors

Saiph Savage is a faculty member at Northeastern University, where she directs the Civic A.I. Lab and is a leading expert on AI for the future of work. Her research explores how AI can be designed with and for workers, especially freelancers, so that technology strengthens their power, protections, and livelihoods. She is a recipient of the NSF CAREER Award, and her research on AI and labor has been recognized by MIT Technology Review's 35 Innovators Under 35, Forbes' list of top AI leaders in Mexico, and UNESCO as one of the most impactful AI projects in the world.

Saiph advises senators and governments in the United States and Mexico, collaborates with presidential offices across Latin America, and serves on the OECD's Global Partnership on AI, shaping international strategies for AI and employment. She studied computer engineering at the National Autonomous University of Mexico (UNAM), where she is now a research collaborator, and earned her Ph.D. in computer science at the University of California, Santa Barbara. Formerly a tech worker at Intel Labs and Microsoft Bing, she now focuses her technical and policy expertise on one mission: ensuring that AI helps workers, especially freelancers, build dignified and sustainable futures.

Pamela Cerdeira is a journalist with more than 25 years of experience and the co-founder of Opinión 51, a groundbreaking media platform created to bring together the most influential women's voices. Its launch marked a historic moment: a space where female columnists shape national conversation with authority, diversity, and intellectual force.

She is a passionate enthusiast of artificial intelligence and an early adopter of emerging technologies. She is known for turning complex ideas into clear, accessible explanations that empower audiences to understand—and use—the tools shaping the future.

Liliana Savage is an expert in AI for freelancers and digital workers. She is a program manager and researcher at the Civic Tech Lab at the National Autonomous University of Mexico (UNAM) and a research affiliate at the Civic AI Lab at Northeastern University. As a UNESCO AI Ethics Expert Without Borders Consultant, she focuses on how AI is reshaping freelance and digital labor in the Global South and how governance can protect and empower those workers. She has also been a freelancer herself for several years, which grounds her research in the daily realities of independent workers.

With a human-computer interaction master's degree from Siegen University in Germany, Liliana specializes in participatory design and inclusive AI technologies that center freelancers and gig workers. Her work includes co-designing AI tools with government workers who support women navigating violence and with migrants, as well as contributing to the Global

Partnership on AI to study how gig workers in Latin America use AI and how policy can better reflect the freelance economy.

Across her projects, Liliana develops technological agendas that improve user experience, economic opportunity, and dignity for freelancers and underrepresented communities, including those impacted by migration, domestic violence, and workforce reintegration. Her research has informed global conversations on ethical AI and digital work at international venues such as the UNESCO Global Forum on the Ethics of AI in Bangkok and UNESCO's Mondiacult in Barcelona. As a Latina woman in tech, she is committed to opening paths for other designers, freelancers, and researchers across Latin America who want to shape the future of work with AI.

Index